PRIVATE LIVES/PUBLIC MOMENTS

READINGS IN AMERICAN HISTORY
VOLUME 2: FROM RECONSTRUCTION
TO THE PRESENT

Dominick Cavallo, Editor
Adelphi University

Prentice Hall
Boston Columbus Indianapolis New York San Francisco
Upper Saddle River Amsterdam Cape Town Dubai London Madrid
Milan Munich Paris Montreal Toronto Delhi Mexico City Sao Paulo
Sydney Hong Kong Seoul Singapore Taipei Tokyo

Editorial Director: Leah Jewell
Publisher: Charlyce Jones Owen
Editorial Assistant: Maureen Diana
Director of Marketing: Brandy Dawson
Senior Managing Editor: Ann Marie McCarthy
Production Project Manager: Lynn Savino Wendel
Operations Specialist: Maura Zaldivar
Creative Director: Jayne Conte
Cover Designer: Bruce Kenselaar
Manager, Visual Research: Beth Brenzel
Manager, Rights and Permissions: Zina Arabia
Image Permission Coordinator: Silvana Attanasio
Manager, Cover Visual Research and Permissions: Karen Sanatar
Cover Art: Joe Jones (1909–1963), "We Demand," 1934, Property of The Butler Institute
of American Art
Full-Service Project Management/Composition: Christian Holdener,
  S4Carlisle Publishing Services
Printer/Binder: R.R. Donnelley & Sons, Inc.
Cover Printer: R.R. Donnelley & Sons, Inc.

This book was set in 10/11 Palatino.

Library of Congress Cataloging-in-Publication Data
Private lives/public moments : readings in American history/Dominick Cavallo, editor.
  p. cm.
  Includes bibliographical references.
  ISBN 978-0-321-29856-0 (v. 1) — ISBN 978-0-205-72368-3 (v. 2) 1. United States—History.
I. Cavallo, Dominick,
  E178.1.P946 2010
  973—dc22   2009017441

10 9 8 7 6 5 4 3 2 1

Prentice Hall
is an imprint of

www.pearsonhighered.com   ISBN-13: 978-0-205-72368-3
                                ISBN-10:   0-205-72368-3

For JoAnn

I pray thee, gentle mortal, sing again:
Mine ear is much enamour'd of thy note;
So is mine eye enthralled to thy shape;
And thy fair virtue's force, perforce, doth move me;
On the first view, to say, I swear, I love thee.

—William Shakespeare, *A Midsummer Night's Dream*

CONTENTS

FOREWORD

Every generation must write a history that speaks to its own time. Today, many of the issues that preoccupy Americans involve private life. For more than a quarter-century, bitter political controversy has raged over abortion, dead-beat dads, domestic violence, gay rights, same-sex marriage, teenage pregnancy, and a host of other issues rooted in private life. This fascinating reader in American history provides essential historical context for understanding recent controversies over "traditional family values." It also helps us recognize that every major event in American history—from colonization to the Revolution, slavery to the Civil War—had a vital, but largely unrecognized, private dimension. It shows students the human meaning of public events—of how African Americans coped with slavery and racial discrimination, how immigrants adapted to new ways of life, how working families coped with the strains of industrialization and economic hardship, and how women have struggled to expand their roles and opportunities.

Equally important, *Private Lives/Public Moments* demonstrates that private choices have profound public consequences. Many of the most important historical developments were the result not of the actions of presidents, legislators, or judges, but of the cumulate decisions of millions of ordinary women and men. The decision to migrate, to protest discrimination, to raise or reduce the birthrate—these private choices have carried immense public implications.

By exploring the private side of American history, *Private Lives/Public Moments* shatters many myths and misconceptions that Americans take for granted. Sensationalized newspaper and television reports have led many Americans to conclude that divorce and family breakdown are recent phenomena. But readers of this volume will quickly learn that this view is wrong. Already, by the late nineteenth century, the United States had the Western world's highest divorce rate. The fact is that families in the past experienced many problems similar to those facing families today: desertion, child abuse, spousal battering, and alcohol and drug addiction.

Let's take another misconception. Many Americans mistakenly assume that the male breadwinner family was always the traditional form in America. In fact, it was not until the 1920s that a majority of children lived in a home where the husband was the breadwinner, the wife was a full-time homemaker, and the kids could go to school instead of working for wages.

The history recounted in this volume decisively demonstrates that American family life has always been diverse, changing, and unstable. America's families have varied in structure and functioning across lines of social classes, ethnicity, and emotional and power dynamics over the course of American history. At the dawn of the twentieth century, single-parent households made up about 15 percent of urban families, as a result, largely, of abandonment and premature death. As recently as 1940, about 10 percent of children lived with neither of their biological parents.

Today, many Americans use the language of crisis and decline to describe private life. Many blame society's ills, including poverty, crime, violence, and substance abuse—on the decline of traditional family values. Many look at the rising age of those entering into marriage, and the high rates of divorce and nonmartial cohabitation, and fear that the marriage is disappearing, that family life is becoming more transient, that women and men are growing more selfishly independent.

Is family life less stable today than in the past? Not nearly as much as some assume. Divorce rates, lower today than a quarter-century ago, are much lower among better-educated and more affluent families than among the poor—suggesting that economic stress is a major contributor to marital instability. Are Americans abandoning marriage? The answer is clearly no. Young people delay marriage for multiple reasons—including the need to complete their education and to enter a satisfying career—but most eventually marry. About 90 percent of Americans marry at some point in their lives and 75 percent of those who divorce eventually remarry. The overwhelming majority of today's children grow up in two-parent households—just as they have throughout American history.

By demonstrating that private decisions have public significance and that public events inevitably color private life, this volume offers a fresh way of thinking about American history. It also provides students with a new way of understanding our own time. Today, many families experience intense stress. This volume helps students understand that these strains cannot be understood apart from broader societal developments. For example, since the mid-1960s, our society has undergone a revolution in women's lives, but it is a revolution that remains incomplete. Even though our society is legally committed to gender equality, in many families responsibility for housework and child care remains unequal. This imbalance is a source of strain in many families.

Since the 1960s, our society has also experienced a revolution in the realm of work. The rapid influx of married women into the paid labor force not only gave women greater economic independence, it also spawned profound work–family conflicts. Professional child care is expensive and highly uneven in quality and is largely unavailable on weekends or during evenings. Many families find it difficult to provide the level of care that they would like for their children. As our population ages, many families are also hard-pressed to care for aging parents.

A "new," post-industrial service economy that began to emerge in the 1970s and 1980s has also carried profound consequences for private life. Today, many adults are on call 24/7, and very few Americans will work for a single employer throughout their work lives. Job insecurity and long work hours, in turn, have inflicted a great deal of stress on our personal lives.

Far from being two separate spheres, the private and public realms are inextricably interconnected. Changes in one domain inevitably affect the other. By showing students how public events have influenced private life and how private choices have altered society as a whole, *Private Lives/Public Moments* does something that is exceedingly rare: it encourages you to look at life, in the present as well as the past, differently.

Steven Mintz
Columbia University

ACKNOWLEDGMENTS

I owe an enormous debt to colleagues, friends, and experts in the field who guided me through the research and writing of this book. They include Mel Albin, David Burner, Jo Cavallo, Dennis Fagan, Dennis Hidalgo, Jeffrey Kane, Peter Katopes, Michael LaCombe, Alan Sadovnik, JoAnn Smith, Martin VanLith, Fred Weinstein, and Glen Zeitzer.

I also appreciated the wisdom, expertise, and insight of the editors and staff at Pearson: Vanessa Gennarelli, Rob DeRosa, and Lynn Savino Wendel. I especially want to thank my editor at Pearson, Charlyce Jones Owen: her focus, drive, creativity, and experience made working on this project a pleasure. Thanks as well to Christian Holdener and Jolynn Kilburg for their fine work in producing this book, and to Sue Nodine for her superlative copyediting.

Finally, I owe a special debt of gratitude to reviewers who read both manuscripts and provided both astute criticisms of their inadequacies and wise council about remedies. They include Sarah Knott, Indiana University; Mary Beth Emmerichs, University of Wisconsin; Don Palm, Sacramento City College; Rachel Standish, Menlo College; Donald C. Elder III, Eastern New Mexico University; Cornelia Sexauer, University of Wisconsin; James H. Williams, Middle Tennessee State University; Jeffrey C. Livingston, California State University; Paula Hinton, Tennessee Tech; David R. Novak, Purdue University; Shirley Teresa Wajda, Kent State University; Joseph Hawes, University of Memphis; Christy Snider, Berry College; Katherine Chavigny, Sweet Briar College; Nancy J. Rosenbloom, Canisius College; William Simons, SUNY Oneonta; Kathleen Carter, Highpoint University; Jacqueline M. Cavalier, Community College of Allegheny County; Peter Levy, York College of Pennsylvania; Jennifer L. Gross, Jacksonville State University; Randi Storch, SUNY Cortland; Leslie Heaphy, Kent State University; Mary Ann Bodayla, Southwest Tennessee State University; Julie L. Smith, Mt. Aloysius College; Alison Parker, SUNY Brockport.

INTRODUCTION

The essays in this book examine the history of the United States by connecting the private lives of its people to the public issues that have had a major impact on the nation's destiny. Perhaps because of their traditions of personal freedom, economic individualism, and family privacy, Americans have a tendency to think of "private" life and "public" concerns as distinct realms of experience. There are cultural and psychological barriers to thinking about the relationships between self and society, family life and public events, private desires and political conflicts. But the premise of this book is that much of what we call "history" is the product of conflict or concord (or some combination of the two) between private aspirations, frustrations, and values on the one side and public issues, events, and policies on the other.

The essays in Volume 2 provide students with historical knowledge about significant *public* events in American history from 1865 to the present. These include Reconstruction, immigration, industrialization, the Great Depression, World War II, the upheavals of the 1960s, and the rise of the New Right in the 1970s and 1980s. But they do so by exploring how those issues and events shaped, and were shaped by, Americans in determined pursuit of their *private* interests: their ambitions and frustrations, their values and fears, their hopes and disappointments.

For example, one advantage of linking private lives to public moments in American history is that it compels us to think about the interdependence of family and society. There is a tendency to imagine family as a sanctuary from the pressures and stresses of the "outside" world (nineteenth-century Americans called the family a "haven in a heartless world"). But the boundary between family and society has always been fluid, though in different ways at different times. Public issues and events impact private lives and decisions. And decisions made privately within families can influence the course of public policies and politics.

An example of this is presented in Chapter 10, "The Great Depression on the Farm: The Dust Bowl." In the late nineteenth and early twentieth centuries, thousands of farm families took advantage of government-sponsored programs to settle on cheap land along the southern portion of the Great Plains. This was clearly a case of public policies influencing private decisions. But these farm families proceeded to plant crops on soil better suited for livestock grazing than farming. Over time, in the aggressive pursuit of the family self-sufficiency and private profit associated with the agrarian myth, they stripped the topsoil from millions of acres. By the 1930s, this led to one of the great environmental disasters in American history, the Dust Bowl. Thousands of farm families were forced from their homes—and from the land they themselves had ruined. They became refugees in their own country, in search of new places to live.

In this example, we see how public policies influenced private decisions, which, in turn, led to disastrous "public" consequences—and to still further "private" decisions. Other essays investigate the family–society connection from different angles. For instance, during World War II some children were exposed to their parents' prejudices against various religious and racial groups. Chapter 12 ("Children and Conflict on the Home Front during World War II") traces the violent public consequences of those "private" feelings; it also questions the common belief that Americans were unified during the war years. In a very different time and setting, Chapter 18 ("The Columbine Shooting: Teenage Male Violence and Contemporary America") analyzes the 1998 Columbine tragedy in the context of the shortcomings both of family life and high school culture as experienced by modern young people.

The history of immigration is another important element of the American experience that is illuminated by weaving private life with public issues. Millions of individuals and families made "private" decisions to leave their homelands in search of opportunity in America. Those decisions had crucial public consequences. For instance, Chapter 5 ("Life and Work for Turn-of-the-Century Chicago Immigrants") explores the economic impact of immigration—on both the families who came to these shores and on that city's meatpacking industry. And racial, ethnic, and religious intolerance toward newcomers frequently resulted in powerful anti-immigrant sentiments and movements. A tragic instance of this is portrayed in Chapter 4 ("The Crusade to 'Purify' America by Driving Out the Chinese"). But political events and social movements also affect the values of newly arrived immigrants and their families. Chapter 19 ("Gender and the Latino Experience in Late Twentieth-Century America") describes how the modern feminist movement of the 1960s and 1970s helped reshape gender roles in Latino immigrant families coming to the United States in the 1980s and 1990s.

The interplay between personal and public views of gender is another theme that provides insight into major events in the country's history. For example, Chapter 3 ("American Manhood and Declaring War on Spain in 1898") discusses perceptions of American masculinity and valor held by members of Congress and how they became part of public discourse in response to the sinking of the battleship *Maine*. Chapter 14 ("Race, Gender, and the Civil Rights Movement: The Struggle in Mississippi") traces the consequences of radically different images of gender held by civil rights activists and white racists.

Finally, a number of essays focus on interactions with various crises that confronted Americans during these years and how they affected—and were affected by—private values concerning gender, religion, and sexuality. Chapter 9 ("The Great Depression in the City: The Housewives' Meat Strike of 1935") details the outrage of married women over the high cost of meat in these years, their powerful protests against it, and their role as housewives in creating their protest movement. In Chapter 11 ("Rosie the Riveter Gets

Married: Women during World War II"), we see how the crisis of war *both* changed *and* reinforced traditional views of married women's proper place in American society. And Chapter 13 ("The Federal Government's Campaign against Homosexuals and Other 'Sex Offenders' during the McCarthy Era") links the Cold War crisis to the issue of sexuality during the 1950s. During that time, federal officials claimed that homosexuals who worked for the government were a threat to national security. Hundreds of loyal and competent government employees suspected of being homosexuals were fired from their jobs.

A brief introduction at the beginning of each essay provides students with a context for the issues raised in the article. At the end of each essay are "Questions for Discussion" and an extensive "For Further Reading" list on the topic.

CHAPTER

1

Freedom?
After the Civil War
Black Women and Their
Families during Reconstruction

Noralee Frankel

In 1865, with the war winding down, a former slave, now a soldier in the Union army, ran across his old master, now a prisoner of war. "Hello, massa," said the black soldier in the dialect of the time, "bottom rail on top dis time." Amid the chaos and destruction of the defeated South, there was some justification for this free man's optimism. Four million slaves had been emancipated after 250 years of bondage. The political and economic power of their former masters was broken. The freed slaves believed the triumphant North would confiscate the plantations they had toiled on for generations without compensation and distribute them to emancipated African Americans. After all, as one African American rightly said, the property owned by their former masters "was nearly all earned by the sweat of *our* brows." Black people would not only become property owners, but would enjoy the full rights and privileges of citizenship, including the right to vote.

None of this happened. In the end, the Reconstruction era, which lasted until 1877, was a bitterly disappointing experience for African Americans. There were moments during the postwar years when former slaves enjoyed the basic rights of citizenship. But they were short-lived. Nothing could compensate black people for the horrors they had endured during slavery. Although Reconstruction was an opportunity to provide African Americans with a measure of equity and justice, it failed. Why?

There are a number of issues raised by this 1874 depiction of life in the South after the Civil War. What do you think are the three most important?

For one thing, it is important to keep in mind President Lincoln's goal in fighting the Civil War. Lincoln's aim in the early years of the conflict was to save the Union, not to free the slaves, much less provide free black people with political rights equal to those of whites. Although personally opposed to slavery, Lincoln was a reluctant emancipator. As he put it, "If I could save the Union without freeing any slave I would do it, and if I could save it by freeing all the slaves I would do it, and if I could save it by freeing some and leaving others alone I would also do that." In other words, emancipation was a war measure and ending slavery a means toward achieving victory. Anything approaching racial equality was never part of this equation. This was evident in Lincoln's plan for Reconstruction—for bringing the South back into the Union after the war. His initial proposal limited voting rights and office holding to white southerners. The slaves would be "free" but would lack basic political rights. A few days before he was assassinated,

Lincoln softened this stance somewhat by advocating the vote for educated African Americans and those who were veterans of the Union army.

Also, in order for Reconstruction to work, the South would have had to be economically "reconstructed." The former slaves possessed neither land nor the money to purchase it. How were they to survive, much less prosper, after the war? They were also educationally disadvantaged. Most could not read or write. Prior to the Civil War, every slave state except Tennessee prohibited teaching slaves to read and write. Under these circumstances, the only way to their economic viability would have been to provide the tens of thousands of emancipated black families with land. That meant either giving them land owned by the federal government or confiscating the property of their former masters (who, after all, were viewed as traitors by the North), or both. Most freed black people expected this to happen. It didn't, and instead they were left to fend for themselves. In the end, as the next essay by Noralee Frankel makes clear, the majority of African American families eventually became sharecroppers on land owned by former slave holders. They were no longer slaves, but the system of sharecropping placed the economic destinies of most southern African Americans in the hands of wealthy white planters who had the power to exploit them.

Finally, in order for the South to be "reconstructed" racially, its tradition of white domination had to be challenged. For a time it was, especially during the period when Reconstruction was controlled by the "Radical" Republicans in Congress. Among other laws, Congress passed the Fourteenth Amendment to the Constitution (approved in 1868) that prohibited states from denying "equal protection of the laws" to any citizen. In 1870 the Fifteenth Amendment went into effect; it prohibited the state and federal governments from depriving any male citizen of the right to vote because of race. (It should be noted that the South did not have a monopoly on preventing blacks from voting; more than 90 percent of black men residing in northern states prior to the Civil War were prohibited from voting as well.) The Civil Rights Act of 1866 outlawed the infamous "Black Codes," laws passed by southern states restricting the freedom of African Americans (they are described in Frankel's essay). And in 1867 Congress passed the Reconstruction Act, which divided the conquered South into five military districts, prohibited former Confederates from voting or holding office, and guaranteed the rights of black people to vote and hold office.

At first, this worked. African Americans voted in huge numbers, and more than 1,500 of them held a variety of political offices in the South. One became governor of Louisiana, fourteen were elected to the House of Representatives, and two were sent to the United States Senate from Mississippi. Hundreds of former slaves became police officers, sheriffs, postal workers, justices of the peace, and state legislators. In other words, Reconstruction could have been effective in undermining the southern tradition of white domination.

But most northerners didn't care about the destinies of black people and were tired of the financial and political costs of occupying the South. In 1877, Reconstruction officially ended. The South, left to its own devices, began the process of reasserting the domination of whites over blacks. Over the next twenty years, it passed laws that deprived African Americans of the basic rights of citizenship, including voting and holding office. Laws were passed mandating racial segregation in public accommodations and education. And where the law fell short in ensuring white domination, terrorist groups like the Ku Klux Klan stepped in.

Noralee Frankel describes the Reconstruction era in Mississippi in the next essay. Although Frankel's work is focused on the post–Civil War black experience in Mississippi, her discussion is relevant to other southern states as well. The Black Codes, Klan violence, sharecropping, and the desperate efforts of African American parents to create a decent life for themselves and their children occurred across the South.

It is hard to imagine a "public moment" in American history that had more of an impact on "private lives" than the emancipation of 4 million slaves. It is equally hard to imagine the disappointment and disillusion felt by African Americans as the promise of Reconstruction turned into the bitter reality of poverty, violence, and second-class citizenship.

Source: Noralee Frankel, *Freedom's Women: Black Women and Families in Civil War Era Mississippi* (Bloomington: University of Indiana Press, 1999), pp. 56–59, 66–72, 76–78, 111–112, 127–131, 138–141. Reprinted with permission of Indiana University Press.

Although most African Americans in Mississippi continued to be agricultural workers, emancipation encouraged them to challenge the conditions under which they worked. Freedwomen performed the same type of work as they had when they were slaves, but freedpeople and former slave owners held conflicting views about the definition of non-slave labor. For African Americans, free labor meant adequate compensation and less white supervision. Blacks contested the insistence of white planters that they make all their labor decisions and their continued use of force.

As 1865 ended, freedpeople were reluctant to enter into year-long contracts as wage laborers because they expected to receive their own land. They also concluded that the labor contracts would limit their control over their own labor. They resisted the insistence of northern and southern whites that they become laborers for whites. Blacks wanted to work for themselves. They preferred to set their own work schedules and construct a greater distinction between public and private life, which laboring for whites permitted.

Employers expected their workforce to continue to labor the same number of hours each day and under many of the same restrictions as slavery. Many former slave owners relied on the threat of violence as a means of controlling workers. Whites even found it hard to adjust to new terminology for their employees. The word "slaves" was erased from W. S. Noble's labor contract of July 11, 1865, and "servants" written in its place.

The agricultural and domestic work of blacks set the scene for struggles with employers, but labor disputes must also be viewed in the context of the larger political struggle for race equity. Historian John Hope Franklin refers to this period (1865 and 1866) as Confederate Reconstruction, a particularly apt phrase for Mississippi. In Mississippi, whites elected former Confederates to office, such as Governor Benjamin Humphrey, a general in the Confederate army. In the fall of 1865, the Mississippi legislature passed restrictive legislation collectively known as the Black Codes. The codes were so named because almost all the provisions applied solely to African Americans. The legislation included restrictions on owning or renting rural land in the state by newly freed African Americans.

These laws reflected the attitude of the majority of white planters toward free labor. Although planters accepted the demise of slavery, they rejected the concept of free labor for African Americans by which laborers freely sold their labor and worked without coercion. This lack of faith in free labor, combined with their need for racial domination, led the Mississippi legislature in 1865 to approve strict vagrancy laws as part of the Black Codes in order to force African Americans to work on plantations. The laws were aimed at African Americans who resisted working for former slave masters.

The vagrancy laws defined African Americans solely in terms of laborers and more specifically in terms of their employment to whites. Targeting African American women as well as men, the vagrancy laws ensured that any African American who left an employer for any reason without permission could be arrested as a vagrant. These laws, reinforced by year-long labor contracts that were strictly enforced, vastly decreased the ability of African Americans to gain higher wages when they signed contracts. Such conditions made African Americans leery of signing labor contracts.

Most freedpeople anticipated that freedwomen would work with their husbands on their own land safe from sexually harassing or violent overseers or employers. The failure to divide and distribute the land of former owners bitterly disappointed freedpeople and forced them to seek employment with former masters. Nevertheless, African Americans continued to petition the government for land "for every man and woman" and they remained reluctant about working for white planters. . . .

During Confederate Reconstruction and for a few years after, the federal government through the Freedman's Bureau . . . continued to supervise free labor and legal marriages of former slaves. Although Congress established the Bureau, in part, to oversee the distribution of land taken from the Confederates, this program ended quickly with [President Andrew] Johnson's restoration of plantations to southern owners. Bureau agents attempted to dissuade African Americans from the tenaciously held belief that the plantations of former slave owners would be divided by the government and that the former slaves were entitled to it.

Bureau agents encouraged the planters to offer higher wages or a greater share of the crops, while agents grimly informed former slaves that the federal government was not giving them their forty acres. Samuel Thomas, the first Freedman's Bureau assistant commissioner in Mississippi, wrote a stern letter on January 2, 1866, "To the Colored People of Mississippi." He explained, "some of you have the absurd notion that if you put your hands to a contract you will somehow be made slaves. This is all nonsense, made up by some foolish or wicked person." He added, "I hope you are all convinced that you are not to receive property of any kind from the government and that you must labor for what you get, like other people." Additionally, he reminded them that "the time has arrived for you [to] contract for another year's labor, I wish to impress upon you the importance of doing this at once. . . . You cannot live without work of some kind. Your houses and lands belong to the white people, and you cannot expect that they will allow you to live on them in idleness." A combination of remonstrations by Freedman's Bureau officials, strict vagrancy laws, and restrictions on available land pushed reluctant African Americans toward contract labor by early 1866. . . .

The factors that influenced the evolution of sharecropping included the failure of land to be distributed, disputes over nonpayment of monetary wages, white supervision and intervention both in labor and family life, and the fundamental nature of the meaning of freedom. The northern concept of wage labor did not work successfully in the south. Freedpeople and planters defined free labor differently. Slavery shaped the responses of both freedpeople and former masters. Planters expected freedpeople to behave with the deference and obedience of slaves. Former slave owners anticipated that they would rule their laborers with absolute authority and reacted vehemently and sometimes violently to any challenge. In contrast, workers separated their lives from those of their employers whenever they could in ways that had been impossible during slavery.

Labor contracts and vagrancy laws kept freed men and women from using market forces to barter for better wages in spite of labor shortages. For example, [Freedman's Bureau] agent John Sunderland reminded freedwomen who worked for Charles Gordon that, under the stringent laws known as the Black Codes passed by Mississippi legislators in 1865, they could be incarcerated as vagrants if they left Gordon without due cause. Bureau agent John Knox dispatched a man to force African American laborers "Betsey and family" to return to their place of employment. Knox believed that workers needed to demonstrate strict obedience to their employers. When workers refused to "obey" a planter's "lawful orders," they failed to live up to "their contract and ought to be discharged," often without payment.

Nonpayment of wages to freedmen and women kept wage labor from becoming the success northerners wanted it to be. According to Freedman's Bureau documents, including complaint books, the largest area of conflict between African American men and women and plantation owners was the unwillingness of planters to pay wages to their workers. . . .

To freedpeople, wage labor seemed too reminiscent of slavery. Male and female workers complained that planters found trivial excuses to dismiss workers after the harvest to avoid paying them. This caused hardships for employees both because they failed to receive wages and because employers forced them to leave their homes on the plantations where they worked and lived. Although workers could be forced off plantations, workers could not leave when they wanted to hire for better wages.

Employers countered the complaints of workers. They justified their refusal to pay wages at the end of the year by arguing that they merely withheld accumulated debts from the pay of workers. Restrictive mobility clauses in the labor contracts as well as the inability or refusal of employers to pay in cash often forced freedpeople to buy from their employers and kept laborers from better priced goods available elsewhere. Planters charged at least 20 percent over cost for these products, although some added as much as 50 to 100 percent. Although these are not unreasonable amounts for modern retailers, the prices were expensive for African Americans. For example, a fifty-cent bar of soap became a relatively expensive luxury for a freedwoman who earned a maximum of $10 a month. . . .

In addition to difficulties over the payment of wages, conflicts between freedpeople and planters erupted over what kind of labor would be performed, when, how, and for whom. These disputes pushed both freedpeople and planters toward sharecropping. Former slave owners tried to continue to organize their workers in gangs, having successfully relied on them during slavery. Laborers resisted the supervision of a gang system. They preferred to contract in smaller units on a certain number of acres of land, sometimes with family members working in squads.

In addition to resisting work gangs as a method to organize and control their labor, African American men and women also vigorously protested the use of force. Although labor contracts forbade physical punishment, white Mississippi employers believed that only force made African Americans obey them. Planters occasionally used it as a punitive measure as well as a warning to other workers. Although some whites used violence more readily than others, former slave owners and overseers (after the war referred to as agents) in Mississippi generally considered physical coercion a permissible way to resolve labor disputes with workers. . . .

According to Freedman's Bureau complaint records, although freedmen received physical punishment more than female workers, a woman's sex, as in slavery, failed to protect her from physical abuse. Freedwoman Mary Connor's employer struck her because she "did not know how to plough." Naomi Smith's employer kicked her for "not washing the clothes clean." When her former master ordered her to build a fire, Harriet Kilgore told him that she "had a backache and was not in any hurry to get up there." Outraged by her defiance, Kilgore beat her. He later justified his action by explaining, with unconscious irony, that she acted as if she "was free and would do nothing he told [her] to." Another former master beat a woman for attempting to leave his plantation, explaining that he had "a right to beat her for she is his slave." In the first two examples, employers beat freedwomen for incompetence, just as they would have during slavery. In the last two examples, employers physically abused their former slaves for asserting themselves as free laborers: One woman set her own slower work pace and showed, in her employer's mind, disrespect and the other woman decided to exercise her right to leave.

In actions that were reminiscent of slavery, employers hit freedwomen with their fists, kicked them, and whipped them with horsewhips and switches. Southern white gentlemen pistol-whipped freedwomen and struck them with canes. From the violent legacy of slave discipline, whites set dogs on disobedient freedwomen. One employer forced a freedwoman to labor in the fields while wearing a chain. The bodily harm inflicted on freedwomen was sometimes grievous. One woman died from "250 lashes." The records are unclear about the punishment of the men who were accused of the whipping. During these violent episodes, southern men insulted African American women with epithets that were theoretically inapplicable to white women of their own class such as "black bitch." The literal reduction of African American women to animals exemplified the desire of whites to demean African American women. Their race, poverty, and class exempted them from southern male chivalry.

White women also resorted to violence against women workers. When white women physically attacked their female employees, they often used household articles. One woman attacked a freedwoman with a pair of scissors, and another "imprinted a hot flat iron" on a freedwoman's face. When a freedwoman was "insulting" to her white female employer whom she felt had cheated her out of part of her wages, her employer hit her with a fire shovel. African American women retaliated when possible. When her employer, Mrs. Scarborough, hit her with a brush broom, Laura Sloan fought back and tossed "a bucket of water on her." Such actions by employers strengthened the desire of African American women to remove themselves as much as possible from working directly for whites. . . .

When freedwomen complained to the Freedman's Bureau about sexual assaults, they most often accused their employers of making unwarranted advances or attempting rape. Ann Woodson accused both her employer and his son of pursuing her. Women and their men both protested such attacks. They pleaded for release of the women from their labor contracts with pay and without penalty.

Although sexual harassment by white men often occurred in a work context, freedwomen were subject to assault from white men other than their employers. White violence toward African American men and women enforced racial domination. Vigilante groups such as the Ku Klux Klan that were formed to repress black equality used gang rape as an instrument of terror and racial control. Although these groups murdered more African American men than women, freedwomen were vulnerable to sexual assault. While in disguise "with their faces blackened," white men whipped an African American man and his wife and then raped her "three times after they beat her."

Such events acted as powerful reminders of the continuation of southern white domination after the war and the fragility of African American women's protection from white assault. Freedwoman Laura Sanders stated that six white men "broke into her house" and three "ravished her and otherwise mistreated her." The attackers picked some of their victims because of their links to political activists. Ellen Parton testified in the early 1870s before the United States Congress Joint Select Committee to investigate the Ku Klux Klan that eight men broke into her home looking for Republican activists, and one "committed rape upon me." She explained, "I yielded to him because he had a pistol drawn, when he took me down he hurt me of course." In addition to being devastating for women, rape served as a surrogate attack on African American manhood, because it reinforced an image of the powerless African American man. Men could not protect their women in spite of emancipation and the women could not protect themselves. In cases such as Ellen Parton's, the assaults also reminded African American men that their support of the Republican Party endangered the entire community. . . .

Regardless of whether or not they involved violence, labor disputes were tied to the definitions of former slaves of the concept of freedom in terms of who controlled African American labor, leisure, and time within the family. Freed men and women were interested in the fundamental question of how emancipation would differ from slavery and how freedom was going to change their work. Disagreements between employers and employees developed over the intention of freedpeople to work fewer hours than they had as slaves. After the war, freedpeople strove to minimize the interference of former slave owners in the domestic and family portion of their lives. Although planters opposed any changes from slavery, freedpeople expected that the needs of African American families would be important components in decisions about how much time freedwomen and their children devoted to outside employment. African American parents wanted to send their children to school rather than to the fields. African American women, who assumed most of the domestic responsibility for their households, needed more time for their families.

Freedwomen wanted their agricultural work to be performed for the benefit of their family and perceived field work, just as much as washing or cooking, to be part of their labor for their family. They did not want to work only for the material betterment of white people but also for their own households. After the war, the link between labor and family strengthened for women as decisions about one had the capacity to influence the other. Ultimately, the desire of freedwomen to set their own schedules for domestic tasks caused men and women alike to resist gang labor and become sharecroppers.

Freedwomen needed more time for their families in part because their private domestic responsibilities increased after the Civil War. Cooking and clothes-making often ceased to be communal activities as they had been under slavery. . . . After emancipation, freedwomen prepared more meals for themselves and their families. When employers gave their workers patches of land, African American women planted gardens and raised produce, including potatoes, squash, and peas, for sale. Although male farm workers on J. G. Colbert's place received pay of one-third of the crop, Colbert gave their wives "three acres of land" for their own use. African American women also raised animals for their families, such as hogs and chickens for food, while men tended to the draft animals. Pigs proved to have the added advantage of being as loyal and affectionate as dogs. (One freedwoman described a sow that she raised "just like one of her children.") In addition to cooking, washing, sewing and gardening, freedwomen took charge of caring for their own children. . . .

As husband and father, a freedman assumed the role of legal head of the family and maintained guardianship of his children. Symbolic of the transfer of family power from slaveholder to father was the universal acceptance of the father's surname by former slave wives and children. Widowed Jane Kendrick explained that "the reason I changed my name to Jane Reece was my husband's father was named Reece and directly after the war every slave had the privilege of choosing their sir names and I chose the name of my husband's father who had chosen the name of Reece."

After emancipation, as freedmen gained the responsibilities of citizens, the male head of household became the family's legal representative and protector. When necessary, African American men went to court on behalf of their families, acting for their wives and siblings as well as their extended kin. When employers refused to pay both husband and wife their wages, or drove families off their plantations, the husband spoke for the family before the Freedman's Bureau agent. . . .

African American men attempted to act as intermediaries between their families and employers. They tried to protect their families against violence. When Richard Bryant's wife's employer severely whipped her, Bryant demanded an explanation. For his efforts, Richard Bryant barely escaped death from an attack with an iron bar. Peter Robinson complained to the Bureau that Gill Gordon struck Robinson's wife to the ground and kicked her. When J. Monroe Palmer beat Abner Abraham's wife, Abraham protested. In retaliation, Palmer "beat him." Men also objected to other injustices, such as when whites insulted their wives. When a Justice of the Peace called William Davis's wife a "damn black bitch," Davis threatened to report him to the federal military officer stationed in the town. African American husbands also resorted to violence to protect their wives. One African American man defended his shooting of a white man, explaining that the man had "abused [his] wife."

Wives rarely voiced complaints on behalf of their husbands in a public forum such as the Freedman's Bureau. African American women represented their husbands only when circumstances kept men from speaking for themselves, for example, in cases when their men were unfairly jailed or very infirm. Instead, women defended their husbands in more informal ways. When necessary, wives refused to reveal the hiding places of their husbands, thereby shielding their men from the Ku Klux Klan. Fearing death at the hands of the Klan, men ran for safety, leaving their wives because, as one man explained, the Klan "don't hurt women unless some of the women is sassy to some of their wives, or speak like a white woman, and they call that sass; then they go and nearly whip them to death." This man felt comfortable leaving his wife because he knew she "wouldn't say nothing; she says nothing, or only so little that you can't take no offense at it—can't get mad." Such loyalty incurred risk. A Klansman hit Ann Burris with his gun when she refused to divulge where her husband had fled, and Klansmen threatened to kill Hester Buford for withholding her husband's location from them. Women left behind were also vulnerable to rape.

In addition to assuming responsibilities as head of the family, African American men exercised certain familial prerogatives. White employers and Freedman's Bureau agents encouraged freedmen to control freedwomen's labor when such behavior reinforced the sanctity of the labor contract or ensured the women's continued participation in the labor force. Thus, employers and the Freedman's Bureau supported a dominant role for African American males when it promoted their own interests. . . .

Although the male head of the African American family maintained legal rights such as custody and right of contract over other family members, his power was less than the law implied. The legacy of the slave experience and racial animosity from whites undermined the authority of the father within the family. Southern whites generally refused to acknowledge the African American man's newly acquired legal privileges over members of his family, especially when the father's rights interfered with the labor supply of white employers or with white male sexual access to African American women. As Thomas C. Holt has argued, "there was a blatant contradiction between the notion that workers would imitate the bourgeois private sphere and the planters' demand that they control the labor of whole families."

The Black Codes that were passed in 1865 in Mississippi in part denied African American men privileges associated with manhood, including land ownership, possession of a weapon, and "civil responsibilities and rights." These policies helped to keep African Americans in an economically and racially subordinate status to white men. Southern whites refused to defer to African American men regarding their families. White expectations of African American subservience also included a concept of work which required African Americans to labor for whites. White belief in African American inferiority ill-prepared whites to accept the creation of an African American patriarchy. According to one Freedman's Bureau agent, Mississippi whites wanted "to establish some relation which evades the simple recognition of the freedom and manhood of the Negro."

The ability of white southerners to dictate labor terms, and, by extension, the structure of the family, to freedpeople was a prominent feature of the postwar labor economy. It was inconceivable to white employers that any African American father or husband would challenge their will. As one Freedman's Bureau agent noted, "The marital relations of the freedpeople is anything but pleasing. Nothing is more surprising than the disregard . . . by the whites in their dealings with them." He elaborated, "If it suits the white man's or woman's convenience to discharge the husband . . . and retain the wife . . . they will." A perplexed Mississippi planter requested that the Freedman's Bureau help him regain a freedwoman employee who left once her husband brought an order from a Bureau agent that authorized the husband to remove her without penalty from the plantation. The employer expressed puzzlement about the freedwoman's action in joining her husband because the woman never "expressed a desire to leave." Similarly, A. F. Mount pleaded with the Bureau to force the spouse of a former hand to return to his place. Mount states simply, "I do not want him. I only want his wife and children." He saw no inherent problem even though his request, if granted, separated the wife and children from their husband and father. . . .

After the war, one of the greatest threats to the African American family and African American parental authority over their own children was the apprenticing of African American children by white planters. The majority of disputes concerning children that freedpeople brought to the Freedman's Bureau involved attempts by southern whites to retain or apprentice African American children. These conflicts combined the issues of African American control over their families and the labor of freedpeople. Special laws passed in 1865 as part of the Black Codes authorized Mississippi officials, which included "sheriffs, [and] justices of the peace" to report African American (defined as "freedmen, free negroes and mulattos") orphans and impoverished children to local authorities so that the probate court could apprentice them. The law also specified "that the former owner of said minors shall have the preference when, in the opinion of the court, he or she shall be a suitable person for that purpose." Former slave owners paid a bond in probate court for the child after following legal procedures that required "due notice" to the parents (if living) "by posting notices in five public places, and by calling [the parent's name] three times at the court house door." Such legal gestures did not protect African American parents from losing their children, especially given the high rate of illiteracy among freedpeople and their unfamiliarity with the law. One woman who swore that she could support her daughter lost her case because she "was ignorant of the requirement of law regarding witnesses" that she needed to fulfill to prove that she could support the child. Apprenticed children remained with the white family until they reached 21 years of age, if male, or 18 years, if female. Immediately after the war if the court declared African American parents destitute or vagrants, it apprenticed the children without parental consent. The courts justified their decisions on the grounds that un-apprenticed, orphaned, or destitute children needed private support to prevent them from becoming a financial burden to the local government. Children were apprenticed in significant numbers during Presidential Reconstruction. According to one historian, "the probate court at Calhoun City apprenticed two hundred and twenty at one term."

In disputed cases between parents and former owners, the Mississippi local courts usually gave the children to whites. In 1865 and 1866, the local government, controlled by Democrats and still sympathetic to the interests of planters, supported the apprentice system as a form of race and labor control.

In contrast, the federal government, usually represented by Freedman's Bureau agents in Mississippi, generally sided with freed families who were trying to regain their children if the families could support them. Although it was committed to keeping former slave families together, the Bureau also wanted to prevent African American children from becoming financially dependent on the federal government. Because the apprentice law allowed whites to break up families and gave them the virtual slave labor of children, Freedman's Bureau agents protested the widespread abuse. As Samuel Thomas [a white Union officer] wrote the head of the Freedman's Bureau, Oliver Otis Howard, the apprentice law "is capable of being made an instrument of oppression to the colored people and is being so used." Former slave masters swore that children who were bonded to them were orphans and tried to convince the courts that parents who claimed them were frauds. Others falsely accused parents of destitution even in those cases where such claims proved highly questionable. J. H. Grace testified in civil court that the mother of the children he wanted to apprentice, all of whom were his former slaves, was mentally deficient and incapable of caring for her children. The court granted him the apprenticeship. When the mother sought aid from a Freedman's Bureau agent, he found her completely competent and bitterly complained to his superior, "better would it have been for them to remain in slavery if they are to be dragged up and apprenticed in violation of law, and against their will and common sense. . . ."

To counteract such as the apprenticeship legislation that discriminated against African Americans, the United States Congress passed the Civil Rights Act in 1866 over Andrew Johnson's presidential veto. The act stated that "citizens, of every race and color, without regard to any previous condition of slavery or involuntary servitude . . . shall have the same right[s] . . . as . . . enjoyed by white citizens." Because the special apprentice laws passed in Mississippi as part of the Black Codes applied only to African American children, the Civil Rights Act effectively nullified the law. Some Bureau agents interpreted the Civil Rights Act as requiring parental consent prior to the apprenticeship of children. To regain custody of their children under the Civil Rights Act, African American parents needed to obtain a writ of habeas corpus in Circuit Court and file it with the probate court. Even with a writ, the courts required parents to prove their ability to support their children. Although the use of habeas corpus expanded after the Civil War, African Americans discovered that the legal system was expensive, slow, and governed by incomprehensible court procedures. . . .

* * *

As historian W. E. B. DuBois pointed out, "Mississippi was the place where first and last Negroes were largely deprived of any opportunity for landownership." Because of the inability of freedmen to obtain land and the unwillingness of former slave owners to pay monetary wages, African American women and their men became sharecroppers as a way to support themselves. When a family worked as a labor unit in the fields, rather than as gangs of men and women, it often received a share of the crop. This system, along with factors such as who provided the tools and draft animals, evolved into the sharecropping system. Sharecropping gradually became the fate of freed men and women, although it developed more slowly in some areas of Mississippi than in others. African Americans were sharecropping as early as 1867, when sharecropping coexisted with monetary and share wages.

Ultimately, sharecropping returned African Americans to a new reliance on whites and crippled them economically by keeping them indebted. The federal government's refusal to give land to freedmen had a profound impact on the extent to which African Americans could be self-employed. Because they could not acquire land, freedpeople expected wages; when they became disillusioned with monetary wages, they negotiated for a share of the crop. The failure of employers to pay monetary wages, and the desire of freedpeople for less white supervision in the fields all led to sharecropping. Sharecropping developed as cotton prices declined and white landowners in Mississippi made little effort to shift to mixed agriculture. It emerged despite the political change from Democratic to short-lived moderate Republican control of the state. Even under the civil rights reforms of the late 1860s and early 1870s in Mississippi that outlawed the Black Codes, African Americans continued to work for whites. Freedwoman Rina Brown recalled that "every thing we got we had to buy it on credit an' den de white man got whut we made."

The inability of Reconstruction to bring about a radical change in the economic lives of the former slaves represented one of the most acute failures of emancipation for African Americans. The lack of economic opportunities ensured that freedpeople remained laborers for whites, unable to achieve upward mobility. To that extent, they felt that freedom had failed them. As one Mississippi woman bitterly stated, "Is I free? Hasn't I got to get up before daylight and go into the field to work?" As the quote points out, formerly enslaved women worked as field hands or domestic workers who performed the same work that they had as slave women. With more resignation, another freedwoman explained, "[D]ere wusn't no difference in freedom cause I went right on working for Miss."

Although sharecropping was far less than what African Americans wanted, the labor system did change from slavery. Although sharecropping did not permit economic self-sufficiency and economic mobility, it allowed more flexibility than gang labor. The use of overseers decreased and workers determined more of their own work schedules.

After emancipation the rural African American family became a stronger unit than it had been under slavery. Black women controlled more of their private domestic lives but they had more familial labor to perform as well as the need to work for wages (in money or shares). . . .

In one sense work and family were more strongly tied together under sharecropping because families often worked in the fields together. But sharecropping was also part of the separation between family and labor as freedpeople removed their family concerns away from white interference. Women's familial concerns informed the labor choices of freedpeople as they tried to separate reproductive from productive work in their dealings with whites. Although they wanted the end of white supervision of both types of labor, they were never totally successful in their attempts to gain control of these two spheres.

Questions for Discussion

1. Why did African Americans expect to receive land—"40 acres and a mule"—after Emancipation? Were their expectations justified?
2. What methods did southern whites use to reassert their control over the lives and labor of newly emancipated African Americans? How effective were they? On balance, was the federal government's response to this situation more supportive of southern whites or of African Americans?
3. What was sharecropping? Why did it evolve? Did it help or hinder African Americans in their quest for economic security?
4. How did African American family life develop after slavery? Why did southern whites oppose powerful family ties among African Americans? What did they do to prevent them?

For Further Reading

Cindy Barden, *The Reconstruction* Era (2002); William L. Barney, *Battlefield for the Union: The Era of the Civil War and Reconstruction, 1848–1877* (1989); La Wanda Cox, *Lincoln and Black Freedom: A Study in Presidential Leadership* (1981); Jane Dailey, *Before Jim Crow: The Politics of Race in Post-Emancipation Virginia* (2000); W. E. B. DuBois, *Black Reconstruction in America* (1935); Eric Foner, *Reconstruction: America's Unfinished Revolution, 1863–1877* (1988); John Hope Franklin, *Reconstruction After the Civil War* (1960); Chungchan Gao, *African Americans in the Reconstruction Era* (2000); Jacqueline Jones, *Labor of Love, Labor of Sorrow: Black Women, Work and the Family, from Slavery to the Present* (1985); Kenneth Kusmer, *The Civil War and Reconstruction Era, 1861–1877* (1991); Leon F. Litwack, *Been in the Storm So Long: The Aftermath of Slavery* (1979); John Solomon Otto, *Southern Agriculture During the Reconstruction Era, 1860–1880* (1994); George C. Rable, *But There Was No Peace: The Role of Violence in the Politics of Reconstruction* (1984); James L. Roark, *Masters Without Slaves: Southern Planters in the Civil War and Reconstruction* (1977); Willie Lee Rose, *Rehearsal for Reconstruction: The Port Royal Experiment* (1964); Nina Silber, *The Romance of Reunion: Northerners and the South, 1865–1900* (1993); Mitchell Snay, *Finians, Freedmen and Southern Whites: Race and Nationality in the Era of Reconstruction* (2007); Kenneth Stampp, *The Reconstruction Era* (1967); Betty Stroud and Virginia Schomp, *The Reconstruction Era* (2006); Allen W. Trelease, *White Terror: The Ku Klux Klan Conspiracy and Southern Reconstruction* (1971); Rick Warwick, *Freedom and Work in the Reconstruction Era: The Freedman's Bureau Labor Contracts of Williamson County, Tennessee* (2006); C. Vann Woodward, *Origins of the New South, 1877–1913* (1951); Richard Zuczek, *Encyclopedia of the Reconstruction Era* (2006).

CHAPTER

2

Resisting "Civilization"
Native American Opposition
to the Federal Education Program

David Wallace Adams

In the years between the end of the Civil War and the conclusion of the nineteenth century, the epic confrontation between Native and white Americans finally drew to a close. For nearly 400 years they had battled for control of the North American continent. Much of that conflict was over land and other natural resources. But it also involved what Americans today would call a "culture war." Whites and Indians had drastically different views about the most basic human values and institutions: gender roles, the ownership of property, work, religion, sexuality, and childrearing. By 1900 Native Americans were subdued, at least militarily. Their various cultures would survive—a revival of Native American values blossomed into the American Indian Movement of the 1960s and 1970s. But the ability of Indians to militarily challenge white America was finished.

In the first half of the nineteenth century, the United States government forcibly removed most eastern tribes to territory west of the Mississippi River. By 1865, the majority of Native Americans resided in the western part of the country. Approximately 250,000 of them lived there, most on the Great Plains. The Great Plains stretched from the western edge of Missouri to the foothills of the Rockies. It was vast, often desolate, mostly flat, and semi-arid. Not for nothing was it known as the "Great American Desert." The landscape was boring, but the weather was frequently spectacular. Cascades of hail the size of grapefruits would alternate with drought and torrid temperatures. Despite these unattractive qualities, Plains Indians such as the

Native American youngsters at the federal government's Carlisle School in Pennsylvania. How do their apparel and general appearance express the federal government's efforts to "civilize" Indian children?

Sioux, Pawnee, Comanche, Cheyenne, Crow, and Arapaho built tribal cultures around a nomadic way of life on this vast landscape. That way of life usually followed the seasonal migrations of huge buffalo herds.

Perhaps as many as 15 million buffalo moved through the Great Plains in 1865. Indians hunted buffalo not only for food, clothing, and shelter, but for a variety of other purposes as well. They turned buffalo hooves into glue, their dried feces into fuel, their bladders and kidneys into containers, their brains into a tanning compound, and their blood into a dessert pudding. And a good deal of Plains Indian religious rituals centered on the buffalo. Gender roles were also linked to the buffalo. The primary roles of Indian males were hunting and warfare; Native women, in addition to raising children, transformed the killed buffalo into nearly 100 different products.

These gender roles appear similar to those of white Americans—women doing domestic chores and men wandering the world beyond the home. But things were not so cut and dried. Unlike their white female counterparts, married Indian women usually owned their families' lodges. They owned most other significant family possessions as well. They also controlled their children's upbringing. As for men, the distinguished historian of the West, Robert M. Utley, has described the four major virtues instilled in young Indian males. Only two of them, bravery and fortitude, prepared them for the male roles of warrior and hunter. The other two virtues, generosity and wisdom, reminded men that their main task in life was not self-aggrandizement, but to help secure the well-being of the tribal community.

In the early years of the nineteenth century the United States government paid relatively little attention to the western tribes. But the annexation of Texas, and the acquisition of California and the New Mexico territory in the aftermath of the Mexican War, changed this situation. The discovery of gold in California in 1848 was a boon to the American economy and a disaster for Native Americans who lived there. In 1845 there may have been as many as 150,000 Indians in California; by the late 1850s, disease and violence reduced the Native population to about 25,000.

As Americans swept across the Great Plains headed for California and Oregon in the 1840s and 1850s, they encountered the Indians. Despite Hollywood movies depicting frequent battles between Plains Indians and white pioneers, interactions between the two groups were wary but usually friendly. And as long as the Great Plains served white people as a highway to the West Coast, and not a place of permanent settlement, most Indians tolerated the situation.

That changed as land-hungry farmers in the East, as well as some immigrant groups, were tempted by the plenitude of farmland on the Plains. The Homestead Act of 1862 opened the floodgates to white settlement on the Great Plains. Those settlements led directly to the reservation system—the government plan to contain Native populations on limited plots of land and to segregate them as much as possible from white communities.

Unwilling to accept limitations on their freedom to travel and hunt on the Great Plains, the Sioux and other tribes resisted the reservation system. They also fought against persistent violations of treaties in which the United States government had promised territory to Indians for "as long as the rivers shall run." And they were outraged by the orgy of slaughter visited on the vast buffalo herds by white hunters. By the mid-1880s, the buffalo population was nearly extinct—reduced from about *15 million* to barely *200*.

Indians won a few spectacular battles, such as the annihilation of Lieutenant Colonel George Armstrong Custer and his 265 soldiers at the Little Bighorn in Montana in 1876. But there was no hope of ultimately resisting the overwhelming military superiority of the United States army. The last major battle of the Indian wars was fought between the Seventh Calvary and a band of Sioux at Wounded Knee Creek in South Dakota in December 1891. Between 150 and 200 Indian men, women, and children were gunned down in the snow. After that, the Sioux joined most other tribes on the Great Plains who had already resigned themselves to reservation life.

This is the context for the following essay by David Wallace Adams. In the 1870s and 1880s, the United States government began a process of dissolving Indian tribal life. The goal was to "civilize" Indians, as officials put it, by "assimilating" them into American culture. Assimilation included ending the Indian tradition of tribal rather than individual ownership of land. In 1887, Congress passed the General Allotment Act (commonly known as the Dawes Act for its Senate sponsor, Henry Dawes of Massachusetts). Reservation land owned by the tribe was to be broken up into individual plots of private property—160 acres of farmland for each adult male, smaller amounts for others. The remainder of the reservation would be open to white settlers. The goal was not only to instill the idea of private property in Indians, but to alter traditional gender roles by transforming Native males from hunters to farmers. Indians who agreed to become landowners could apply for American citizenship. As a result of the Dawes Act, over time tribes on the Great Plains lost more than 80 percent of their land to whites.

The essay by David Wallace Adams deals with a related attempt to undermine Native American culture: forcibly taking Indian children from their parents and sending them to government-run schools. Indian schools were designed to "civilize" Indian children by making them Christians (the rules stipulated that the "Sabbath must be strictly observed"); "Americanizing" them (they had to speak English and were punished for using their native languages), preparing them for low-level work and traditional white gender roles (vocational training for boys, "domestic science" for girls), and drawing them away from their parents and tribal values ("Kill the Indian and save the man," as one white educator put it).

Indian parents who refused to send their children to the schools could be deprived of their government-provided food. Nevertheless, as Adams demonstrates, many Native American parents did resist the forced removal of their children.

Source: David Wallace Adams, *Education for Extinction: American Indians and the Boarding School Experience, 1875–1928* (Lawrence: University Press of Kansas, 1995), pp. 209–222.

The Indian agent Eugene White would never forget the day one seven-year-old Ute boy was enrolled at Uintah Boarding School [in eastern Utah]. The induction should have gone smoothly. Even though the lad was brought in "wild as a jack rabbit," he was delivered to the school by his father, normally a strong indicator that the boy would be cooperative. As a matter of procedure, White turned the youngster over to Fannie Weeks, the school superintendent, and Clara Granger, the matron, and invited the boy's father into the office for a bit of friendly conversation. It was all a matter of routine. The father would seek assurances he had done the right thing in bringing the boy in; the agent would praise him for his intelligence and foresight in doing so and would promise to watch over the boy like his, the agent's, very own son.

All was proceeding according to script until, as White later recounted: "I heard a tremendous disturbance break out up at the schoolhouse. Tables and chairs were being hurled about, women were screaming, children were running in every direction." When White reached the schoolhouse he could scarcely believe the scene before him. In one part of the room Superintendent Weeks was almost in a "swoon." "Her dress was torn, her face badly scratched, and two-thirds of her hair missing." In another stood Mrs. Granger, "her face and neck showed several ugly fingernail scratches, one ear was bitten almost off, and her nose was swollen to ridiculous size, and bleeding profusely." Meanwhile, crouched upon a corner woodbox was the silent but defiant culprit, "the worst scared little animal I ever saw."

Calm restored, White reconstructed events. After the boy had been turned over to the two women, they had "petted" and fed him, all the while coaxing him, in a tongue he had never heard before, to speak to them. Then Miss Weeks turned to other duties, and Mrs. Granger was to lead him to the storeroom for a new set of clothing. When Mrs. Granger

> stopped to take his hand, the little fellow sprang up on her shoulders and went to snatching, biting, and pulling hair like a real wildcat. Of course, when Miss Weeks heard the screaming she rushed heroically to the rescue of Mrs. Granger. In trying to pull the boy loose she bent Mrs. Granger over the table. The little Indian jumped off on the table, kicked Mrs. Granger on the nose, leaped upon Miss Weeks' shoulders and commenced to pluck her head. She struggled and screamed tremendously at first, but in a little while she dropped on her hands and knees and commenced to pray. When she sank entirely to the floor the little fellow

jumped off, ran to the far corner of the room and climbed up on the woodbox. The ladies said he did not utter a word—did not even whimper—during the melee, and did not look at all mad, but just seemed to be scared almost to death.

What is one to make of this episode, especially considering the fact that the defiant youth eventually became "one of the brightest and most amiable children in school"? Is it possible that once acclimated, the boy found boarding school life completely agreeable? Perhaps, but not necessarily. As will be shown shortly, the fact of resistance need not take such dramatic form. What was the reason for the boy's rebellion? Was it simply a matter of fear or the pain of being separated from his father? Was it possibly a reaction to the cultural assault about to be performed? Perhaps both of these. One wonders also if the boy's eventual cooperation was elicited by virtue of the fact that his father had voluntarily brought him to school. How different would the young Ute's adjustment have been if the agent had been compelled to take him by force?

Although the evidence for this particular episode is incomplete, the historical record on student response in general makes one thing abundantly clear: students, often in collaboration with their parents, frequently went to great lengths to resist. . . .

PARENTS' RESISTANCE TO THE SCHOOLS

The opposition of Indian parents to white schooling was both deeply felt and widespread. "The Indians have a prejudice against schools," the agent at Sac and Fox Agency reported in 1882, and another agent complained, "The Crows are bitterly opposed to sending their children to school and invent all kinds of excuses to get the children out or keep from sending them." Similarly, the Lemhi in Idaho were said to be "constantly at rebellion against civilizing elements," of which the school was a prime irritant. The problem, the agent lamented, was that the Indians in his charge had "not yet reached that state of civilization to know the advantages of education, and consequently look upon school work with abhorrence." Frustrated over recruitment problems, the superintendent of one school could only conclude that the average Indian had as much regard for education "as a horse does for the Constitution."

When parents refused to enroll their children in school, agents normally resorted to either withholding rations or using the agency police. When one agent at Fort Peck met with resistance, he sent the police to round up the children, denied rations to the parents, and then, to drive the point home, locked several of the most intractable fathers in the agency guardhouse. In any event, the forced procurement of children was usually unpleasant business. In 1886, the agent in Mescalero Apache reported:

Everything in the way of persuasion and argument having failed, it became necessary to visit the camps unexpectedly with a detachment of police, and seize such children as were proper and take them away to school, willing or unwilling. Some hurried their children off to the mountains or hid them away in camp, and the police had to chase and capture them like so many wild rabbits. This unusual proceeding created quite an outcry. The men were sullen and muttering, the women loud in their lamentations, and the children almost out their wits with fright.

Resistance to the annual fall roundup took a variety of forms. Most dramatic were those instances when an entire village or tribal faction refused to turn over their children. Sometimes parents simply slipped away from the main camp for several weeks until the pressure for students had let up. Another response was to offer up orphans or children living on the fringe of extended kinship circles. Occasionally, resistance took the form of bargaining. This occurred on those reservations where the school-age population was in excess of dormitory space, thus allowing tribal leaders and agents to negotiate a family quota until the school was filled. In other instances, the whole matter was simply dropped in the lap of tribal policemen, who in turn might put the agonizing question to a mother—Which child to give up, which to hold back? In his memoirs, Frank Mitchell readily admits that he was the first child to be given over because he was the "black sheep" of the family. Indeed, he argues that when Navajo policemen were looking for children, they consciously avoided taking the "prime." Rather, "they took those who were not so intelligent, those the People [tribal members] thought could be spared because of their physical conditions, and those who were not well taken care of."

Even after children were enrolled, parents still found ways to oppose the school. In the face of a particularly obnoxious school policy, or in time of crisis, parents were known to withdraw their children en masse or to encourage runaways. Sending delegations to the agency, drawing up petitions to Washington, and catching the ear of an inspector were other methods of protest. From the Indian Office's point of view, the most insidious form of resistance was the conscious efforts of tribal leaders to undermine the school's teachings during vacation periods by enculturating youth in the curriculum of traditional culture, a phenomenon that . . . was one of the major reasons for policymakers' preference for off-reservation schools. And finally, after 1893 some parents took full advantage of their legal right to deny transfer of older students to off-reservation institutions.

What prompted such resistance? . . . Conquered and colonized, Native Americans were hardly of a mind to view government policies, including that of compulsory education, as benign.

If nothing else, the policy of forced acculturation exacerbated an age-old characteristic of native life, tribal factionalism. "Upon close study," [Western novelist] Hamlin Garland observed in 1902,

Each tribe, whether Sioux, or Navajo, or Hopi will be found to be divided into two parties, the radicals and the conservatives—those who are willing to change, to walk the white man's way; and those who are deeply, sullenly skeptical of all civilizing measures, clinging tenaciously to the traditions and lore of their race. These men are often the strongest and bravest of their tribe, the most dignified and the most intellectual. They represent the spirit that will break but will not bow. And, broadly speaking, they are in the majority. Though in rags, their spirits are unbroken; from the point of view of their sympathizers, they are patriots.

Although Garland's analysis fails to do justice to the complexity of tribal opinion, it does offer a major motivation for resistance, namely, that a significant body of tribal opinion saw white education for what it was: an invitation to cultural suicide. If white teachings were taken to heart, almost every vestige of traditional life would be cast aside. At the very least, whites expected Indians—and here, of course, the extent of the list differed with cultures—to abandon ancestral gods and ceremonies; redefine the division of labor for the sexes; abolish polygyny [taking of more than one wife]; extinguish tribal political structures; squelch traditions of gift giving and communalism; abandon hunting and gathering; and restructure traditional familial and kinship arrangements. Across campfires, tribal elders weighed the issues. And many, like this Papago parent, asked:

> Now, are we a better people than we were years ago when we sang our own songs, when we spoke to the Great Spirit in our own language? We asked then for rain, good health and long life. Now what more do we want? What is that thought so great and so sacred that cannot be expressed in our own language, that we should seek to use the white man's words?

When such attitudes translated into a complete indictment of white ways, the agent's call for students was almost certain to meet with staunch resistance.

But opposition to schools did not always spring from a comprehensive rejection of white ways. It might just as well represent opposition to some selective aspect of the school program: punishing children for speaking their native tongue, pressuring them to convert to Christianity, forcing them to perform manual labor. Especially obnoxious to some was the school's manner of disciplining Indian children, and even more, the practice of dressing and drilling them like soldiers. One of the reasons given by Spotted Tail [a Sioux chief] for withdrawing his children from Carlisle [a federal Indian school in Pennsylvania] in 1880 was his discovery that [U.S. Army officer Richard Henry] Pratt had turned the school into "a soldier's place."

Parents also were certain to dig in their heels if they suspected that a superintendent was unusually mean-spirited. In early 1890, for instance, it appears that one of the major reasons for the Navajo's refusal to fill the agency school at Fort Defiance was the widespread belief that Superintendent

G. H. Wadleigh, nicknamed "Billy Goat" by the local Navajos, was mistreating their children. In a special investigation, one Navajo mother testified how her eight-year-old son, Henry, was confined in the school belfry for two days, only to be released in leg irons. In this condition the boy ran away, and his mother found him

> crawling on his hands and knees. His legs were tied up with iron shackles. I picked up and carried him in my arms. When I got my boy home—the Billy Goat came after the boy, and said he wanted to take him to school again. I told him to take the iron strings off of my son Henry, and I would let him go—he took the iron strings off and left my house returning to the school leaving my son with me, telling me not to tell the agent. Next day I sent the boy back to school—he is there now.

One of the [Indian] headmen in the area, Sour Water, frankly told the inspector that Billy Goat Wadleigh was a major cause for parents holding back their children. "I told Mr. Wadleigh," the old man related, "that we put our children into school to learn to read and write. That we did not want our children whipped. That the school was no jail for them.". . .

Many parents also had suspicions that boarding schools posed a threat to their children's health. When an agent at Uintah went looking for students in 1900, one of the major reasons for opposition was the school's high death rate. Still, by November the school had managed to boost its enrollment to sixty-five. And then, in the words of the agent, "came the catastrophe"—an epidemic of measles. After word reached the villages, parents swooped down upon the school and carried their children off to camp, turning them over to medicine men. Upon hearing that the Indians planned to burn down the school, the agent called in a troop of cavalry. Meanwhile, the school staff listened to the "tom-tom and the barbarous howl of the medicine men at night, and the death wail from the same wickiup [Indian hut] in the morning." A few students were coaxed back again and things began to improve until it was announced that the children were to be vaccinated. Not waiting for their parents this time, the frightened students bolted for home, and there they stayed until the year's end.

Parents especially associated off-reservation schools with death. In 1889 Washington received word from the Navajo Agency that since two boys of a leading chief had died at Carlisle, "no Navajo will listen to a proposition to send a child of his to an eastern school." By 1891, the Spokane, who had lost sixteen of twenty-one children sent to eastern schools, also were fed up with off-reservation schools. "I made up [my] mind that my people were right in being afraid to send the children away," one chief declared. "My people do not want to send their children so far away. If I had white people's children I would have put their bodies in a coffin and sent them home so they could see them. I do not know who did it, but they treated my people as if they were dogs.". . .

The bottom line was that parents resented boarding schools, both reservation and off-reservation, because they severed the most fundamental of human ties: the parent-child bond. The reservation school, by taking the child for months at a time, was bad enough; the off-reservation term of three to five years was an altogether hellish prospect, especially if the child had been shipped off without the parent's consent. "It has been with us like a tree dropping its leaves," one distressed Navajo parent protested in council.

> They fall one by one to the ground until finally the wind sweeps them all away and they are gone forever. The parents of those children who were taken away are crying for them. I had a boy who was taken from this school [Fort Defiance] to Grand Junction. The tears came to our eyes whenever we think of him. I do not know whether my boy is alive or not.

THE CRISIS AT FORT HILL

In 1892 the Indian Office experienced a year of crisis. During the course of that year several tribes of the Far West—Navajo, Hopi, Apache, Bannock, Shoshone, and Southern Ute—made a defiant stand against compulsory schooling. Not surprisingly, these acts of resistance came in the last year of [Baptist minister] Thomas J. Morgan's term [1889–1893] as Commissioner of Indian Affairs as that year marked the peak of the government's efforts to enroll children in school. As Morgan soon discovered, it was one thing to convince Congress to build schools but quite another to fill them. In 1892 the question facing Morgan was, in a supreme test of will between the Indian Office and Indian parents, if withdrawing rations and sending out the police failed to accomplish their objective, could his superiors be counted on to enforce attendance?

The situation was particularly critical at Fort Hall, Idaho, home to nearly a thousand Northern Shoshone and half as many Northern Paiute, called Bannock. Although the reservation had been established in 1867, the Fort Hall Indians had been largely ignored until the early 1880s, when the government began instructing them in agriculture. But plowing the earth did not come easily, especially to the formerly nomadic, buffalo-hunting Bannock. In 1885 the agent concluded that the Bannock were both "intractable and very improvident." Rather than till the soil, they held fast "to the primitive idea that they were not made to work, resisting stubbornly every effort to induce them to improve their condition.". . .

In 1880 the Fort Hill Boarding School opened its doors. . . . The problem was enrollment; only 62 [of a possible 200 students] were in attendance. One-half to two-thirds of the Indians at Fort Hall wanted no part of the school, and with this fact in mind, Agent S. J. Fisher, with the help of a school supervisor, began beating the bushes for students in January 1892. Lecturing parents in [tribal] council and rounding up a few orphans boosted the enrollment to 88, still far below an acceptable figure.

But Fisher pressed ahead, informing Morgan in March that "things are assuming a more serious aspect every day." Fisher reported that he had personally "taken quite a number of school children by force," but it hadn't been easy. On one occasion, he had even been compelled "to choke a so-called chief into subjection" to get hold of his children. The new crisis, Fisher went on, stemmed from the complete breakdown of the police system [usually staffed by Indians]. In particular, the five Bannock policemen had recently declared in tribal council that they would no longer force parents to give up children. Hearing of this statement, Fisher called the policemen to his office and ordered each to produce a Bannock child by the end of the week or face dismissal. When no children were brought in, Fisher, true to his word, discharged them. At that point, one of the policemen, who was also a "war chief," announced that no other Bannock would serve on the police force. This proved to be no idle threat, and Fisher could not induce any other Bannock to wear a badge. . . .

Why such opposition to the school? Actually there appear to have been several reasons. Surely a major factor was the threat that white education posed to traditional ways. In the words of the agent, Fisher, before moving to the reservation, the Bannock had been a "wild, restless, and nomadic" people, and the path to status and manhood had included stealing horses, war, and hunting, certainly not the plow. Hence, "there are a good many Indians on this reservation," proclaimed one observer, "who would much rather see their children with painted faces and decorated with feathers, spending their time in idleness about the camps than attending school."

By 1890 this aversion to the "new way" had been intensified because of the ghost dance. Many Indians in the Fort Hall area had been practicing a version of this dance since 1870, and a new "Messiah craze" now increased old revivalist longings. The ghost dance religion promised much: if the Shoshone and Bannock would but carry out prescribed rituals and remain true to tradition, the white man would vanish, deceased tribesmen would spring to life again, and the hills would be full of deer and buffalo. The impact of the movement on the school was catastrophic. As the school superintendent explained at year's end, when the envisioned paradise failed to arrive in late summer, "the defense of the medicine men was that too many parents were sending their children to the white man's school."

J. S. Leonard, special Indian agent, concurred that the "religious fanaticism" of the ghost dance religion was a primary cause of opposition to the school.

The medicine men predicted during the winter that great floods would destroy the whites, and curiously enough there have been unprecedented rains this spring, which has so emboldened the most fanatical that they are prepared to resist any efforts to stop the dances, extend farming operations, or to put their children in the school. The coming of the Indians' Messiah, according to the revelations of the medicine men, is conditioned upon the firm resistance to white man's ways. While I am of the opinion that only a few of the whole number would resort to violence, yet a great majority are dominated by the medicine men. Many of those whose children are in school, seek to take them out, and no runaway is permitted to return to the school.

A second reason for resistance was the school's poor health record. Indeed, School Superintendent George Gregory, in a letter to Morgan in late 1892, cited the "unusual amount of sickness" and the "large number of deaths" as the primary reason for parent opposition. In November 1890, scarlet fever had swept through the dormitories, striking down sixty-eight children. During the next two months, eight children died in school and another thirty, removed from the school by their parents, died at home, dropping the enrollment from 105 to 68. And that was not the end of it. In 1892 the agency physician reported that "quite a number of school children have died during the last year from various diseases but principally consumption [tuberculosis]." In self-defense, Fisher assured Washington that sanitary conditions were excellent. What he failed to mention was what government physicians actually knew to be the case: dormitories were hotbeds of contagion. Fisher, meanwhile, assessed the situation by saying that "these Indians are so badly blinded by superstition that it is impossible to reason with them." But such excuses did little to alter the fact that many of the Indians at Fort Hall viewed the school as a death house.

There is also a third possibility: parents were holding children back in protest of white encroachment and treaty violations. The Indians at Fort Hall had much to complain about. In 1888 President Cleveland had signed a bill negotiated and ratified a year before that sold some 1,600 acres to the Union Pacific for its Pocatello station, where a small but thriving white community had settled on reservation land [in violation of a treaty]. The following year saw implementation of a treaty, originally negotiated in 1880, that sold some 297,000 acres to whites who had illegally settled on Shoshone-Bannock land. Meanwhile, the Indians harbored grievances over the failure of the government to keep whites off the reservation. In a petition sent to Washington in 1895, Shoshone-Bannock chiefs protested the fact that white farmers were stealing their water, cutting their timber, and homesteading on reservation land. Although this petition was drafted three years after the crisis of 1892, it surely represented long-standing resentments. Moreover, when Inspector William Jenkin went to investigate events at Fort Hall in November 1892, his report to Washington made a direct connection between treaty violations by whites and the Indians' resistance to schools. After noting that the Indians pay "no attention to the treaty clause wherein they agree to send children to school," he observed that they were quick to "refer to the violations of the treaty by the whites." Indeed, "they refer to themselves as nations, and ask that all obligations beneficial to them be observed.". . .

Meanwhile Morgan was presented with the problem of how to fill the school. On March 11, 1892, scarcely a week after Agent Fisher had requested troops, Morgan recommended to Secretary of the Interior John Noble that the necessary military support be detached to Fort Hall. Noble, in turn, sent the recommendation to President [William] Harrison. In early May, Morgan received the following memorandum from the president: "I do not like to resort to extreme measures in these cases, and hope that this matter can be successfully managed by the agent and his police. Of course if resistance to the authority of the agent continues I will reconsider the question.". . .

Morgan was astounded. If the situation at Fort Hall had been an isolated instance of Indian defiance, perhaps patience would have been in order, but the Navajo, the Hopi, and the Ute were also creating problems. It was time to take a stand. . . . Morgan pounded away at a single theme: the entire civilization program was in jeopardy unless the government renewed its commitment to place all Indian children in school, at gunpoint if need be. . . .

The Indian Office, Morgan wrote, was "confronted with a crisis." Although the "rights of parents" should not be tread on lightly, "I do not believe that Indians like the Bannock and Navajos of Arizona—people who, for the most part speak no English, live in squalor and degradation, make little progress from year to year, who are a perpetual source of expense to the Government and a constant menace to thousands of their white neighbors, a hindrance to civilization and a clog on our progress—have any right to forcibly keep their children out of school to grow up like themselves, a race of barbarians and semi-savages.". . .

Meanwhile, the situation at Fort Hall would not go away. The issue finally came to a head in 1897, when a new agent, F. G. Irwin, sent out the police (now back in force) to round up more students. In this case, however, the police proved to be a bit overzealous and brought in a kicking, screaming fourteen-year-old girl who claimed to be married. The furious husband and several younger men shortly descended upon the school, disarmed and humiliated the police, and left with the grieving bride. The situation grew decidedly worse when a group of old women protested that almost all of the older girls in school were married. Next, a number of Indians began interfering with police attempts to round up students. Agent Irwin then did what Fisher had done five years before: he called for a troop of cavalry. This time, however, the request was granted.

On Sunday, September 26, 1897, some forty-three men of Troop F, Fourth Cavalry, boarded a train at Boise for Fort Hall Agency. A crowd assembled to watch as railroad cars were loaded with baggage, horses, pack mules, thirty days' rations, rifles, and ammunition—200 rounds for each man. "When the train pulled out," a reporter for the *Boise Statesman* recorded, "nearly every member of the departing troop had promised one or more [Indian] scalps for his friends upon his return." As it turned out, there would be no opportunity for taking scalps. Just as Morgan had predicted, the mere sight of the troops was enough. Some 40 students were collected in a single day, and by year's end, the school boasted an all-time high enrollment of 207 students. After the show of force, Superintendent Hosea Locked reported in 1898, "The opposition soon melted away, and some of the worst Indians seemed reconciled and in favor of the school."

Questions for Discussion

1. The stated purpose of Indian schools was to "Americanize" or "assimilate" these children. From your point of view, how was this strategy similar to, or different from, attempts to Americanize the children of European immigrants during those years?
2. Why did Indian parents oppose the government schools? Were they united in this opposition? What was the ghost dance, and how did it enhance Indian resistance?
3. How did white authorities justify Indian schools and forced removal of children from their parents?
4. What was the difference between on-reservation and off-reservation schooling? Which did government officials favor?

For Further Reading

Ralph K. Andrist, *The Long Death: The Last Days of the Plains Indians* (1964); Kingsley M. Bray, *Crazy Horse: A Lakota Life* (2006); Dee Brown, *Bury My Heart at Wounded Knee* (1971); Colin Calloway, *One Vast Winter Count: The Native American West before Lewis and Clark* (2003); Leonard A. Carlson, *Indians, Bureaucrats and Land: The Dawes Act and the Decline of Indian Farming* (1981); Paul H. Carlson, *The Plains Indians* (1998); Brenda J. Child, *Boarding School Seasons: American Indian Families, 1900–1940* (2000); Steven Conn, *History's Shadow: Native Americans and Historical Consciousness in the Nineteenth Century* (2004); Vine Deloria Jr., *Custer Died for Your Sins* (1969); Robert V. Hine, *The American West* (1984); Tom Holm, *The Great Confusion in Indian Affairs: Native Americans and Whites in the Progressive Era* (2005); Frederick A. Hoxie, *A Final Promise: The Campaign to Assimilate the Indians, 1880–1920* (1984); Helen Hunt Jackson, *A Century of Dishonor* (1985); Robert W. Larson, *Gall: Lakota War Chief* (2007); Patricia Limerick, *Legacy of Conquest: The Unbroken Past of the American West* (1987); Janet McDonnell, *The Dispossession of the American Indian, 1887–1934* (1991); Clyde A. Milner, Carol A. O'Connor, and Martha A. Sandweiss, eds., *The Oxford History of the American West* (1994); Jon Allen Reyhner and Jeanne M. Oyawin Eder, eds., *American Indian Education: A History* (2006); John Williams Sayer, *Ghost Dancing the Law: The Wounded Knee Trials* (1997); Alan Trachtenberg, *Shades of Hiawatha: Staging Indians, Making Americans, 1880–1930* (2004); Clifford E. Trafzer and Jean A. Keller, eds., *Boarding School Blues: Revisiting American Indian Educational Experiences* (2006); Robert A. Trennert Jr., *The Phoenix Indian School: Forced Assimilation in Arizona, 1891–1935* (1988), *Alternative to Extinction: Federal Indian Policy and the Beginnings of the Reservation System, 1846–1851* (1975); Robert M. Utley, *Lance and Shield: The Life and Times of Sitting Bull* (1993), *Cavalier in Buckskin: George Armstrong Custer and the Western Military Frontier* (1988), *Frontiersmen in Blue: The United States Army and the Indian, 1848–1865* (1981), *Custer and the Great Controversy: The Origin and Development of a Legend* (1998), *The Indian Frontier of the American West, 1846–1890* (1984).

CHAPTER

3

American Manhood and Declaring War on Spain in 1898

Kristin L. Hoganson

On February 15, 1898, an explosion ripped through the United States battleship *Maine* as it sat anchored in the waters just off Havana, Cuba. The blast killed 266 American sailors and ignited a furious cry for revenge within Congress, the press, and the general public. They accused Spain of planting the explosives, and called for war. In April they got their wish. In addition to war, the *Maine* tragedy set off a year-long series of dramatic events that launched the United States on a course that many thought a betrayal of its anticolonial ideals. On February 9, 1899, the Senate approved a treaty that ended the war with Spain and made the United States a colonial power. It now controlled a group of overseas islands: Cuba, Puerto Rico, Guam, and the Philippines. What happened?

Cuba and Puerto Rico were the last remnants of a once-sprawling Spanish colonial empire in the Western Hemisphere. Cuban nationalists were especially resentful of Spanish control of their island and, over the decades, had staged periodic revolts. They did so again in 1895, and this one turned especially brutal. In 1896 Spain sent General Valeriano Weyler to put down the rebellion. To undermine the rebel's base of support among Cuban peasants, Weyler forced thousands of rural families to move into Spanish-controlled towns. This "reconcentration" policy led to the deaths of thousands from disease, starvation, and brutal treatment. It also created outrage in the United States and widespread support among Americans for Cuban independence.

This 1900 cartoon shows pacifist and presidential candidate William Jennings Bryan branding President William McKinley an imperialist. Based on evidence presented in the article, was that a fair description of President McKinley's role in events leading up to war with Spain?

Recently elected President William McKinley resisted calls for intervention. Although sympathetic to the Cuban rebels, McKinley was focused on reviving the American economy in the aftermath of the devastating depression of 1893. He also questioned whether the United States army and navy were prepared for war. In January 1898, however, as conditions worsened in Cuba, McKinley sent the battleship *Maine* to Havana in case Americans living there had to be evacuated.

When the *Maine* exploded the following month, chants of "Remember the *Maine*, and the Hell with Spain" were heard around the country. McKinley again resisted a rush to war, instead appointing a commission to investigate the cause of the explosion. He suspected that the blast was accidental, caused by an internal explosion in the ship's coal bunkers. (Modern investigations of the explosion support this view.) And he knew that the last thing Spain wanted was war with the United States. But most were convinced the Spanish were behind the deed. When McKinley's commission concluded that the blast was external rather than internal, cries for revenge against Spain became irresistible. On April 25, 1898, Congress passed a declaration of war and McKinley signed it. It included an amendment stating that the United States had no territorial designs on Cuba and would not annex that island.

The war lasted about ten weeks and, despite nearly 3,000 American deaths, most agreed with diplomat John Hay when he called it "a splendid little war." But the proposed peace treaty generated controversy. McKinley said of his fellow Americans that imperialism was "foreign to the temper and genius of this free and glorious people." But in treaty negotiations in Paris, the United States insisted that Spain cede control of Puerto Rico, Guam, and the Philippine Islands. Also, despite its claim that Cuba would not be annexed, the United States insisted on gaining legal control of that island as well.

Those who favored these demands did so for a variety of reasons. Some believed the United States was now a world power and should join other major nations in the hunt for control of resources in Africa, the Middle East, Asia, and the Caribbean. Others wanted overseas markets so American farmers and manufacturers could sell their surplus products. Still others insisted that the United States had a God-given "mission" to uplift the people of the world by bringing them the blessings of American institutions and values. "What America wants," said one, "is not territorial expansion, but expansion of civilization. We want, not to acquire the Philippines for ourselves, but to give the Philippines free schools, a free church, open courts, no caste, equal rights to all."

Opponents to the proposed treaty countered by organizing the Anti-Imperialist League in 1898. Like those who favored annexation, the League's members had diverse points of view. Some who opposed the treaty were racists; they did not want people of color from Asia and the Caribbean as potential citizens of the United States. Others, like the writer Mark Twain, the educator John Dewey, and the social reformer Jane Addams, argued that imperialism was a betrayal of American traditions. The proposal to gain control of the Philippines was especially vexing to this group. What value, they asked, did control of a cluster of islands 7,000 miles away have to Americans? Especially when the Philippine people were themselves intent upon independence. As Mark Twain put it, "We don't intend to free, but to subjugate, the people of the Philippines."

Nevertheless, in February 1899, the Senate approved the Treaty of Paris—by a single vote. The people of the Philippines rebelled against American control, and the United States embarked upon its first—though not its last—guerilla war in Southeast Asia. Three years of brutal warfare ensued between Philippine guerillas and well-armed American soldiers. More than 125,000 American troops saw combat, and 4,000 died. Approximately 20,000 Philippine combatants were killed, along with between 200,000 and 5 million Philippine civilians. Many of the civilians died in "relocation" camps set up by American forces. Like the Spanish reconcentration program in Cuba, Americans wanted to separate Philippine peasants from the guerila forces many of them supported.

The next essay, by Kristin L. Hoganson, is a fascinating portrait of events leading up to war with Spain. Hoganson shows that many members of Congress wanted war with Spain (they were called "jingoes," or those who favor an aggressive foreign policy). Jingoes were convinced that President McKinley's reluctance to go to war indicated he was less than a "man"—and they were not shy about saying so. That McKinley had volunteered for service during the Civil War, and was cited for bravery in combat, did not matter.

Hoganson uses gender stereotypes that existed in the late nineteenth century as a means of shedding light on the debate leading up to war. For Hoganson, the various political and economic issues involved in the war debate, including sincere sympathy for the Cuban rebels, were real. She places those issues within the context of Victorian-era gender ideals as a way of demonstrating that cultural values, including ideas about gender, inform the ways in which politicians approach public policy issues, including war. Members of Congress did not want to appear "weak" or "unmanly" in the aftermath of the *Maine* disaster. And insofar as McKinley urged calm and caution, he was accused of being less than a man. As Theodore Roosevelt, an assistant secretary of the navy at the time (and soon to be president after McKinley's assassination in 1901), put it: McKinley had "no more backbone than a chocolate éclair."

Source: Kristin L. Hoganson, *Fighting for American Manhood: How Gender Politics Provoked the Spanish-American and Philippine-American Wars* (New Haven, CT: Yale University Press, 2000), pp. 68–69, 70–74, 76–78, 84, 90–94, 99–101, 105–106.

CONGRESS AND WAR

On the night of February 15, 1898, the U.S. battleship *Maine*, which had been sent to Havana to protect American citizens after an outbreak of riots, exploded and sank in Havana harbor. Two hundred and sixty-six men died in the disaster. President McKinley responded to the crisis by appointing a court of naval inquiry. The court's report, submitted on March 25, attributed the explosion to an external source. Although the commission admitted that it could not determine who was responsible, suspicion came to rest on Spain. Not only did Spain have a reputation for perfidy, but, to many Americans, it appeared that only the Spanish government had the technological capabilities to commit such an act. Americans were outraged at the thought of the Spaniards striking in the dark without giving the sleeping crew a chance to fight. "Splendid sport, indeed! How chivalric!" exclaimed one senator, who, well-versed in the chivalric paradigm for understanding the Spanish-Cuban war, interpreted the incident as yet another manifestation of Spanish treachery.

Americans who blamed the disaster on Spain regarded it as a challenge to American men, particularly because Spain refused to apologize or offer reparations and instead suggested that the men of the *Maine* were at fault. Sen. Richard R. Kenney [Democrat of Delaware] captured the leading sentiment of the day in his response to the supposed Spanish insult: "American manhood and American chivalry give back the answer that innocent blood shall be avenged, starvation and crime shall cease, Cuba shall be free. For such reasons, for such causes, America can and will fight. For such causes and for such reasons, we should have war."

The desire to assert American manhood and chivalry was highly conspicuous in Congress, the most bellicose branch of government in the early months of 1898. As it waited for the investigators' report on the cause of the incident, Congress passed a $50 million defense appropriation to move the U.S. military to a wartime footing. Congressmen were eager to show their support for the measure. The Senate did not debate the issue at all, passing the $50 million bill without discussion or an opposing vote. In the House, which also passed the bill unanimously, one word surfaced repeatedly in the discussion over the appropriation—*honor*. On the Democratic side of the House, Rep. John F. Fitzgerald [Democrat of Massachusetts] announced he would vote for the appropriation "to defend the honor and maintain the dignity of this Republic. [Great applause.]" From across the aisle, Rep. Stephen A. Northway [Republican of Ohio] proclaimed that, if necessary, "we will vote to spend not only this appropriation, but millions more in defense of our country and our country's honor. [Applause.]". . .

Although *honor* had a female component—in 1895 the *Century Dictionary* defined it as "loyalty and high courage in men and chastity in women, as virtues of the highest consideration"—in the context of the debate over war in 1898, *honor* implied male courage rather than female virtue. It referred to a male code of behavior; being honorable meant being manly. Congressmen showed that they connected the chivalrous standard of honor with ideals of manliness by declaring the opposites of honor were effeminacy and childishness. As Rep. John J. Lentz [Democrat of Ohio] questioned, would the nation defend its honor or "remain impotent"? Earlier Lentz had associated dishonor with childishness: "We have not yet awakened to realization of what 'national honor' means when we can go waddling and wabbling along, day in a day out, refusing to hear the cry of the people—'Remember the *Maine*!'"

That congressmen connected manliness and honor is also shown by their tendency to use the word *honor* alongside words that evoked manly qualities, such as *bravery, liberty, glory,* and *manhood* itself. Sen. George F. Hoar

[Republican from Massachusetts] implied that honor was related to manhood when he expressed fears that "manhood and courage and honor will follow athletes to Yale" if Harvard men did not repudiate Charles Eliot Norton, a professor who discouraged Harvard students from enlisting. At times, congressmen substituted the word *manhood* for *honor* with no perceptible change in meaning, as in a speech by Rep. James R. Mann [Republican from Illinois]: "We do not fight for a fancied slight; we do not fight for a commercial wrong; we do not fight for an increase in territory; we do not fight because our commercial spirit has been outraged; we do not fight because our land has been invaded; we fight because it has become necessary to fight if we would uphold our manhood." In sum, as used in Congress in 1898, *honor* referred to a male code of valorous and self-respecting behavior. Honor was an attribute of a potent, mature, and chivalrous man, of a man who wielded power, who was poised to fight.

The militant understanding of honor that guided the war debate reflected the new standards of passionate manhood that were in the ascendance in the late nineteenth century. As E. Anthony Rotundo and other men's historians have noted, at the end of the century, older standards of self-controlled manhood were giving way to ideals that exalted aggression, toughness, and physical prowess. Late-nineteenth-century standards of manhood valued combativeness; new words like *sissy, pussy-foot,* and *stuffed shirt* expressed the rising disfavor with self-restraint. According to the new standards, it was not so much his specific objectives that signaled a man's character but his willingness to fight for whatever he believed in. An advertisement published in the *Boston Journal* at the time of the war debate conveyed this point. The pitch for Dr. Pierce's patent medicine (which promised to cure white-livered men) ran as follows: "A woman judges a man from appearances. If he is energetic and forcible she doesn't always stop to reason why. She . . . applauds the man who fights bravely. He may win, he may lose; but he must never flag; he must fight.". . . The valorization of militant qualities in men benefited jingoes after the *Maine* disaster, as an appreciative editorial from the *Rochester Democrat and Chronicle* attests: "We may call these war orators 'hotheads,' but what would a nation be without hotheads?". . . .

The congressmen who cited honor as a rationale for war were highly vested in the term because it represented their self-worth and identity as men. They used the concept of honor to connect deeply held individual ideals to public policies. What made this tactic effective was the widespread conviction that the standards that guided individual men should be the standards that guided nations. This certainty led jingoist congressmen to draw on a man and nations analogy to argue for war. The analogy was often only implicit in jingoes' pro-war arguments, but at times they stated it straightforwardly. As Rep. Lorenzo Danford [Republican of Ohio] maintained, "No man ever went to the assistance of a weak and defenseless fellow-being who was being tortured by a brutal master and did not feel that he had done a good act, and did not receive the encouragement and plaudits of manly men; and so, no nation that goes to the relief of an oppressed people but will grow in the respect of other nations, and what is better than all, in the self-respect of his own people." In his men and nations analogy (clearly a reference to U.S. intervention in the Spanish-Cuban War), Danford suggested that intervention would reflect positively on both American men and their nation, for the virtues admired in one were the virtues admired in the other.

Taking the men and nations analogy to heart, jingoist congressmen applied their personal standards of behavior to international affairs. One congressman who concluded that violence was the only appropriate response to the *Maine* incident was Representative William Sulzer [Democrat of New York]. "I am no jingo crying for war for the sake of war," he said, "but there are things more horrible than war. I would rather be dead upon the battlefield than live under the white flag of national disgrace, national cowardice, national decay, and national disintegration." Sulzer invoked the specter of male cowardice and disgrace to convey the magnitude of the nation's cowardice and disgrace should it fail to intervene. . . . "I have no sympathy with those rash, intemperate spirits who would provoke war simply for the sake of fighting," said Rep. Joseph W. Bailey [Democrat of Texas], "and yet I would rather follow them, and suffer all the miseries and misfortunes their heedlessness would bring than to follow those other contemptible and mercenary creatures who are crying out for 'peace at any price.' [Great applause.]" Bailey elaborated on this point in a later speech: "If in order for a man to preserve his equanimity and to appear cool he must allow insults to pass unanswered, then I prefer to be classed with those who lose their heads. I would infinitely rather lose my head in resenting an insult than to lose my self-respect by submitting to be insulted." Believing that the nation should live up to his personal code of conduct, Bailey called for war.

The conviction that an affront to honor mandated combat led jingoist congressmen to conclude that submitting the *Maine* and Cuban independence issues to arbitration would be unacceptable. "There can not be and must not be any arbitration," Rep. William C. Arnold [Republican of Pennsylvania] said to loud applause. "Our honor is at stake and our flag insulted. If I insult any gentleman in this house should there be arbitration to decide and inform that gentleman whether or not he has been insulted?". . .

What made a militant defense of honor particularly appealing to jingoes was their assuredness that such a noble undertaking would foster a greater sense of brotherhood in American men. Rep. Mason S. Peters [Populist of Kansas] conveyed this idea in his statement that war would bring men from different parties together "as one man in defense of our country's honor." Other congressmen predicted that war would lead wealthy men to enlist alongside poor men and northern men to serve alongside of southerners. The remarks of Rep. Reese C. De Graffenreid [Democrat of Texas] illustrate the conviction that war was an opportunity to foster brotherhood: "The boys who wore the blue and the boys who wore the gray, reconciled and reunited in the great and grand bonds of true brotherhood and love, side by side, heart by heart, and hand in hand, will go marching on with the one purpose, the one intention, and one exclamation, that is, woe, irretrievable woe, shall betide that country, that nation, and that people against whom a brother American's blood shall cry to us from the ground.". . .

Along with reminding American men of their common citizenship, war promised to draw attention to the differences between men and women. . . . Rep. Joseph Wheeler [Democrat of Alabama] declared that war would enable American men to recapture a bygone era, an era in which mothers "taught their sons that the highest possible honor and greatest possible privilege was to fight for [their] country, its safety and its honor . . . that an ounce of glory earned in battle was worth more than a million pounds of gold." After the applause had died down he continued: "This is the teaching which we must continue to impress upon our children, and it is the best heritage we can give to those who are to follow us. This and this alone will cause the flag of our country to continue to soar higher and higher and the prestige of this great Republic to extend its power for good in the farthest corners of the earth. [Applause.]" Wheeler believed that war would restore an imagined past in which women dedicated themselves to their families and men won political authority on the battlefield, a past in which women respected men because of their fighting capacities and male honor reigned supreme in public life. . . .

The most vivid demonstration of the belief that action was the manly response to a slight of honor was the hullabaloo in the House on April 13. On that day, according to the *New York Times*, the House was in a state of "frenzied excitement as it considered the prospect for war. Representative Robert B. Henderson [Republican of Iowa] "made an impassioned appeal to the men of the American Congress to act like men. The remark was met with a storm of hisses." Democrats and Republicans accused each other of playing for political advantage. In the discussion, Rep. Charles N. Brumm [Republican of Pennsylvania] called Rep. Charles L. Bartlett [Democrat of Georgia] a liar. "Instantly," ran the description in the *New York Times*, Mr. Bartlett reached for a large bound copy of the *Congressional Record* in the desk before him, and, raising it aloft, hurled it at his adversary. It fell short and then the two antagonists rushed for each other."

The House was immediately in an uproar. Some of the ladies in the galleries screamed. Congressmen crowded into the aisles, "clinching, tugging, hauling at each other like madmen. It was like free fight in the street." Congressmen Bartlett and Brumm tried to "get at each other over the benches, but they were borne back by friends." In the end, the Speaker commanded the sergeant at arms to restore order. Armed with the great silver mace, he "repeatedly charged the thick mass of struggling members, but was as often swept aside." Another House employee was "felled by a blow on the jaw." Finally, a dozen "muscular members" of the House separated the belligerents and a semblance of order was restored. As the House again considered the resolution before it, Representative Henderson said the Republicans were "overwhelmingly in favor of action, not talk." His Republican colleagues applauded his pronouncement. The brawl in the House suggests that congressmen's aggressive personal standards of honor helped make fighting seem a legitimate, if not a desirable, option for the nation. Congressmen who saw violence as an appropriate response to personal insults viewed war with Spain as an appropriate way to resolve international disputes.

Not surprisingly, those who opposed U.S. intervention in the Spanish-Cuban War responded to the outbreak in Congress with horror. After the incident, the Boston reformer Henry B. Blackwell questioned, "How can we expect a Congress which in grave national emergency resorts to blows and personal violence, to exercise national self-restraint and intelligent adaptation of means to ends?" Blackwell interpreted the nation's path toward war as the result of misguided standards of manly behavior. An ardent women's suffrage supporter, he thought the war debate demonstrated the need to enfranchise women. That, he opined, would shift the tone of political debate from aggressive posturing to intelligent reflection. As the language of honor drowned out other ways of viewing the war issue, thus leading the nation into war, his daughter, Alice Stone Blackwell, the editor of the pro-suffrage *Woman's Journal*, cited the war debate to prove suffragists' point that Congress did not represent American women. "Congress is composed exclusively of men," wrote the younger Blackwell, "the chosen representatives of all the men of the nation. Assuming for the sake of argument that war is . . . utterly inexcusable . . . it is a Congress of men that has declared it. We must all admit that there is much division of opinion among the women of our acquaintance, while Congress is practically unanimous for war."

Alice Blackwell's assertion that the jingoist Congress did not represent American women appears well-founded, for women were more visible on the anti-interventionist side of the debate than the jingoist side. Politically active women who belonged to such groups as the WCTU [Women's Christian Temperance Union] may have sympathized with the Cubans, but . . . activist women generally viewed the prospect of war between the United States and Spain as a reflection of male values. The lack of modern polling data for this period makes it difficult to gauge the sentiments of women (and of men, for that matter) who did not take public stances on the issue, but it does seem likely that women were less enthusiastic about war than men because women experienced the dictates of honor differently. If a women and nations analogy had guided political debate, war would have seemed absurd, for chivalric traditions did not teach women to respond to insults with violence. To the contrary, one mark of a true woman was that she did not engage in fisticuffs. Furthermore, as the protected class in the chivalric paradigm, women had little reason to think that the *Maine* issue had bearing on their self-worth and identity as women. Unlike men, they were under little pressure to assume a bellicose stance.

In contrast to women, men faced considerable pressure to assume a bellicose stance on the *Maine* issue because of the standard of honor. Jingoes regarded honor not only as a guide for their own behavior, but also as a potent political tool. They realized that honor signified the manly character so necessary for wielding political authority and thus invoked the term to push their associates toward war. . . .

Jingoes' efforts to present war as the manly course of action can be seen in Rep. David A. De Armond's [Democrat of Missouri] claim that warlike sentiments represented "as assertion of American manhood by American representatives." It can also be seen in pleas exhorting men to act like men by supporting war. Representative Sulzer conflated fighting with manly character in his appeal: "Let us be men. Let us do our duty. Let us be true to our people and to our constituents." Rep. Samuel B. Cooper [Democrat of Texas] suggested that fighting was as necessary to men's honor as marriage was to women's in his assertion that men from his state would "rush to the nation's defense as swiftly and as cheerfully as ever maiden rushed to the marriage alter. . . ." By portraying themselves as honorable men and their opponents as "nervous old ladies," jingoes inside and outside of Congress equated martial policies with manly character. . . .

Jingoes' concerted effort to paint the *Maine* issue as a choice between fighting and dishonor proved so persuasive that few congressmen expressed strong opposition to war in congressional debate. Because congressmen faced so much political pressure to support war, much of the argument against it was developed not on the floors of Congress but in the press and among the wider public. When it came time to vote on a declaration of war, both houses of Congress voted unanimously in favor of it—the Senate in a closed executive session, the House in a resounding chorus of ayes that sparked a round of applause and some cheers from the floor and the galleries. The congressmen who had reservations put them aside lest they or their nation appear less than completely committed to honor.

PRESIDENT MCKINLEY'S "BACKBONE" AND WAR

Those who believed that the manly response to Spanish insults was war won a significantly wider following after the *Maine* disaster. . . . McKinley appointed a court of naval inquiry and urged Americans to suspend judgment until the investigators had reported on the cause of the explosion. Yet even after the investigators submitted a report saying that an external mine had triggered the explosion, McKinley continued to urge restraint. He praised the country for its self-control as he continued to seek a peaceful solution to the conflict. He told his callers that he wanted to avoid war. Instead of assuming a belligerent stance in his message to Congress of March 28, he asked for continued deliberation. Through the American minister in Madrid, McKinley tried to settle the issue without resorting to war. He asked Spain for an armistice in Cuba, negotiations between Spain and the Cuban insurgents mediated by the United States, and a revocation of the Spanish "reconcentration" policy [forced removal of rural Cuban peasants into towns controlled by Spanish forces] that had caused so much suffering in Cuba. He hinted at the need for Cuban independence but did not demand it outright.

When the Spanish government replied on March 31, it offered to arbitrate the *Maine* incident, abolish reconcentration, and submit the Cuban problem to an insular parliament. But Spain would not suspend hostilities or accept American mediation. After the Spanish reply, McKinley prepared another message to Congress, which he delivered on April 11. In this message, McKinley still did not ask for war. He asked for discretionary power to use the nation's military force, but he kept the possibility of further negotiations alive. Jingoes voiced disappointment at his continued restraint.

McKinley's adversaries responded to the president's refusal to declare war by questioning his manhood. Editorials from the *Atlanta Constitution* illustrate this tactic. One described McKinley as a "goody-goody man" a disappointment in comparison to more militant versions of manhood. Another said that the Cuban crisis revealed McKinley's inability to fill the executive chair. "At this moment there is great need of a man in the White House," it opined. "The people need a man—an American—at the helm." A later editorial continued the theme. It said the people wanted a "declaration of American virility." Only the president, it concluded, was indifferent to the people's demands.

Across the country, anti-administration newspapers joined in the chorus. The *New York Journal* looked forward to seeing "any signs, however faint, of manhood in the White House." "There are manly and resolute ways of dealing with treachery and wrong. There are unmanly and irresolute ways," said a *New York World* editorial which argued that McKinley had not been manly and resolute in his speech to Congress on March 28. The *Chicago Tribune* called McKinley's Cuban policy "a weak, ineffectual, pusillanimous policy," thereby impugning the character of the president. . . . These papers wielded the aggressive working-class standards of manliness that were gaining popularity among middle-class men in the late nineteenth century to contend that the president's self-restraint indicated a lack of manly fiber. They downplayed the moral dimension to manliness and proposed that a real man settled disputes with force; he did not hesitate to use military power.

The press was not alone in questioning the president's manhood. Constituents wrote to their congressmen to complain about McKinley's character. One voter heatedly declared, "It is the verdict of the people that we have an executive whose timidity and lack of nerve and bravery and appreciation of American honor and dignity unfit him for the presidency in such a crisis." Bellicose congressmen agreed that McKinley was not demonstrating enough manliness. Sen. John W. Daniel [Democrat of Virginia] accused the administration of having lost the "virile instincts of the American people." Sen. George Turner [Populist of Washington] described the administration's response to the crisis as "lame, halting, and impotent," characteristics that seemed as likely to refer to the president as to his policies. "He wabbles, he waits, he hesitates. He changes his mind," said Rep. William Sulzer . . . in disgust.

The critics' various complaints—that the president was weak, indecisive, effeminate, cowardly, and ineffectual—were encapsulated in the contention that he lacked backbone. Theodore Roosevelt's remark that "McKinley has no more backbone than a chocolate éclair" is the best-known evaluation of McKinley's spine, but it was by no means the only disparaging one. In early April the president of a Wisconsin savings bank groused in a letter to Sen. John C. Spooner [Republican of Wisconsin], "Our president has no back-bone." A few days later, a New Hampshire man wrote his senator, [Republican] William E. Chandler, that McKinley should step aside because he did not have "the nerve and the backbone to resent such damnable insults." After commenting that the president did not seem to have "sufficient back-bone even to resent an offense as gross as this," the *New Orleans Times-Democrat* said all was not lost, for Congress could declare war without him. . . .

Realizing that the crisis lent weight to the aspersions cast upon McKinley, the president's allies responded by attributing to him qualities—such as bravery and strength—that even his opponents associated with man-hood. The president's self-control, wrote one supporter, demanded more courage than "any which is needed amid the excitement of battle." The *Los Angeles Times* praised McKinley for his "stamina, nerve, and backbone," and the *Baltimore Sun* applauded his "firmness and strength of character" and said that at times the "moral courage not to fight" should be valued more highly than the "physical courage to fight." As the positive references to McKinley's courage, strength, and backbone indicate, McKinley's defenders drew on the same terms used by his critics. They, too, recognized the impor-tance of appearing manly to wielding political power, and hence they tried to refute the slurs against McKinley. . . .

Significantly, those who championed McKinley drew on old middle-class ideals of manhood that placed more emphasis on self-control, moral virtue, courage of convictions, and strength of principle than on violent out-breaks or bellicose posturing. They applauded McKinley's "firmness and strength of character" and cited the president's "dignity," "firmness," and "statesmanlike" behavior to prove that he had the manly character necessary to lead. The restrained version of manliness that many McKinley loyalists endorsed was consistent with their circumspect approach to international relations. Those who valued mental and moral rather than physical power in the leaders were more likely to consider the president's course to be, as one adherent described it, "wise, manly and just."

As he contemplated how to respond to the sinking of the *Maine*, McKinley faced a number of issues: humanitarian concerns, the interests of American businessmen in Cuba, the impact of a war on the entire American economy, and the potential for coaling stations and strategic bases. Added to these were concerns for his reputation and credibility as a leader and the implications of his image for his party. McKinley suffered the constraint of being a first-term president in a political system that valued a military style of manliness in leaders. McKinley was deeply sensitive to public opinion. As he assessed the tenor of the war debate, he undoubtedly realized that his perceived cowardice in foreign affairs was undermining his credibility as a leader, and that it threatened to sink his administration along with the *Maine*.

The president had good reason to be apprehensive about charges of cowardice because, regardless of his youthful Civil War record, he was not universally esteemed as a great military hero or forceful leader. The up-and-coming Theodore Roosevelt was not alone in thinking that despite his military record, McKinley was "not a strong man." The sedate McKinley did not embody the new standards of active, athletic, aggressive manhood. He had never enjoyed hunting, and when he tried fishing once as president, in his frock coat and silk hat, he capsized the boat and ruined his shoes and pants. The clean-shaven McKinley was the only president between Andrew Jackson and Woodrow Wilson not to have a beard or mustache, signs of masculinity.

On March 30 McKinley burst into tears as he told a friend that Congress was trying to drive the nation into war. He remembered the Civil War [in which he fought] as a horrible conflict and had hoped that international arbitration would replace war as a means of settling international disputes. McKinley did not want war, but neither did he want to wreck his presidency. Aware of his growing reputation as a spineless leader and recognizing that Republican legislators would be unwilling to go along with his new peace initiative, McKinley drafted a message in early April that put the Cuban matter into the hands of the infamously bellicose Congress. . . .

On April 19 Congress submitted a resolution to the president authorizing him to intervene to end the war in Cuba. McKinley felt he had no choice but to sign, although he knew the resolution would surely lead to war. Spain immediately severed diplomatic relations with the United States. On April 22 the United States imposed a naval blockade of Cuba; on April 24 Spain declared war; and on April 25 McKinley asked Congress to declare war. Congress did so eagerly, predating the start of war to April 21.

McKinley's scanty personal records mean that arguments about his motives (gender-based or otherwise) ultimately must be based on conjecture. But even though McKinley did not record his rationale, the debate over his backbone shows that gendered ideas about leadership limited the range of politically viable options available to him. McKinley's backbone became a central issue in the debate over war because political activists, whether Republicans, Democrats, or Populists, believed that manly character mattered in politics. Men from across the country agreed that the character of the nation's leaders attested to the acceptability of their policies, and following the *Maine* disaster, increasing numbers of men demanded a militant leader. Aware of the links between manhood, military prowess, and political power (indeed, eager to take advantage of them in the campaign of 1896), McKinley reached the logical conclusion that war was politically imperative. His decision to join the jingoes was less a reflection of his courage or cowardice, strength or weakness, than an acknowledgment that the political system he operated in would not permit any other course of action.

Questions for Discussion

1. According to the author, how did congressmen's views about honor and manhood help lead the United States into war with Spain? Do you agree with her argument?
2. How were ideas about honor applied differently to women and men?
3. Both the defenders and detractors of President McKinley used terms such as "manhood" and "backbone." How did each group define these terms?
4. As described in this essay, the executive and legislative branches acted as though they had a co-equal role to play during the *Maine* crisis, the war debate, and the declaration of war. In your opinion, would that be true today?

For Further Reading

Michael Adams, *The Great Adventure: Male Desire and the Coming of World War I* (1990); Harriet Hyman Alonso, *Peace as a Woman's Issue: A History of the U.S. Movement for World Peace and Women's Rights* (1993); Gail Bederman, *Manliness and Civilization: A Cultural History of Race and Gender in the United States, 1880–1917* (1995); Benjamin Beede, ed., *The War of 1898 and U.S. Intervention, 1898–1934* (1994); Robert L. Beisner, *Twelve Against War: The Anti-Imperialists, 1898–1900* (1968); H. W. Brands, *Bound to Empire: The United States and the Philippines* (1992); Brian Damiani, *Advocates of Empire: William McKinley, the Senate, and American Expansionism, 1898–1899* (1987); John M. Dobson, *Reticent Expansionism: The Foreign Policy of William McKinley* (1988); Peter Filene, *Him/Her/Self: Sex Roles in Modern America*, 3rd ed. (1998), Frank Freidel, *The Splendid Little War* (1958); Lewis L. Gould, *The Spanish-American War and President McKinley* (1982); Rebecca Grant and Kathleen Newland, eds., *Gender and International Relations* (1991); David Healy, *Drive to Hegemony: The United States in the Caribbean, 1898–1917* (1988); Michael Kimmel, *Manhood in America: A Cultural History* (1996); Brian McAllister Linn, *The Philippine War, 1899–1902* (2002); Paul T. McCartney, *Power and Progress: American National Identity, the War of 1898, and the Rise of American Imperialism* (2006); G. J. A. O'Toole, *The Spanish War: An American Epic—1898* (1986); Nell Irvin Painter, *Standing at Armageddon: The United States, 1877–1919* (1987); David Pugh, *Sons of Liberty: The Masculine Mind in Nineteenth-Century America* (1983); Harvey Rosenfeld, *Diary of a Dirty Little War: The Spanish-American War of 1898* (2000); Anthony E. Rotundo, *American Manhood: Transformations in Masculinity from the Revolution to the Modern Era* (1993); Joseph Smith, *The Spanish-American War: Conflict in the Caribbean and the Pacific, 1895–1902* (1994); David Trask, *The War with Spain in 1898* (1981); David Traxel, *1898: The Birth of the American Century* (1998).

4

The Crusade to "Purify" America by Driving Out the Chinese

Jean Pfaelzer

Between 1849 and 1882, approximately 250,000 Chinese entered the United States. The Chinese were not strangers to the Western Hemisphere. Since the early nineteenth century, hundreds of thousands of them had worked as indentured servants, or close to outright slaves, in the Caribbean and South America. More than 150,000 Chinese "coolies" (an English translation of the Chinese word *kuli*, meaning "bitter labor") worked in the Cuban sugar fields; more than 80,000 worked the mines of Peru. But most of those who came to the United States as part of the Gold Rush after 1848 did so voluntarily. The reception they received, culminating in the Chinese Exclusion Act of 1882, is among the most shameful episodes in American ethnic history.

The written characters in Chinese for "San Francisco" mean "Gold Mountain." It was the lure of gold that inspired the first major influx of Chinese. About 15,000 came to the gold fields of northern California in the 1850s. Anti-Chinese sentiment surfaced quickly. In 1854, the California Supreme Court ruled that Chinese testimony against white persons was not admissible in court. Among other things, this left Chinese immigrants vulnerable to white violence. Most Chinese were forced out of the gold-mining business. Whites developed the stereotypes that clung to the Chinese well into the twentieth century—they worked cheaply, lowered wages, and "took" jobs from whites; they were lazy, sexually indulgent, and smoked opium; they were "sneaky" and "mysterious." And they were not Christians.

This political cartoon depicts Uncle Sam "cleansing" the country by kicking out the Chinese. Why were words such as "cleansing" and "purifying" used in the contexts of immigration in general and Chinese immigrants in particular?

It is impossible to know exactly how many Chinese were victims of violence between 1850 and 1900, but it is safe to say hundreds were murdered. In 1871 in Los Angeles, rioting whites lynched twenty-one Chinese men and stabbed two others to death; in 1885, twenty-eight were killed in Rock Springs, Wyoming, while the rest of the Chinese community was expelled and their homes burned; in 1887, the mutilated bodies of thirty-one Chinese were tossed into Oregon's Columbia River. During these years, organized boycotts against Chinese businesses were common, as were laws designed to prohibit the employment of Chinese in various occupations.

Anti-Chinese sentiment was not only common among whites of all classes, it was out in the open and respectable. This was especially true in

California, where two-thirds of Chinese immigrants settled. In 1880 the governor of California declared March 4 a legal holiday. The purpose of the holiday was to rally whites throughout the state to assemble for anti-Chinese demonstrations and parades.

While most whites in the West wanted Chinese immigration halted, many employers did not. Farmers and railroad companies were especially impressed by the dedication and effectiveness of Chinese workers. For example, as many as 15,000 Chinese men worked on one of the most monumental engineering feats of the nineteenth century: the transcontinental railroad project. The owners of the Central Pacific Railroad valued Chinese workers because they took on and accomplished the most dangerous jobs—including drilling and demolition of solid rock in the Sierra and Rocky mountains. They were valued by the railroad for other reasons. Unlike white workers, the Chinese did not drink or fight (though they liked to gamble after work). They kept in shape by eating balanced, traditional Chinese meals, mainly fish and fresh vegetables; white workers mostly ate beef, potatoes, and butter. Also, the Chinese kept themselves clean. They washed every night after work; most Americans in those days bathed once a week.

Between 1,200 and 2,000 Chinese workers lost their lives building the Central Pacific—the bones of more than 1,200 of them were returned to China for burial. As the owners of the Central Pacific noted, the project could not have been completed as quickly or as efficiently without the labor of Chinese immigrants. On May 10, 1869, the Union Pacific, heading west, met the Central Pacific, heading east, at Promontory Point, Utah. The country was officially linked by rail. There were no Chinese in photographs celebrating the momentous event.

The demand for Chinese workers inspired the Burlingame Treaty of 1868. The United States and China agreed to unlimited mutual immigration—although without the possibility of citizenship. But the overwhelming hostility of whites toward the Chinese created an atmosphere that eventually ended immigration from China. In 1870, Congress passed a law that limited citizenship to white persons and "aliens of African nativity" (in other words, to African Americans who lived in the country prior to the Civil War and their descendants). The law was designed to exclude Asian immigrants from becoming citizens. The Page Act of 1875 (discussed in the next essay) prohibited most Chinese women from entering the country. And in 1882, Congress enacted the Chinese Exclusion Act, which put an end to almost all immigration from China for ten years. It was later extended indefinitely.

While some Chinese managed to enter the country each year, the Exclusion Act achieved its main goal: lowering America's Chinese population. In 1880 approximately 105,000 Chinese lived in the United States; in 1900 there were 89,000 and by 1920 only 61,000. The Act did not end violence against the Chinese. Organized attempts to forcibly remove Chinese from West Coast cities and towns occurred regularly throughout the 1880s. Chinese often resisted these assaults, arming themselves for self-defense.

They also mounted legal challenges to discriminatory laws. For instance, they challenged the constitutionality of the 1882 Exclusion Act—but it was upheld by the United States Supreme Court. Exclusion of Chinese immigrants remained in force until World War II. In a friendly gesture toward its wartime Chinese ally, in 1943 the United States officially revoked the Chinese Exclusion Act of 1882.

In the following essay Jean Pfaelzer describes a fascinating aspect of the anti-Chinese fever that gripped the United States in those years. In addition to their fears about competing with Chinese workers, Americans also believed that the Chinese would undermine the nation's moral and physical health. Specifically, they were afraid that Chinese women would infect white men with sexually transmitted diseases. Ultimately, they believed the presence of Chinese would destroy the American family. Public policies seeking to limit Chinese immigration were linked to fears about personal "pollution" of one sort or another.

It should be kept in mind that many of the Chinese women brought to the United States between 1850 and 1882 were prostitutes. As Pfaelzer points out, most of these women were sold into sexual slavery in China, often as very young girls. Pfaelzer also shows how many of them resisted and tried to escape this bondage.

It is also important to remember that the vast majority of Chinese immigrants were men. The presence of huge numbers of men living without women helped create a "market" for prostitution. For instance, in 1880 there were fewer than 5,000 Chinese women in the country. Put another way, there were twenty-one Chinese men for every Chinese woman.

Source: Jean Pfaelzer, *Driven Out: The Forgotten War Against Chinese Americans* (New York: Random House, 2007), pp. 89–106, 110–111.

On Sunday, April 30, 1876, a doctor in Antioch [California], a small town near the confluence of the Sacramento and San Joaquin Rivers, announced that seven young "sons of respectable citizens" were under his treatment after visiting a Chinese house of prostitution. When parents heard that their boys had syphilis, they quickly gathered a group of about forty town residents, divided into teams of five, and marched to Chinatown, which was built on the edge of town by the docks.

The enraged parents pounded on the doors of each of the brothels—the Chinese "dens" or "green mansions"—and warned the Chinese women to leave town by three o'clock that afternoon "or trouble would ensue." The women tied up their clothing and bedding in scarves or shawls and stuffed whatever they could into baskets. With their few belongings swinging from heavy shoulder poles, they trudged to the pier.

As the mob grew, rather than wait for the next steamer bound for San Francisco, the women climbed into a fishing boat and set sail down the San Joaquin River toward Stockton. Also onboard was the local Chinese contractor, probably the pimp or the owner of several of the women. As the laden boat pulled out, the townspeople of Antioch watched from the dock, grimly pleased.

Despite the town's rage it is likely that many of the Chinese women desperately wanted to remain in Antioch. Like other Chinese prostitutes in western rural towns, many had fled from slavery in San Francisco to the river town, forty miles to the northeast. If they were shipped back to San Francisco, they faced a return to sexual slavery.

On that bleak Sunday afternoon, the white parents forced only the Chinese women out of town; the Chinese men, mostly gardeners, fishermen, and launderers, were, for the moment, allowed to remain. The residents decided not to "disturb the serenity of the Sabbath" until church was over. But that night the town congratulated itself on driving out the prostitutes "in a dignified manner."

The next afternoon, word flew through the town that the Chinese women had returned. By eight o'clock that evening, Chinatown was on fire. The new fire department ignored the blaze and refused "to stay the progress of the fire fiend." Although Antioch's Chinatown was a jagged row of wooden shacks, it probably could have been saved, as the segregated quarters had been built along the river at Smith's Landing and were connected to the water through narrow tunnels. But as the town watched, all but two buildings collapsed. Terror-stricken, most of the Chinese men fled into the night.

The next morning volunteers demolished the last two buildings in Antioch's Chinatown. The remaining Chinese paid twenty-five cents each for a ticket and boarded the side-wheeler *Amador*, the next steamer bound for San Francisco. The local paper cheered, "Antioch is now free from this disreputable class."

The purge of the women and the torching of Chinatown capped years of racial contempt in Antioch. Most of the Chinese had immigrated to Antioch from the Pearl River delta in China, in Guangdong Province. They were river people, skilled in building dirt levees against floods and in farming marshlands and bottomlands. Passengers and freight to and from the Sacramento delta traveled mainly by the water, and during the heyday of the paddle-wheel steamboats, Chinese passengers were required to stay below in the hold on the "China Deck"—the most dangerous place onboard. If the ship's boiler blew, a constant threat on riverboats, few Chinese passengers would survive. In October 1865 the boiler exploded on the steamship *Yosemite*, and of the 150 travelers drowned or burned to death, 100 were Chinese.

Antioch expressed its contempt for its Chinese residents with codes geared toward segregation, harassment, and, ultimately, expulsion. To enforce segregation, Ordinance 33 imposed a one hundred dollar fine, an amount equal to two months' salary for most white men, on any person caught watching an opium smoker. Chinese people could not own land, and a curfew required that they be off the streets by sunset. If a Chinese man violated the curfew, a town officer could cut off his queue [long braids of hair worn by Chinese men]. . . .

The Antioch purge soon spread south to El Cerrito, where many Chinese men were fired from the Starr Flour Mill and from the Vigorite Powder Works at Point Isabel, where they produced dangerous explosives. As news of the [1877 anti-Chinese] Kearney riots in San Francisco reached north into the delta towns, other Chinese working along the river prepared to flee. By 1877 all the Chinese at the Black Diamond coal mines were let go and forbidden to return, even as "washmen." That year fruit growers on the fertile delta mud islands and along the marsh banks of the Sacramento River met in the little town of Isleton and agreed "not to rent or lease land to Chinamen, nor hire them to perform labor upon our ranches."

The eviction of prostitutes galvanized the movement to drive out rural Chinese by purging the women. In the early spring of 1886, during the Chinese roundups in Humboldt County, Sheriff Eugene Demming arrested Chinese women in the lumber town of Arcata and charged them with prostitution. With their bonds set at the exorbitant sum of five hundred dollars, they remained in prison until the trial. On April 16 the women were shipped out of Arcata under Demming's guard. Newspaper coverage and legal documents end the women's story with their expulsion. But what happened to these enslaved women, whose status was so fragile? What became of the Chinese prostitutes forcibly driven from Truckee later that year?

The notion of impure Chinese bodies infecting the young white manhood of the United States provided a powerful physical metaphor for the "cleansing" that would take place. (The issue of the subsequent contagion to white wives was always patent and always repressed.) The Antioch roundup was also anchored in the assumption that Chinese women were slaves, bodily commodities who could be sold, moved, removed.

THE PROSTITUTE TRADE

In the nineteenth century, brothels were often called "convents," "hotels," or "green mansions." In a short poem a Chinese prostitute in California decried her few choices:

> A green mansion is a place of filth and shame
> Of lost chastity and lost virtue
> Most repulsive is to kiss the customer on the lips
> And let them fondle every part of my body
> I hesitate, I resist
> All the more ashamed, beyond words
> I must by all means leave this troupe of flowers and rouge;
> Find a nice man and follow him as his woman.

Chinese prostitutes shipped back to San Francisco would likely be returned to a street-level "crib," where kidnapped girls were often held, usually by a member of the Chinese Six Companies [an alliance of elite Chinese merchants and contractors]. Locked in cages or tiny chambers facing busy Jackson or Dupont Street, they were forced to solicit men who passed by; then their owners or madams would open the pen and draw a curtain while the girl serviced her customer, white or Chinese. Soon the city would move the cribs to back alleys, hidden from the view of downtown customers and merchants.

Generally, the top price for sex was seventy-five cents. A "lookee" cost between a dime and a quarter and was pitched to the popular belief that there were anatomical differences between Chinese and Caucasian women. . . .

In 1869 the *San Francisco Chronicle* called the growing trade in Chinese prostitutes "the importation of females in bulk," reporting that "each China steamer now brings consignments of women, destined to be placed in the markets." Some Chinese girls arrived in heavily padded crates, billed as freight, and Chinese brokers bribed custom and immigration officials in San Francisco to let them enter. Others were sent by ship captains and then placed or sold by contractors. Some made their own way to rural towns by trains or wagons; others entered from Canada or disembarked in coastal towns, landing in hidden bays or coves up and down the Pacific coast. Often they followed the routes of Chinese men. In response to demands for prostitutes from Chinese miners and vegetable growers, brokers sent many Chinese women into interior mining and lumber towns under the guard of special agents. There the women were sold to the "trade" or to individual men at rates ranging from two hundred to five hundred dollars "per head."

Most Chinese prostitutes in the American West had been in bondage since a young age, sometimes since infancy. Many were "go-away girls," female babies who were sold, abandoned, or fastened to the wall of the city of Chaozhou, a prefectural city twenty miles from the port of Shantou. There a newborn baby girl could be disposed of—deposited in a basket where anyone wishing to own a female child was at liberty to remove her and do with her as he liked. Most Chinese prostitutes came through San Francisco, imported by criminal societies that by 1860 had taken control of the trade. Brokers in China procured the girls, kidnapping them off the streets or purchasing them from destitute families and selling them at great profit in San Francisco. The enslaved children were brought to the United States by large syndicates that owned as many as eight hundred girls, ranging in age from two to sixteen.

Wealthy Chinese individuals, male and female, paid about eighty dollars to a broker for a girl in China, or between four hundred and a thousand dollars if they bought her in an organized slave sale in San Francisco, often in a designated cellar in Chinatown. After the Exclusion Act of 1882, a one-year-old girl cost a hundred dollars, a girl of fourteen—often termed a "daughter"—cost twelve hundred. The designation of "daughter" usually meant that the girl was part of the *mui tsai* or "little sister" system under which impoverished parents sold a young daughter into domestic service, usually stipulating that she be freed through a marriage when she turned eighteen. During her time as a bond servant, she earned no wages, was not free to leave her "employer," was usually overworked, often suffered physical abuse from her mistress, and was sexually available to her master or his son.

To get around the Thirteenth Amendment and laws banning indentured contracts, buyers often paid the purchase price to the girl, who turned it over to her new owner as she marked or signed a contract indenturing herself. In a typical contract a girl promised to "prostitute my body for the term of _____ years. If, in that time, I am sick one day, two weeks shall be added to my time; and if more than one day, my term of prostitution shall continue an additional month. But if I run away from the custody of my keeper, then I am to be held a slave for life." Since sickness included periods of menstruation, the length of a prostitute's contract was inevitably extended indefinitely. Despite the abolition of slavery, the sale of humans endured in the West. . . .

Estimates of the number of Chinese prostitutes in San Francisco in 1870 vary from about one thousand to sixteen hundred. The figures are uncertain because they depended on women's willingness to risk self-disclosure, the political goals of local census enumerators, the desire in the public imagination to eroticize the Chinese community, and a widespread intention among whites to downplay the number of Chinese families. . . .

CONTAGION AND IMPURITY

What began when one community purged its Chinese prostitutes quickly became an all-out rout. Chinese women, both desired and despised by whites, were thought to carry within them the power to taint the physical and moral purity of the nation. The infection of the children in Antioch evoked the era's fears of epidemics of diphtheria, tuberculosis, and cholera and raised concerns about the health, safety, and stability of a family.

The belief that perhaps 90 percent of the Chinese prostitutes in San Francisco, for example, were at some time infected with venereal diseases encouraged towns up and down the coast to expel Chinese women or pass anti-prostitution ordinances that had little to do with the ethics of trafficking in female slaves. Rather, the codes and the roundups often followed a civic investigation or newspaper account of young white boys, usually aged from ten to twelve, frequenting the "cribs" or brothels in rural Chinatowns. Generally it was the infection of white males, rather than the enslaved status of the Chinese women or the risk of contagion to white women or Chinese men, that prompted civic action.

The dangers of syphilis were indeed real throughout California, and the blame returned again and again to Chinese women. During the California State Senate investigations of Chinese immigration in 1876, a series of doctors testified to the prevalence of the disease among Chinese prostitutes and its impact on white society. The testimony of Dr. Hugh Huger Toland, a member of the San Francisco Board of Health, haunted the national press and the minds of thousands of white parents when he reported cases of a particularly virulent strain of syphilis in white boys as young as five who, he claimed, contracted the disease from Chinese prostitutes.

The anti-Chinese forces had found a new and powerful rationale in medical language and concepts of racial contamination. By the mid-1870s, physicians were making dire claims about the inevitable transmission of syphilis from Chinese prostitutes to white males and, with quiet implication, to white wives, as though contagion flowed only in one direction. The pulpit, press, and medical profession declared that all Chinese women were of "the most abject and satanic conception[s] of human slavery and the source of contamination and hereditary diseases.". . .

In an evangelical era, the presence of Chinese prostitutes confirmed the infidelity of married white men and their easy repudiation of Christian morality. Syphilis predicted the fate of the family and the fate of the family-less man in the West. To white women, Chinese prostitutes defiled the Christian ideal of chastity; to white men they represented the frontier promise of freedom from marriage. But syphilis visibly exposed the sexual double standard for men and women even as most medical discussions of the disease excluded its transmission between spouses. Still, the cure was to round up and drive out Chinese women. . . .

By the mid-1870s it was well-known that syphilis was transmitted sexually, but it was also thought to be hereditary. Physicians did little to lessen the idea that all Chinese bodies carried the disease and that their very presence could infect whites. In 1878, for instance, the *Medico-Literary Journal* warned that if Chinese servants were allowed to raise white children, or cook, clean, and launder in white homes, syphilis would spread from the inevitably afflicted Chinese body into the entire household. Yet even in towns that had purged the Chinese, advertisements in popular newspapers for a "secret formula" for curing syphilis and other venereal diseases testified to how common it was in white prostitutes, who continued working their trade after their Chinese competition was sent away on ship, wagon, or foot, and in white men who had transmitted it to their wives.

By targeting sexual relations between Chinese prostitutes and white men, physicians, journalists, cartoonists, and politicians blamed Chinese women for the new forces challenging the ideal if illusory American home. As women left the farm and family to work outside the home, they initiated public demands for better pay, for a fifty-four hour workweek, for sanitation, for the vote, and for job safety, exposing the myth of the protective cult of true womanhood. Emigration from Ireland and eastern Europe was bringing thousands of single men and women to industrializing America, as factory work and night shifts pulled both men and women from their homes. Millions of workers lived in tenement housing similar to the "Chinese dens" mocked in editorials and cartoons. The Victorian family was already teetering precariously in the West, where there was a large ratio of white men to white women and an even larger ratio of Chinese men to Chinese women.

The purge of the prostitutes in Antioch also played to fears about the seductive female body, fears intensified in rural California by the low number of white women in the Pacific Northwest. Many white women seized on the image of the diseased and enslaved Chinese prostitute to distinguish their own limited status and uphold an image of their own virtue. . . .

THE PAGE ACT OF 1875

The task of vilifying Chinese women fell to ministers, of criminalizing them to town councils, of banishing them to police and to mobs, but the task of controlling their immigration fell to Congress. Between 1870 and 1874 the California legislature tried to criminalize the entry of "lewd and debauched" Asian women by threatening steamship companies with heavy fines for transporting unmarried women. But only Congress, ruled the federal courts, had the authority to exclude the "pestilential immorality," and in 1875, at the urging of California, it passed the Page Act. The Page Act prohibited the immigration of any Chinese woman who was not a merchant's wife and any "Mongolian" woman who entered the country for the purpose of prostitution.

Why target the Chinese women in the West when, in fact, there were so few? In 1855 only 2 percent of the Chinese population in the United States was female; by 1875 it was about 4 percent, or one Chinese woman for every twenty-one Chinese men. These skewed ratios had an overlay of causes, including the U.S. government's policy of keeping the Chinese population both low and temporary by preventing the entry of Chinese women and by assaulting those already here.

But other social and global factors were also at play. News of kidnapped and enslaved Chinese women forced to work as prostitutes on Gold Mountain [as the Chinese called California] kept thousands of Chinese women from migrating. Many other Chinese women chose to remain in China, fearful that their husbands might have concubines or other wives in the United States. Further, a Chinese woman was trained to follow the "three obediences"—obey her father at home, her husband after marriage, and her eldest son if she was widowed. Unlike a man, a Chinese woman had no right to divorce or remarry, even if her husband died. A man, however, was permitted to commit adultery, to divorce, to remarry, to practice polygamy, and to discipline his wives as he saw fit. Foreign missionaries in China also discouraged Chinese women's emigration, depicting life in the United States as depraved, promiscuous, and dangerous. Thus Chinese women were reluctant to emigrate, and Chinese men were forced to return to China, albeit temporarily, to have a family. . . .

Most of the Chinese women who immigrated to the American West as prostitutes came under the control of the Chinese Six Companies, based in San Francisco. The companies arranged for their procurement, shipping, and sale and controlled the urban brothels. Information about how Chinese women were kidnapped or sold into "sexual slavery" is mostly still hidden to history. But Chinese women made every effort to escape San Francisco, Sacramento, and Seattle, to live in remote towns outside the command of the Six Companies and settle into the familiarity of village life. . . .

Concern over Chinese prostitution was part of a larger American fascination with the sexuality of Chinese women and men. Although half of the Chinese men who immigrated to the United States were married, cartoons in popular magazines and in trade cards alluded to their homosexuality, suggesting that Chinese men disregarded marriage, family, and respectable womanhood. These hostile caricatures may have derived from homophobic fears surrounding crowded all-male mining communities, small-town boardinghouses, and tent camps where men cooked and sewed for themselves.

Before the Chinese Exclusion Act of 1882, 90 percent of Chinese immigrants were single men. In the rural towns that expelled the Chinese these numbers were even more skewed. Yet the Chinese women who entered, prostitutes included, formed the fabric of Chinatown, and foreshadowed an established, rooted Chinese society in the West.

The Page Act of 1875—passed in the midst of a depression, a rise in anti-Chinese violence, and the collapse of the myth of domesticity—sought to erase Chinese women from the social cartography of the United States. The act prevented the "landing" of anyone for a fixed "term of service within the United States for lewd and immoral purposes." In fact, the Page Act would have prevented the entry of 90 percent of the Chinese women already living in the United States. Now, by banning admission of all Chinese women except merchants' wives, the U.S. government hoped to force thousands of men to return to China. The Page Act sought to make sure that another ethnic minority would not endure in the West. . . .

Another brutal tactic that prevented Chinese women from emigrating was the seizure of their children, whose parentage was questioned, a case poignantly described in the 1909 story "In the Land of the Free," by Sui Sin Far (Edith Maude Eaton), the first Chinese American fiction writer. This is the tale of a desperate Chinese woman valiantly trying to prove that her son was conceived during a home visit by her husband, a merchant legally entitled to bring his family into the United States. U.S. Customs officers could place the children of Chinese immigrant women in orphanages or foundling homes or even put them up for adoption to white families.

The shadow of the Page Act fell on all Chinese women, for it presumed that their primary work was the sale of sex. Indeed during the 1860s and 1870s most Chinese women in the United States worked as prostitutes. In San Francisco in 1860, over 90 percent of Chinese women worked and lived in brothels; in 1870, the number dropped to just over 60 percent, perhaps because hundreds of prostitutes had either died or managed to work off the terms of their indentures. It is estimated that by 1880, following the Page Act, between 21 and 50 percent of Chinese women in the United States were prostitutes.

The Page Act itself acted as a purge. It forced the overall ratio to fall from seventy-eight Chinese females per one thousand Chinese males in 1870 to forty-seven per one thousand in 1880. The number was low enough to risk the future of Chinese America—as the law intended. . . .

Nonetheless, despite pressures to remain in China with their husbands' families, despite obligations to their own primary families, despite hardships of traveling with small children, and despite the Page Law, Chinese women did emigrate. Resenting their second-class status in their husbands' families in China, tired of waiting for their husbands' visit or no longer believing their promises of permanent return, many Chinese women traveled, sometimes on foot, sometimes alone, to the port cities and boarded the crowded ships bound for San Francisco or Seattle. Many had entered quickly arranged marriages with Chinese men about to depart for the United States, and these adventurous women barely knew the husbands who awaited them.

Although in the 1870s the U.S. government was still willing to accept Chinese laborers as transient workers, by attempting to prevent the entry of Chinese women and thus the entry of Chinese children, it sundered Chinese family life and community. By 1880 there were more than 75,000 Chinese men in the United States and fewer than 4,000 Chinese women. The Page Act allowed the flow of single Chinese male laborers to continue, a workforce cheaply housed in bunks or tents. It protected rural townships from paying for schools for Chinese children. But as white workers came to realize that without women and children Chinese men would work longer hours and for less money than what might constitute a "family" wage, the Page Act fueled the racial anger of the new labor movement. The Knights of Labor and the Workingman's Party saw the paradox: single Chinese men accumulated money in California to send home, save, invest, and spend—sometimes on prostitutes. . . .

The journalistic, evangelical, and political attention to Chinese prostitutes has obscured the everyday lives of other Chinese women who entered the United States, who worked and bore children, built communities during rough times of intimidation, contributed to the family wage, faced harassment, and ultimately endured expulsion. . . .

Like anti-miscegenation laws directed against African Americans during the postbellum period, the Page Act sought to regulate who would constitute the body politic. Chinese expectations of permanent lives in the United States—expectations tied to naturalization and citizenship—were limited by gender. At the time, the Constitution provided that if a baby was born within the United States, or if a foreign women married a male citizen of the United States, citizenship followed. Until 1875, a Chinese woman who married a white man could sooner or later become an American citizen. The Page Act both foiled this possibility and banned citizenship for Chinese men who married white female citizens or immigrants (e.g., from Ireland, France, or Germany) who had the right to become citizens.

In 1870 Congress specifically allowed persons of African descent to become naturalized, but not those of Asian descent. The Exclusion Act of 1882 clarified Congress's intent: no state or federal court could naturalize a Chinese person. A Chinese American citizenry was not to be. Granted, citizenship in the late nineteenth century did not guarantee the vote or the right to testify [in court], sit on a jury, or hold property; citizenship did not bestow liberty, autonomy, or civic standing. Nonetheless, it defined identity and belonging. But by limiting the immigration of women, the federal government invoked sexual relations to achieve ethnic cleansing.

In 1907 Congress ended any confusion about whether an American woman would risk her citizenship by marrying a Chinese man, declaring "that any American woman who marries a foreigner shall take the nationality of her husband." This act echoed miscegenation laws passed between 1861 and 1913 in California, Arizona, Idaho, Montana, Nebraska, Nevada, Utah, and Wyoming. These laws criminalized or voided marriages between Chinese—indeed, any people of color—and whites. In short, the American legislative system attempted to stop any chances of a growing Chinese America. Even so, Chinese women kept coming.

Questions for Discussion

1. The white Americans discussed in this essay believed Chinese immigrants, especially women, were a grave threat to the moral and physical health of their society and families. What evidence did they produce to support these claims?
2. In what ways were white stereotypes of Chinese similar to or different from those aimed by African Americans and Native Americans? How do you account for these similarities and differences?
3. How did the "trade" in female prostitution work among the Chinese? Did it start in the United States? Why did it thrive in this country?
4. How did the "owners" of Chinese prostitutes evade American laws against enslavement and indentured labor?
5. What was the Page Act? Did it succeed in its aims?

For Further Reading

John Bodnar, *The Transplanted: A History of Immigrants in America* (1985); Sucheng Chan, *Asian Americans: An Interpretive History* (1991), *This Bittersweet Soil: The Chinese in California Agriculture, 1860–1910* (1986), ed., *Entry Denied: Exclusion and the Chinese Community in America, 1882–1943* (1991); Yong Chen, *Chinese San Francisco, 1850–1943* (2000); Roger *Asian America: Chinese and Japanese in the United States Since 1850* (1988), *Coming to America: A History of Immigration and Ethnicity in American Life* (1990), *Not Like Us: Immigrants and Minorities in America, 1890–1924* (1997); Wallace Hagaman and Steve Cottrell, *The Chinese Must Go: The Anti-Chinese Boycott in Truckee, 1886* (2004); John Higham, *Strangers in the Land: Patterns of American Nativism* (1955); Maxine Hong Kingston, *The Woman Warrior: Memoirs of a Girlhood among Ghosts* (1989); Walton Look Lai, *Indentured Labor, Caribbean Sugar: Chinese and Indian Migrants to the British West Indies, 1838–1918* (1993); Huping Ling, *Surviving on the Gold Mountain: A History of Chinese Women and Their Lives* (1998); Charles McClain, *In*

Search of Equality: The Chinese Struggle Against Discrimination in Nineteenth-Century America (1994); George Anthony Peffer, *If They Don't Bring Their Women Here: Chinese Female Immigration Before Exclusion* (1999); Jean Pfaelzer, *Driven Out: The Forgotten War Against Chinese Americans* (2007); Lucy E. Salyer, *Laws Harsh as Tigers: Chinese Immigrants and the Shaping of Modern Immigration Law* (1995); Elmer Sandmeyer, *The Anti-Chinese Movement in California* (1991); Alexander Saxton, *The Indispensable Enemy: Labor and the Anti-Chinese Movement in California* (1971); Nayan Shah, *Contagious Divides: Epidemics and Race in San Francisco's Chinatown* (2001); Margit Stange, *Personal Property: Wives, White Slaves and the Market in Women* (1998); Graig Storti, *Incident at Bitter Creek: The Story of the Rock Springs Chinese Massacre* (1991); Ronald Takaki, *Strangers from a Distant Shore: A History of Asian Americans* (1989); Benson Tong, *Unsubmissive Women: Chinese Prostitutes in Nineteenth-Century San Francisco* (1994); Judy Yung, *Unbound Feet: A Social History of Chinese Women in San Francisco* (1995), *Unbound Voices: A Documentary History of Chinese Women in San Francisco* (1999).

5

Life and Work for Turn-of-the-Century Chicago Immigrants

James R. Barrett

"You could literally taste it." That is how the writer Upton Sinclair described the stench of slaughtered animals that hovered over Chicago's meatpacking district. Sinclair knew that odor well. He had lived in the Chicago neighborhood, known as Packingtown—the center of the nation's meat-processing industry—for nearly two months while doing research for his 1906 novel, *The Jungle*. The book was a powerful indictment of meatpacking corporations. Sinclair was most concerned about the exploitation of workers by giant packers like Swift and Armour. But his novel also portrayed graphic, stomach-turning scenes of how those companies processed and sold rancid, vermin-infested meat.

Most of the 40,000 meatpacking workers who lived in Packingtown and attracted Sinclair's attention were immigrants and their children. Between 1870 and 1920, more than 26 million immigrants arrived in the United States. Until 1890, most came from northern and central Europe; they were mainly Protestant, although significant numbers of Irish and German Catholics came as well. By the time Sinclair wrote *The Jungle*, most immigrants were coming from southern and eastern Europe, as well as Mexico. They were overwhelmingly Catholic, Jewish, and Christian Orthodox. In the first decade of the twentieth century alone, nearly 9 million came to America. In 1910 the foreign born accounted for almost 15 percent of the population. One-third of the population was immigrants and their American-born children.

Immigrants working in the Armour Company's meatpacking plant in Chicago. Note the age difference in the two photographs. Can you guess why the workers in the second photograph are much younger than those in the first photograph?

Chicago attracted more immigrants than any city except New York. Well over half of the 2.1 million people living in Chicago in 1910 were immigrants and their children. Through the 1880s, the Irish, Germans, and Canadians dominated immigration to the city; by the turn of the century, the bulk of Chicago's immigrants were Hungarian, Polish, Lithuanian, Slavic, Greek, Scandinavian, and Italian. They were attracted by construction jobs in the bustling downtown area and by work in huge manufacturing firms—like the McCormick farm-equipment company and the Pullman railroad car factory.

No Chicago industry employed more workers than the slaughterhouses. The Armour Company alone had 6,000 employees in 1910. More than 45,000 worked in the sprawling Union Stock Yard complex, southwest of downtown. Stockyard pens could hold 450,000 hogs, cattle, and sheep. The work was brutal and dangerous.

On the "killing floor," for example, live hogs were hung upside down, attached to a moving overhead cable, and then systematically "disassembled." After one worker slit the hogs' throats, another scalded them with hot water, then others scraped and gutted them. Then the hogs were decapitated. The meat was refrigerated, an innovation of the 1870s. Their blood and waste matter was pumped into the Chicago River. Their fat was made into lard, their horns and hoofs into glue. Their intestines, stuffed with poor-quality, chemically treated meat (sometimes including parts of rats and roaches), were made into sausages. Regardless of what the labels claimed, processed and packaged meats could be almost anything. As a rhyme from those years put it:

Mary had a little lamb
And when she saw it sicken
She shipped it off to Packingtown
And now it's labeled chicken

Working in Packingtown's slaughterhouses was even more dangerous than eating its processed meats. Hundreds of stockyard workers were maimed and killed each year by on-the-job accidents. Workers' compensation was rare, the hours long (fifty-five to sixty hours per week), and the wages low. Most of those who worked in the meatpacking industry earned on average about 15–20 cents an hour. In 2005 dollars, that would add up to about $3.00 an hour. Put another way: a slaughterhouse worker earning 18 cents an hour who worked a sixty-hour week for forty-four weeks (most industrial workers were laid off for at least eight weeks each year without pay) earned about $475 a year in 1900 dollars. That would be about $8,000 in 2005 dollars. In other words, most of those working in Chicago's meatpacking industry—like the majority of skilled and un-skilled American industrial workers at the time—earned wages that could not support their families.

These were low wages, but they were higher than immigrants could have made in their native countries. That's why they came to the United States. And while the cost of housing was high, those on tight budgets could find bargains on consumer items. Many saloons offered a "free lunch" with the purchase of a "nickel" beer. A nickel bought rides on Chicago streetcars and New York subways; hot dogs and ice cream cones also cost 5 cents.

Nevertheless, there were vast gaps in wealth and income among American families. Perhaps 40 percent of workers earned incomes that were at or barely above the poverty level; another 40 percent were below that level. At the same time, in 1900, approximately 70 percent of the nation's wealth was owned by a mere 10 percent of its households. Also, the number of millionaires rose from a handful in 1865 to more than 4,000 in 1890. There was no income tax at the time.

This situation had two major consequences. One was massive labor unrest and violence in the late nineteenth and early twentieth centuries. Between 1877 and 1905, more than 7 million workers went on strike (in a total American population of less than 100 million). In the general railroad strike of 1877, a hundred workers were killed by police and "private deputies" hired by the railroads. Chicago was the scene of massive labor discord and violence during these years. That included the Haymarket explosion in 1886, the strike at the Pullman factory in 1894, a stockyard strike in 1904, and a work stoppage by the city's textile workers in 1910.

The other major consequence of poor wages for industrial workers was what James R. Barrett in the following essay calls the "family economy." Because most male breadwinners earned poor wages, everyone else in the family had to work in order to make ends meet. Barrett describes the division of labor in the Packingtown family economy. He also shows that most immigrants tried to live in Packingtown neighborhoods with members of their own ethnic and religious groups. This was what scholars call "chain migration," in which migrating individuals followed family members or friends already in the United States. Finally, while Barrett portrays the health hazards and other dangers of living in the shadow of Chicago's stockyards, he also shows how immigrant families successfully transplanted their native cultural values to their New World surroundings.

Source: James R. Barrett, *Work and Community in the Jungle: Chicago's Packinghouse Workers, 1894–1922.* Copyright 1987 by the Board of Trustees of the University of Illinois. Used with permission of the University of Illinois Press.

Packingtown was but one portion of a solid industrial belt running north and south along the branches of the Chicago River from the city's central business district. On the South Side the industrial landscape included vast expanses of railroad freight yards with their warehouses and car shops, a network of canals serving a dozen lumberyards, the huge McCormick plant of International Harvester Corporation, a number of foundries and machine shops, breweries, and several coal yards and electrical generating stations to keep the whole complex in operation. Farther south lay the blast furnaces and rolling mills of South Chicago. Just north of Thirty-ninth Street, a number of box manufacturers, packing companies, and rendering plants drew upon the stockyards for their economic survival and on the surrounding neighborhoods for their labor supply.

One became aware of Packingtown long before stepping down from the streetcar near the great stone gate of the Union Stockyards. The unique yards smell—a mixture of decaying blood, hair, and organic tissue; fertilizer dust; smoke; and other ingredients—permeated the air of the surrounding neighborhoods. Smoke belching from the shacks of the largest plants all but obscured the other dominant structures in the South Side skyline, the steeples of the various ethnic churches. . . .

Just south and west of the yards, tucked amidst the smoke and garbage, parking plants and car shops, was a community of forty thousand people. The advantage of living here was obvious from the common laborer's point of view—one could walk to work. In an industry where employment depended in large part on one's ability to stay close to the plants, waiting for the word from the foreman or special policeman, this was an important consideration. In turn, ethnic communities thrived in this forbidding environment, and so the laborer could expect to find a comprehensible language and familiar cultural institutions there as well as emotional and economic support in the struggle for existence.

Notwithstanding such important considerations, the combined effects of the casual labor system and the close proximity of the neighborhood to the yards and packing plants undermined the quality of life in Packingtown. By 1900 nearly all of the streets in Hyde Park [a middle-class South Side suburb not far from Packingtown] were paved, for example, while Packingtown's roads, with the exception of Forty-seventh Street and Ashland Avenue, were dirt. The working-class community also had far fewer sewerage facilities than its neighbors, and its main business district consisted largely of saloons. With an average family income at the turn of the century of less than one-fifth of Hyde Park's, Packingtown had more than fourteen times the number of families on relief. By the First World War, physical conditions had improved somewhat, but the neighborhood remained polluted and unhealthful.

Living in the shadow of the packing plants and working in their damp cellars and cutting rooms meant not only irregular employment at low wages but often disabling illness and death. The industry's effects on the physical environment are best reflected in the health statistics for the neighboring communities. Although Packingtown's population was less than twice the size of Hyde Park's in the years from 1894 to 1900, its death from consumption, bronchitis, diphtheria, and other contagious diseases ranged from two and a half to five times those for the middle-class neighborhood. As in so many other urban communities of the era, tuberculosis was the big killer, accounting for more than 30 percent of the 429 adult deaths during 1908 and 1909. Packingtown was widely thought to have the highest tuberculosis rate in the city and one of the highest in the country. Infant mortality rates for the period around the turn of the century were also disproportionately high. Packingtown averaged less than three and a half times Hyde Park's number of children under six but almost five and a half times its mortality figure for those in that age group. By 1900, the situation was actually worse. One of every three infants died before the age of two, a rate seven and a half times that for the lakefront ward that included Hyde Park.

Not included in such health statistics are the thousands of injuries which became a part of the new mass-production process, including many peculiar to meat-packing. In one house alone, Swift and Company, 3,500 injuries were reported for the first six months of 1910, and this number included only those requiring a physician's care. According to the director of Armour's welfare department, one of every two of the company's 22,281 workers was injured or became ill at work during 1917. Armour's Chicago plant averaged twenty-three accidents per day. Each job had its own dangers: the dampness and cold of the pickling room and hide cellar; the sharp blade of the beef boner's knife; the noxious dust of the wool department and fertilizer plant; the wild charge of a half-crazed steer on the killing floor. And those dangers intrinsic to the work itself were exacerbated by the speed with which it was carried on. The result was frequent idleness due to accidents and disease. In a total of 284 households studied by the U.S. Commissioner of Labor in 1905, thirty-four family heads (12 percent) noted periods of unemployment, averaging about 12.4 weeks, as a result of accident or illness on the job. At work or at home, a butcher workman or -woman faced death and disabling illness simply by virtue of his or her occupation and social position. . . .

The typical Packingtown tenement was a dilapidated two-story wooden structure divided into four or more flats. Each flat consisted of four dark, ill-ventilated rooms shared by the family and its borders. An "average" household included 6.7 people—the parents, two children, and two or three borders. There were exceptions—a good number of widows; some families who had taken in grandparents; even a flat shared by eight men, one of whom cooked and cleaned while the others worked. But the overwhelming majority of households comprised nuclear families who took in borders of their own nationality. The degree of congestion in the flat had a direct relationship to the family's economic condition as well as to its stage in the family life cycle. Poorer families with all their children still at home were forced to take in more borders, thereby aggravating the congestion. Predictably, the most crowded parts of the neighborhood were those inhabited by the greatest number of borders, and these were also the blocks with the highest rates for tuberculosis and infant mortality. . . .

Packingtown became increasingly congested under the impact of successive waves of "new immigrants"—unskilled workers from agricultural backgrounds in eastern Europe. Between the turn of the century and the end of the First World War, the original Irish and German pioneers were largely displaced by Slavic people, particularly Poles and Lithuanians. . . .

The old immigrant (German, Irish, Canadian) groups declined in cumulative percentage of the population from 55.5 in 1900 to 28 in 1910, while the new immigrant groups (Polish, Lithuanian, Slovak, Hungarian) rose from 18.5 percent to 48 percent of the population over these same years. The 1910 sample also included several Slovene and eastern European Jewish families. A 1905 census by the U.S. Commissioner of Labor and a 1909 University of Chicago survey both demonstrate a disproportionate concentration of eastern European families, notably Poles and Lithuanians, in those parts of the neighborhood immediately adjacent to the stockyards. The massive immigration following the turn of the century transformed the ethnic character of the neighborhood, then, creating a community which was quite mixed ethnically but increasingly dominated by new immigrants. The *size* of the population also grew dramatically, crowding more and more people into the stifling tenements. In the first decade of this century population increased by 75 percent and continued to grow until by 1920 over fifty-seven thousand people were living "back of the yards. . . ."

Throughout the early twentieth century social life in the community flowed along paths shaped by a strong ethnic identification among the various nationalities. One striking indication of this division was the almost total absence of interethnic marriages. Of 284 households surveyed in 1905, only five were inhabited by interethnic couples: one Polish/Russian, one Polish/Bohemian, one English/Irish, one German/Bohemian, and one Polish/Slovak. At the most intimate level of social relations, then, ethnicity ruled; sexual contact across nationality lines was extremely rare, at least among the first generation.

If it was rare for someone of one nationality to marry someone of another, this was because people's personal lives were divided from one another, on the surface at least, by the organizations and culture which they created for themselves. Soon after arrival in the community, each ethnic group established its own church, so that despite the neighborhood's overwhelming adherence to Roman Catholicism religion was not a unifying force in Packingtown. In addition, the Lithuanian and Polish Catholic and German Lutheran parishes all maintained their own schools, where children were taught in the native tongue rather than in English. A 1912 study found that the community's nine parochial schools had an enrollment more than twice that of the public elementary schools. As late as 1918, a sample of nine hundred of the community' children showed that about two-thirds were still educated in the parish schools, which were organized along ethnic lines.

Fraternal, economic, and political groups were all characterized by the same ethnic division. The Bohemians in particular were joiners, and they developed an impressive array of voluntary organizations. By 1902 there were over 30 savings and loans and 259 benefit societies, as well as 35 gymnastic clubs, 18 singing societies, 5 bicycling clubs, and 4 drama groups. It seemed to Hull House [a local social settlement] investigators that every Bohemian man and woman belonged to at least one order or beneficial society; some belonged to several. Many of these organizations maintained their headquarters in the vicinity of the yards, though the real heart of Chicago's Bohemian community was a couple of miles north in Pilsen, on the near southwest side of the city. The Bohemians were also more divided than other ethnic communities between Roman Catholics and freethinkers, anticlerical radicals who emphasized education and other forms of self-improvement and battled constantly against the Church's influence. . . .

Each of the other major ethnic groups in the community rivaled the Bohemians in extent of voluntary organization. The eastern Europeans created extensive networks based on their parishes, the focal points of Slavic community life. Both the Lithuanians and Poles established fraternal orders, savings and loans, and nationalist organizations in addition to an array of religious and social groups which knitted each parish together. Both communities were rent by the same clerical/freethought conflict that divided the Bohemians, though the Polish and Lithuanian freethinkers were clearly in the minority. Each community also fostered an active socialist movement. The Lithuanian Socialist Alliance, which eventually became the Lithuanian Language Federation of the Socialist Party, was particularly strong, providing a network of cultural activities for the community's radicals. Every shade of political opinion seemed to be represented, and each faction published its own newspaper. There were local Democratic and Republican organizations among both Lithuanians and Poles, and Bohemian Democratic and Socialist clubs and other groupings, but all conformed to the dominant ethnic divisions within the community.

Finally, there were ties to the old country itself. In some cases the link was too strong to be broken by emigration. For these people the stay in America was a brief sojourn, or perhaps part of a pattern of cyclical migration; one's goals and identification remained focused on the Old World. While the new immigrants of the late nineteenth and early twentieth centuries generally showed a strong tendency toward remigration, the phenomenon was particularly common among certain Slavic groups. National figures for 1908 to 1923 show that about two Poles left the country for every five who arrived. Chicago *Polonia* [Polish language newspaper] had a term to describe those in continual migration to and from the Old World— *obiezyswiaty*, or "globetrotters." Polish remigration was especially high in the years just before World War I, when the outward flow very nearly approximated that of arrival. While the figure for Lithuanians in the 1908–23 period was a bit lower than that for Poles (one leaving for every four who arrived), the rate for Slovaks was actually higher (one leaving for every two who arrived). There are no detailed data for Packingtown immigrants in particular, but the fact that there was a complete travel service for immigrants operating out of a neighborhood bank suggests that the paths between Chicago's South Side and eastern Europe were well worn. It was possible to arrange the whole trip right in the neighborhood. . . .

One of the greatest testaments to ethnic cohesion in Packingtown is the slow progress that formal "Americanization"—English instruction and naturalization, for example—made in the community. The Citizenship School at the University of Chicago Settlement was proud of its English and civic classes for adult immigrants, but in 1909 enrollment stood at only 122, a tiny fraction of the community's foreign-born. Studying the problem among packinghouse workers in the same year, Immigration Commission investigators found that only 27.7 percent of the Poles, 21 percent of the Lithuanians, and 11.7 percent of the Slovaks studied were fully naturalized [i.e., United States citizens], and the fact that the study included only immigrants who had been living in the country five years or more means that it probably overestimated the number of naturalized citizens in the work force considerably. The packers' own First World War study showed that 32 percent of the men and 67 percent of the women surveyed could not speak English. Only one-fourth of the men were citizens, and 43 percent had not even taken out first papers in the naturalization process, despite the fact that they had lived in the United States an average of fifteen years. Census figures for 1920 suggest that even the nativism of the war years had little effect; the proportion of aliens in most parts of the neighborhood remained high. Clearly, formal efforts at Americanization were not reaching the vast majority of the foreign-born in Packingtown. . . .

At least one social institution certainly bridged some of the ethnic divisions in the community—the saloon. Considerable attention has been focused recently on the obvious cultural importance of the working-class saloon. But it would be difficult to imagine a situation in which it played a more vital role in the life of the community than it did in Packingtown. The Twenty-ninth Ward, which included Packingtown, had five hundred saloons at the turn of the century, twenty-five times the number in Hyde Park. . . . The saloon played an important role in the social contacts between recent immigrants and the more assimilated butcher workmen who had worked in the industry for decades and provided the leadership for early labor organizations.

As the most important commercial base in the community, saloons provided one of the few avenues of upward social mobility for those hoping to escape the packinghouses. Many saloonkeepers along "Whiskey Row" on Ashland Avenue, for example, were retired butcher workmen who had been financed by breweries. In exchange for an agreement from the prospective saloonkeeper to sell only his brand of beer, the brewer paid the rent and license fee, provided the fixtures and beer, and even helped to find a suitable location. A special assessment was levied on each barrel of beer and in this way the saloonkeeper gradually reimbursed his brewer. By 1907 an estimated 80 percent of Chicago's saloons were brewer-financed. This arrangement made it relatively easy for some better-paid workers to enter the liquor trade.

Saloonkeepers were not only the community's single most important group of businesspeople. They also offered important services for the great mass of packinghouse workers who were not on their way up. Since they provided practically the only halls in the community, saloons hosted weddings, dances, and other festivities and offered meeting places for fraternal groups, other ethnic organizations, and, later, union locals. Another service provided was check cashing. One writer estimated that 95 percent of all stockyards checks were cashed in saloons. The one at Forty-third and Ashland Avenue, for example, cashed over forty thousand dollars' worth of paychecks each month. For such service, the saloonkeeper kept the odd change [from each check] and the patron was expected to stand a round of drinks. The saloon was also a cafeteria. Since the packers provided none, the worker faced the option of eating his lunch amid the blood and filth of the killing floor or walking across Ashland Avenue to a saloon where he could get a hot lunch for the price of a beer. Then there were the less tangible benefits of saloon socializing—newspapers, fellowship, perhaps even a bit of music. It is not difficult, then, to understand why saloons thrived in the community. . . .

THE STANDARD OF LIVING AND THE FAMILY ECONOMY

What standard of living did this employment [meatpacking] allow? The question is important not only to gaining a fuller understanding of the lives of packinghouse workers, but also because thousands of workers shared the kind of working conditions faced by common laborers in packing—irregular employment, low wages, accidents, and industrial disease. . . .

The neighborhood's physical environment provides some indication of living standards, but we must analyze the finances of Packingtown's families in order to understand how work affected family life. The nature of work in the industry, for example, greatly increased the burden of responsibility on married women and mothers by drawing them into the plants. It truncated education and significantly narrowed the future prospects for the community's children. And it tied all into a complicated local economy which allowed the family to survive, while actually subsidizing the industry's employment system and wage structure.

Wages for most male packinghouse workers were extremely low. The common labor rate, the wage earned by at least two-thirds of the labor force, fluctuated between 15 cents and 20 cents per hour from the turn of the century until 1917. Workers won important gains in real wages during the First World War, but these largely disappeared during the postwar depression. Real earnings, moreover, were far lower than these rates suggest, because of the irregularity of employment. . . . Thousands of laborers in cattle- and hog-slaughtering gangs were laid off for two or three months during the slow summer season and for shorter periods at other times of the year. As the number of cattle fell off, the packers reduced gang size and skilled men often took over common labor jobs at reduced wages. Light cattle shipments at the end of the week also meant that many laborers could not count on more than three days' work each week even during the busier season. Thousands of workers, always more than were needed, milled around the Union Stockyards gates and the employment offices of the various packers. They were called to work only when the killing was about to begin and sent home once it was finished. . . .

As a result of low wages and high unemployment, the earnings of male family heads in Packingtown came nowhere near meeting their families' minimum budget requirements. A meticulous 1911 study by University of Chicago Settlement House investigators estimated the average weekly wage for laborer husbands at $9.67, while the estimate for minimum weekly expenditures needed to support a family of five . . . was $15.40. . . . When *all* sources of income were considered, 30 percent of the 184 families in the study showed budget *deficits.* Estimates did not include such "extraordinary" expenses as weddings, funerals, injuries, or prolonged illness. In a Catholic community with a very high infant mortality rate, such expenses were probably not so extraordinary, and workers often borrowed money to bury their little ones. A wedding, a funeral, or a doctor's bill could present the prospect of stark privation.

How did Packingtown's families survive on a day-to-day basis? The answer, of course, is that family heads' earnings comprised only a portion of family income (54.4 percent in the 1911 University of Chicago study). As in so many other working-class communities of this era, Packingtown's families relied on a complicated local economy aimed at supplementing the insufficient earnings of family heads. Husbands searched for alternative employment in slack periods. Wives took in borders and sometimes engaged in marginal employment within the home. Children left school early for factory work. Some residents even fell back on the "resources" of the neighborhood, scavenging to make ends meet. . . .

Families with teenage children sent them to work in the stockyards or in the surrounding factories and plants. . . . Most women packinghouse workers until the First World War were the young, single daughters of butcher workmen. Not only did most of these young women work because of financial necessity, but they were frequently primary breadwinners. The 1906 Illinois Bureau of Labor Statistics Report showed that 55 percent came from families where fathers' earnings were either impaired, because of disease, injury, or some other cause of chronic unemployment, or nonexistent, because of desertion, divorce, or death. These young single women were joined by their brothers. Children contributed significantly to family income throughout the early twentieth century. . . .

This integration of children into the family economy was not new to the experience of eastern European immigrants. In the Polish community, for example, a high premium was placed on obedience, love, and respect for one's parents, and contributions to family support represented one way of expressing such familial loyalty. Children had always played an important role in the economic life of Polish peasant society, and in the course of industrialization young Polish migrants frequently contributed their earnings to support parents and siblings back home.

Yet it is probably misleading to describe the family strictly in terms of harmonious familial cooperation based on traditional values. Such an approach obscures the tensions which developed between generations under the wage labor system in American cities. . . .

Once they had experienced wage work, young Polish-American women sometimes resisted the complete control of earnings by their mothers. Very few refused to support their families, but many insisted on keeping a portion of their earnings for fashionable clothes and for recreational activities which their parents considered wasteful. The fancy hat became a symbol on both sides of this generation gap. In eastern Europe no woman below the middle class wore one, but the streets of Packingtown were full of them. To the Slavic mother, the hat represented the corrupting influences of the big-city environment and a threat to traditional values; to her daughter, it was a badge of her status as an American working girl. [Louise] Montgomery [in her 1913 study of Packingtown women] found that many girls clamored to leave school for the packing plant or candy factory, partly to help their families but also to win a measure of the independence which the work symbolized for them. Such evidence suggests that these immigrant families were in a state of flux. While continuing to espouse traditional values, they were forced to adapt to their new environment and the changes in consciousness it produced.

In contrast to those of children, wives' wages for industrial work provided little or no supplement to Packingtown's family income before World War I. In 1905 (even after the entrance of women into several departments during a strike), very few wives worked in the yards or anywhere else outside the home. Those who did claim earnings tended to be engaged in irregular non-industrial work of some kind. Out of a sample of 280 wives that year, only six reported an income. One was a midwife, two took in washing "occasionally," and two collected firewood. The sixth, clearly the exception, was a newly arrived forty-five-year-old Lithuanian woman who worked in the yards. She had no children and only one boarder and earned a dollar a day making sausage.

Some scholars have explained the failure of certain groups of immigrant women to take up industrial work in terms of the limited employment available to them. Steel mill towns and other heavy industry areas offered few jobs for women. But unlike a steel mill town, Packingtown and the neighborhoods surrounding it offered considerable employment for women from the late nineteenth century on. Others have argued that some immigrant women avoided industrial employment for cultural reasons. Such work would have violated deeply held traditional peasant values regarding the role of [married] women in the family. In Packingtown, however, wives' rejection of wage work crossed all ethnic lines and included Polish women who showed a strong proclivity for industrial work in other communities. Why did so few of Packingtown's wives and mothers choose wage work?

There may, in fact, have been a number of reasons, but the most compelling one was economic. As a money-making proposition, the work which wives did in the home—cooking, washing, and caring for the needs of borders—was far more lucrative than employment in the yards, considering the low wages and irregularity of women's work there. In the yards a woman could not expect to earn, on average, more than six or seven dollars a week; she could earn about thirty dollars per week, minus the cost of extra food, by taking in three male lodgers and cooking for them at the prevailing rates.

Descriptions of the family economy also show that the mother occupied the crucial position of managing the family budget, collecting payment from the boarders and the wages of all family members, doling out each person's share, and making do with what was available. This was certainly the case in Packingtown. A mother could make a greater financial contribution to the family's maintenance, while performing what were probably viewed as her family duties of childrearing and caring for the home, by taking in boarders than by going to work in the yards.

Questions for Discussion

1. Describe the work and housing conditions in Packingtown. How did these circumstances affect the health of residents?
2. Given these poor living conditions, why did so many packinghouse workers live there?
3. How does the idea of the "melting pot" stack up with the attitudes of immigrants described in this essay? How frequently did eastern European immigrants return to their countries of origin? Why?
4. What was the immigrant "family economy"? How was it related to male breadwinner wages in the meatpacking industry?
5. Why did most Packingtown wives refuse to work outside the home?

For Further Reading

Jane Addams, *Twenty Years at Hull House* (1910); Paul Avrich, *The Haymarket Tragedy* (1984); James R. Barrett, *Work and Community in the Jungle: Chicago's Packinghouse Workers, 1894–1922* (1987); David M. Brownstone and Irene M. Franck, *Facts About American Immigration* (2001); Stanley Buder, *Pullman: An Experiment in Industrial Order and Community Planning, 1880–1920* (1967); Jeffory A. Clymer, *America's Culture of Terrorism: Violence, Capitalism, and the Written Word* (2003); William Cronon, *Nature's*

Metropolis: Chicago and the Great West (1992); Perry Duis, *The Saloon: Public Drinking in Chicago and Boston* (1983); Philip S. Foner and David R. Roediger, *In Our Time: A History of American Labor and the Working Day* (1989); James Green, *Death in the Haymarket* (2006); Herbert Gutman, *Work, Culture and Society in Industrializing America* (1977); Rick Halpern, *Down on the Killing Floor: Black and White Workers in Chicago's Packinghouses* (1997); Rick Halpern and Roger Horowitz, *Meatpackers: An Oral History of Black Packinghouse Workers and Their Struggle for Racial and Economic Equality* (1996); Dirk Hoerder, ed., *"Struggle a Hard Battle": Essays on Working-Class Immigrants* (1986); Roger Horowitz, *"Negro and White, Unite and Fight!" A Social History of Industrial Unionism in Meatpacking, 1930–1990* (1997); Edward Kirkland, *Dream and Thought in the Business Community, 1860–1900* (1964); Donald L. Miller, *City of the Century: The Epic of Chicago and the Making of America* (1996); David Montgomery, *Citizen Worker* (1993); Karen Sawislak, *Smoldering City: Chicagoans and the Great Fire, 1871–1874* (1995); Thomas J. Schlereth, *Victorian America: Transformations in Everyday Life, 1876–1915* (1991); Upton Sinclair, *The Jungle* (1906); Robert Spinney, *Chit of Big Shoulders: A History of Chicago* (2000); David O. Stowell, *Streets, Railroads, and the Great Strike of 1877* (1999); Louise Carroll Wade, *Chicago's Pride: The Stockyards, Packingtown, and Environs in the Nineteenth Century* (2002).

6

Life and Leisure for Turn-of-the-Century New York City Immigrants

Kathy Peiss

There was more to immigrant and working-class life than the struggle to make ends meet or surviving hazardous living conditions. As Kathy Peiss demonstrates in the next essay, immigrants in New York, especially the men, took advantage of the city's enormous variety of outlets for leisure, recreation, and sociability. Immigrants brought some of these leisure activities with them, like gymnastics, from their native lands; others, such as baseball, saloons, and amusement parks like Coney Island, were American creations. Economic opportunity inspired immigrants to come to the United States. But the country's vibrant, bustling cities offered them an opportunity to enjoy life as well.

To be sure, New York City in 1900 was a densely populated, difficult place for working-class and immigrant families. It was by far the nation's largest city, with 4.7 million residents in 1910 (Chicago was second with 2.1 million). More than 70 percent of New York's residents were immigrants and their children. Many lived on Manhattan's Lower East Side, the focus of reformer Jacob Riis's 1890 book *How the Other Half Lives*. Riis's photographs and narrative exposed horrible living conditions in what was perhaps the most densely populated neighborhood in the world at the time. The Lower East Side had thirty-seven blocks with at least 3,000 inhabitants; more than 400,000 people lived between the Battery and Houston Street. Of the city's

The nearly all-male crowd at the 1906 baseball game in New York's Polo Grounds. According to the author, why were some recreational activities segregated by sex while others were not?

81,000 residential dwellings, 35,000 were dilapidated tenements with at least 1.5 million people living in them. They were poorly ventilated, often without direct sunlight, and frequently lacking adequate indoor plumbing. None had electricity—as late as 1907, only about 8 percent of the country's residential buildings were wired for electricity.

But once they left their apartments, New Yorkers found an electric atmosphere in the city's streets and its commercial entertainments. Few, if any, working-class New Yorkers enjoyed paid vacations in 1900. But that did not stop them from having fun after work and on their days off. For immigrant men, the saloon, as Peiss shows, was a major source of social life. New York had more than 10,000 licensed saloons, one for every 551 residents. By comparison, Chicago had one for every 335 people, San Francisco one for every 218, and Houston one for every 198. The country had more than 215,000 licensed drinking establishments in 1897—and perhaps as many as 50,000 illegal ones.

In addition to the male-dominated saloon there was the gender-integrated world of vaudeville. Depending on the number and quality of the acts, admission to vaudeville shows cost between 25 cents and a dollar. Vaudeville offered women and men hours-long variety shows that included animal acts, dancing, sentimental songs, and ethnic humor. Those who were young and unmarried might prefer dance halls, where they could meet one another. Dance halls were common in immigrant and working-class neighborhoods. But New Yorkers did not have to go indoors to have fun. The city streets provided equally stimulating entertainment—for free. Simply strolling through packed sidewalks was a form of entertainment: dodging legions of hustling pedestrians, many dressed in old-country clothing, as they hunted for bargains in markets that sold ethnic foods and listening to a chorus of conversation, gossip, and sales pitches in Chinese, Yiddish, Italian, Greek, and English.

A new form of commercial entertainment that enjoyed immense popularity among Americans at the turn of the twentieth century was the amusement park. None was more famous or attracted more people than New York's Coney Island. Begun in 1895 on Brooklyn's scenic southern ocean shore, Coney Island was a series of theme parks. Its main "business," according to one of its officials, was "amusing the million." And the million came: according to surveys done at the time, most Manhattan working-class and immigrant families made at least one or two trips to Coney Island every season. They could do so fairly cheaply. One of Coney Island's parks, Steeplechase, offered a combination deal of twenty-five rides for 25 cents. Individual attractions cost a nickel or dime. They included wild rides on new contraptions like roller coasters and Ferris wheels, or customers could jump into the Human Whirlpool, a large saucer-shaped bowl that tossed screaming riders further to its rim as it gathered speed. Families could enjoy the beach in the day time and be dazzled at night by the 250,000 electric lights that illuminated the park.

As historians John Kasson and Thomas Schlereth have pointed out, Coney Island was a refuge for immigrant and working-class families. For a few hours, it freed them from the everyday burdens of work and tenement life. Perhaps as important, the informal atmosphere of Coney Island encouraged people to shed the reserve and proprieties of "normal" life. It was a place where "ordinary" folks could let their hair down by wearing (relatively) revealing swimsuits at the beach or by immersing themselves in the illusions and fantasies of the "fun house." They were not only having "fun"; they were in charge, at least for the day.

Most social reformers frowned on such "fun" and on working-class entertainment in general. They considered saloons and dance halls immoral, unhealthy, and a danger to family stability. Social reformers were especially interested in providing uplifting forms of entertainment to the children of immigrant and working-class families.

For example, prominent reformers, including Lillian Wald and Jacob Riis in New York and Jane Addams in Chicago, advocated the creation of adult-supervised playgrounds for the children of immigrants, especially males. Reformers hoped supervised play would lure young males away from the moral and physical dangers of street life and be a safe haven for them after school. Equally important, Progressives like Riis, Addams, and Wald believed baseball, basketball, and other team games helped reduce animosity among children from different ethnic and religious backgrounds. During these games, children became "teammates" working together toward a common goal. Reformers also believed these games, if properly supervised by trained adults, would instill "American" values like hard work, "fair play," and democracy in children of immigrants. Thanks to their efforts, between 1900 and 1911, more than 1,500 municipal playgrounds employing more than 4,000 "play directors" (most of them teachers working after school and during summers) were constructed in 200 cities.

Reformers had their agendas. But the essay by Kathy Peiss demonstrates that when it came to recreation and leisure, immigrants and working-class families had their own agendas—and acted on them. This is an important issue because it shows that immigrants were far from "lost" or helpless in the New World. Nor did they leave their cultural and personal values on Ellis Island. They brought them into the streets, saloons, tenements, workplaces, and play spaces—and into the fabric—of American life.

Another important issue raised by Peiss deals with the way most immigrant groups segregated the world of male and female leisure. For the most part, married women and men went their separate ways when it came to work and leisure. According to Peiss, immigrant men's work and leisure activities brought them into a male-only public world of companionship. Their wives mostly lived within the narrow confines of the tenement's domestic sphere.

Source: Kathy Peiss, *Cheap Amusements: Working Women and Leisure in Turn-of-the-Century New York* (Philadelphia, PA: Temple University Press, 1986), ch. 1.

Americans in the late nineteenth century perceived New York City's population as split into two classes, typified by the ostentatious mansions of Fifth Avenue and the squalid tenement slums of Mulberry Bend. Images of the elite "400" and the impoverished "other half," created by photographers and poets, cartoonists and crusaders, indelibly shape our understanding of the metropolis. Yet this picture oversimplifies the complex texture of Manhattan's culture, particularly that of its working-class inhabitants. The social worlds of the poverty-stricken day laborer, unionized craftsman, stylish young saleswoman, and boardinghouse keeper were often dissimilar, and diverged further according to ethnic and religious background. Patterns of working-class leisure were likewise kaleidoscopic: a neighborhood's facilities for recreation ranged from sparse to numerous; Old World celebrations and home-centered conviviality competed with commercial amusements; long hours of arduous labor left many without leisure, while others enjoyed the city's variegated nightlife.

As Jacob Riis graphically demonstrated, poverty was a pervasive fact of working-class life in turn-of-the-century New York, whose population was heavily dominated by immigrants and their children. In the 1880s, a majority of Manhattanites lived at the subsistence level, and the depression of the 1890's brought further hardship to the laboring poor. Already over-crowded working-class districts in lower Manhattan swelled with a massive influx of eastern and southern Europeans. Although living standards rose after 1900, many barely survived, uncertain of employment, scrambling to make ends meet.

The income of laboring families varied considerably. Two extensive budget studies covering the period from 1903 to 1909 indicate that the typical working-class family, comprised of four to six members, earned on average eight hundred dollars a year, or fifteen dollars a week. In fewer than 50 percent of the households was the father the sole means of support. "An income of above $700 or $800 is obtainable as a rule only by taking lodgers or by putting mother and children to work," observed Robert Coit Chapin in his investigation of working-class expenditures. Unusually high rents, resulting from urban density, consumed the wages of the poor. Food was usually purchased daily, at higher cost than buying in bulk, and diets were often limited in variety and nutrition.

Nevertheless, working-class standards of living improved in the period from 1880 to 1920, particularly after 1900. A British study in 1911 warned not to confuse the lower East Side's density with squalor: "Poverty is not so much in evidence; shops are bright; there is no lack of places of amusement; restaurants of some pretensions are not hard to find." Many were able to move out of the crowded slums of lower Manhattan to uptown addresses and newly built tenement apartments. The death rate dropped 30 percent in this period, a sign of improved sanitation and health conditions. Skilled workers in particular made important gains in wages and hours of labor, having organized many of New York's major industries, including the engine-operating, printing, building, and metal-working trades. The American-born children of Irish and German immigrants who had poured into Manhattan in the nineteenth century were coming of age and gaining a modicum of social mobility. Even the migrants from eastern Europe and Italy had established their communities on a firmer footing by 1900, the Russian Jews in particular organizing an extensive cultural and political apparatus. . . .

The most common forms of recreation, especially among families living on the margins of self-sufficiency, were free. Streets served as the center of social life in the working-class districts, where laboring people clustered on street corners, on stoops, and in doorways of tenements, relaxing and socializing after their day's work. Lower East Side streets teemed with sights of interest and penny pleasures: organ grinders and buskers [street singers and entertainers] played favorite airs, itinerant acrobats performed tricks, and baked-potato venders, hot-corn stands, and soda dispensers vied for customers. In the Italian community clustered in the upper East Side, street musicians and organ grinders made their melodies heard above the clatter of elevated trains and shouting pushcart vendors, collecting nickels from appreciative passers-by. Maureen Connelly, an Irish immigrant, remembered listening to the German bands that played in Yorkville and the men who would sing for pennies in the tenement yards. "Something was always happening," recalled Samuel Chotzinoff of his boyhood among lower East Side Jews, "and our attention was continually being shifted from one excitement to another."

This multilayered world allowed different groups to construct their own amusements. For many, the after-dinner stroll to a park or window-shopping on Grand Avenue or the Bowery became a ritual. "Every night the brightly lighted main thoroughfares, with their gleaming store windows and their lines of trucks in the gutters, provide a promenade for thousands who find in walk and talk along the pavement a cheap form of social enter-tainment." Sunday diversions might even include visits to tenement construction sites, "to wonder at and admire the light rooms, the bath tubs, and the other improvements."

Parks, too, were a popular form of entertainment for working-class families, particularly among the average wage-earners, who could ill afford excursions or theater trips. An outing to Central Park on a Sunday was con-sidered a special family treat, while the neighborhood parks, squares, and playgrounds were places for daily relaxation. On hot summer nights in Jackson Park, close to the East River, "the men were in their undershirts. The women, more fully dressed, carried newspapers for fans. Hordes of barefoot children played games, weaving in and out of the always thick mass of promenaders."

Although working-class tenements were usually cramped and dark, the home also served as an important social center for family recreation. In the lower East Side, Jewish kinfolk and neighbors gathered together in tene-ment kitchens for everyday socializing and observance of religious holidays. Christian families likewise celebrated yearly festivals, decorating their homes according to the traditions of their homelands at Christmas and Easter. Neighbors from the Old Country joined together for regular social evenings in the home, as in this typical Hungarian gathering:

> In the Grubinsky kitchen they sit in a circle, husbands and wives
> together. Martin Grubinsky and his wife are each at work on cane
> weaving. The babies play on the floor in the middle of the circle.
> Perhaps a pail of mild beer is handed around once or twice, but
> not too often.

Italian friends often met in the home to drink homemade wine, play cards, and socialize. House parties for birthdays or other occasions were also popular. In the West Side Irish districts, revelers enjoyed popular songs, fancy dance steps, masquerading, minstrelsy, and alcohol at the typical house party. . . .

The close quarters of the tenement house engendered particular forms of sociability. Immigrant neighbors who had not learned—or could not afford—the American notion of privacy congregated in the hallways, left their doors open to talk between apartments, and used the airshaft to facilitate conversation. For Italian women, settlement worker Lillian Betts observed, a "tenement house hall in New York is the substitute for the road of her village.". . .

As a recreational space, the home often brought together working-class wives and husbands. [Journalist] George Bevan's extensive 1913 study of male recreation indicates that married men spent about half their leisure time with their families. Men who labored long hours tended to pass their evenings at home recuperating from their toil, while those who worked an eight-hour day spent Saturday afternoons at home. Indeed, two-thirds of the skilled workers reported that they took their recreation with their families, either at home or on outings. The behavior of these craftsmen and mechanics may well have been influenced by the popularization of domestic ideals in the labor press, which not only affirmed women's place in the home but advocated a close family life.

Although the evidence suggests that informal, everyday leisure often was enjoyed within a familial context, closer examination indicates that much working-class social life was divided by gender. Highly skilled workers may have accepted the canons of domesticity, but other men frequently took their recreation apart from wives and children. . . .

Workingmen could turn to a highly visible and extensive network of leisure institutions to which women had marginal or problematic access. Many of these forms of amusement were commercial ventures and included poolrooms and billiard halls, bowling alleys, shooting galleries, and gymnasia. Others were organized by working-class men themselves. Baseball teams, for example, were formed by workingmen's clubs, factory employees, and street gangs throughout the tenement districts. Urban spaces such as cigar stores, barber shops, and street corners were colonized by men as hangouts for socializing and relaxing. The most popular forms of workingmen's recreation, however, were the saloon, lodge, and club, places in which male camaraderie resonated with workingmen's economic and social concerns.

Dominating the space of most tenement neighborhoods, the saloon exemplifies workingmen's public culture. Over ten thousand saloons were in business throughout greater New York in 1900. Saloons tended to be spread out along the wide avenues that ran the length of Manhattan, as well as such commercial downtown streets as the Bowery. The mixed land use in most working-class neighborhoods ensured that saloons, located on the ground floor of tenements and close to factories and businesses, would be central meeting places for men. Most street corners had at least one bar catering to local patrons. In the 15th Assembly District, for example, an area bounded by 43rd Street, 53rd Street, Eighth Avenue, and the Hudson River, almost one-half of the ninety-two street corners were occupied by saloons, and sixty-six taprooms were scattered along the blocks.

Alcohol obviously provided a major attraction for working-class customers who sought to forget tedium, toil, and poverty. George Bevans found that men who labored the longest hours, and thus had the least leisure time, paid the most visits to saloons. Similarly, men who earned low wages, disproportionately attended saloons. Noted one mechanic: "Men who get small wages and are in uncertain employment become easily discouraged when they think of the needs at home. They go to the saloon to drown their despondency and trouble."

More importantly, the saloon united sociability, psychological support, and economic services for workingmen. Their bright lights, etched glass, and polished fixtures, their friendly atmosphere, appearance of abundance, and informal conviviality marked a sharp contrast to crowded tenements and exploitative workplaces. Workers packed saloons on the Bowery and Division Streets on their way home from the factory, seeking "a 'half-way' stopping place where, over a schooner of beer, the men talk over the work of the day and plan for the evening. At nightfall these places are thronged four or five deep about the bar." A man could get a free lunch with a five-cent beer and enjoy the good fellowship of the barkeep and patrons in the bargain. If he wanted a job, a loan, or simply the news, the workingman headed for the saloon. Italian men, for example, met in waterfront cafes on President Street to drink wine and play cards as they waited for information on incoming ships and day labor jobs on the docks. One regular informed [social settlement activist] Lillian Wald that "the fellows just kind of talk about jobs when they're sitting 'round in the saloons, and sometimes you pick something up."

For newly arrived immigrants, saloons offered a wealth of important services to help in the adjustment to the New World. One saloon, for instance, advertised that it supplied Serbians, Croatians, and Hungarians with a large meeting room, money barter, steamship tickets, employment, board, and lodging. In another advertisement, the owner of a hall and bar assured his countrymen of a well-organized social life:

Popular wine-beer hall and coffee house.

The well-liked meeting place of Hungarians. . . .

Comfortably arranged furnished rooms.

First class Hungarian kitchen.

Billiard, also dance hall, comfortable

For meetings further for weddings and balls. Those from the [mother] country receive proper elucidation.

Although the saloon was often termed the "poor man's club," most workingmen also frequented a fraternal society, mutual benefit association, or lodge. Such voluntary organizations combined recreation and camaraderie with economic services, including protection against sickness, disability, and financial emergencies. These forms of working-class self-activity were necessary adaptations to an industrial society that had few social welfare provisions. . . .

Even more common [than fraternal societies] were the mutual benefit societies and lodges organized by immigrants. Insurance was considered a primary obligation of the breadwinner, and contributions to mutual aid associations were often heavy. German immigrants formed Unterstutzung Vereinen, sickness and death benefit societies, which were organized by occupation or place of origin. Numerous Italian societies, estimated at from two to three thousand, thrived in greater New York, each composed of immigrants from a single town or island. The Societa di Mutuo-Soccorso Isola Salina, a typical benevolent order, limited its membership to those born on the island and required an initiation fee based on age. For monthly dues of one dollar, the member would receive a physician's attention, a steamship ticket to Italy for medical reasons, a funeral, and death benefits paid to his widow.

The Jewish East Side was similarly "honey-combed with Clubs and Societies," ranging from national organizations and large Hebrew orders to numerous small societies consisting of émigrés from a particular locality. The Kehillah, or governing structure of New York's Jewish community, estimated in 1918 that over one million Jews were involved in fraternal orders. . . .

The activities of workingmen's voluntary organizations intertwined with the world of the saloon. Fraternal lodges and clubs regularly used the second-story halls and back rooms of saloons for meetings and entertainment. In Magyar Hall, a saloon patronized by Hungarians and Czechs, the "upper floors are occupied for meeting rooms, where different societys [sic] and workmen circles meet. . . ." The close relationship between the commercial interests of the saloon and the voluntary associations of workingmen provided a foundation for the public social life of working-class communities.

At the same time, the interlocking network of leisure activities strengthened an ethos of masculinity among workingmen. This male culture is most clearly revealed in the social practices of the saloon. . . . Bars often encouraged rowdy behavior and vulgar language less acceptable in other areas of social life. . . .

Gambling often played an important role in the social life of the saloon. At the Sport Café, a "resort for respectable Italian workingmen" near Pennsylvania Station, men shot pool and played cards for drinks. . . . The presence of widespread prostitution also defined saloons as male worlds. Vice investigations of the day provide ample evidence that respectable working-class drinking coexisted with soliciting in the back room. George Kneeland's extensive study of prostitution found that in one-seventh of the 765 bars studies, streetwalkers met customers in the back rooms. . . .

In contrast to this male public culture, the leisure activities of married women were more limited and confined. While workingmen had a broad network of ethnic, class, and commercial institutions available to them, their wives often experienced a dearth of pleasure in their lives. Louise Bolard

More's study of Greenwich Village is typical of investigators' observations: "The men have the saloons, political clubs, trade-unions or lodges for their recreation while the mothers have almost no recreation, only a dreary round of work, day after day, with occasionally a door-step gossip to vary the monotony of their lives." One of the few detailed descriptions of married women's leisure reveals its ephemeral quality, orientation toward the home, and reliance on informal kin and friendship networks for sociability:

> Many women spend their leisure sitting on the steps of their tenements gossiping; some lean out of the window with a pillow to keep their elbows from being scraped by the stone sills; others take walks to the parks; some occasionally visit relatives or friends; and their is, once in a while, a dinner party; but, on the whole, except for the men, there is little conscious recreation.

The constraints on married women's leisure time were in large part shaped by the work rhythms of the home. The scheduling of household chores, of cleaning, cooking, and child care, did not permit the clear differentiation between work and leisure experienced by most workingmen, whose labor was timed to the factory clock and the bosses' commands. These scheduling problems were compounded by inadequate plumbing in the tenements, poor municipal sanitation, and the inability to afford simple labor-saving technology. When asked by an interviewer if her mother had worked for a living, Maria Cichetti's reply cataloged the non waged labor of working-class wives: she had used a coal fire to heat her irons, handled big iron pots in cooking, chopped wood in the cellar, baked her own bread, and borne thirteen babies. Many women also took in boarders to make ends meet, multiplying their household burdens.

Women's work continued long after men's had ceased. In a typical evening scene in an East Side home, while "the mother is attending to her household work, the father is reading a paper, or he may be watching the children at play." A common form of working-class recreation involved reading and discussing the news, particularly the Sunday editions of the *New York Journal* and the *World*, but "the women have no time to read the papers, except the fashion or society notes, or some famous scandal or murder case." Women had to fit their entertainment into their work, rather than around it. Washing and laundry, supervising children at play, or shopping at the local market, women might find a few moments to socialize with neighbors. . . .

The distribution of resources among family members also restricted women's participation in recreation. As we have seen, household budgets allowed only small sums for family recreation, but a substantial portion of the breadwinner's income was allocated as spending for personal use. Husbands retained the right to remove whatever spending money they desired before contributing the rest to the household. Workingmen spent about 10 percent of their weekly income on personal expenses, the bulk of it on beer and liquor, tobacco, and movie and theater tickets. While some husbands removed only transportation and lunch money from their pay envelopes, others abused the privilege: "The husband brings his wages to his wife at the end of the week or fortnight. He gives her the whole amount and receives back carfare and 'beer money' or he gives her as much as 'he feels like' or 'as much as he has left after Saturday night.'"

The issue of spending money was a constant source of tension within the working-class family. Wives voiced opposition to men's drinking up their wages in saloons, rather than committing their earnings to the household. Women in Greenwich Village agreed that "a good husband should turn over to his wife all his wages, receiving one or two dollars a week for his personal use." Whatever the outcome of this weekly negotiation, the designation of the breadwinner's spending money as *personal* allowed men to pursue a social life based upon access to commercial, public recreation. Married women, however, received no spending money of their own. Although they controlled the household's purse strings, this power was mitigated by the constant pressure to make ends meet, and family needs usually governed their expenditures. Even a married woman's own income, earned by keeping boarders or taking in laundry, was usually spent on the home and family, on clothing for the children or better-quality food, rather than personal recreation. "The usual attitude toward any expenditure for pleasure," Louise Bolard More noted, "is that it is a luxury which cannot be afforded.". . .

The grinding rhythms of household labor and limited access to financial resources closely circumscribed many women's social participation. "The lives of women are very narrow," noted one observer, "and they have few interests outside their homes." Indeed, many women sought to make the home into a center for recreation, an alternative to the saloons and streets. Working-class wives carefully decorated their small tenement quarters, even designating one of the multipurpose rooms the "parlor." Surprised observers discovered that "the comforts of life are found in the vilest tenements." Heavy overstuffed furniture, cheap lace curtains, carpets, and bric-a-brac crowded the more prosperous working-class home. Respectability was denoted by one's furnishings, even when purchased on the installment plan. Families would get themselves into such debt that, for some, "the only recreation [was] the display of their furniture." Having a piano or organ in the front room, and lessons for the children twice a week, fulfilled the dreams of many proud mothers. Poorer women spruced up their tenement quarters with a variety of room decorations paid for in grocer's coupons and trading stamps. Gaudily colored religious prints, portraits of Lincoln and Washington, and advertising posters mingled indiscriminately in the tenement parlor: "Pictures of every kind are prized, cheap lithographs, bill-posters, portraits of circus performers and cigarette girls, which are companioned by bleeding hearts, saints, angels and heads of Christ."

Some women hardly left their tenement houses. In trying to attract married women to its programs, the College Settlement found it difficult to dislodge the "habit of staying indoors," a tendency fixed by the burdens of child care and housework and exacerbated by lack of money. Henry Moscowitz, a lower East Side resident and civic leader, reported that many mothers went out no more than twice a week: "Complaints, serious complaints, are made, 'Why don't you come to visit me?' and they say 'We live so high up [in walk-up tenements] we seldom come.'" This pattern seems to have been especially prevalent among Italian women, reinforced by the strong tradition of the sheltered female. While Andrea Boccci's father went to a Prince Street saloon every night, her mother never went out: "If one of her friends would be sick, she would go and help them out, but otherwise she would stay at home.". . .

As many recent historians have argued, cultural traditions and "ways of seeing" indigenous to particular national groups were the lenses through which immigrant working-class families responded to a new industrial and urban environment. Familial values, attitudes toward women's roles, and resistance and adaptation to the workplace were all filtered through such traditions. These also shaped working-class patterns of recreation. Germans, for example, encouraged mixed-sex participation in an amusement usually considered a bastion of male prerogative by taking family groups to huge beer gardens. Such beer halls, where all indulged in drink, song, and socializing, catered to respectable and well-behaved crowds of women and men. Italian men, in contrast, took their everyday recreation apart from the family, but joined their wives and children to commemorate saints' days. The festival tradition remained an important part of Italian life in New York, an opportunity to honor the patron saint of their Old World home with parades and fireworks.

Native-born and "Americanized" immigrant groups tended to frequent commercial amusements and spend the most money on recreation. George Bevans, for example, traced workingmen's leisure activities by national origins and found distinctive differences. German men took their leisure most often with their families. The British-born worker could usually be found in the saloon or union hall. Russian Jews were most likely to spend their evenings in didactic pursuits, at public lectures, libraries, and night schools. In contrast, American-born workingmen, who were most often sons of immigrants, used their leisure time in clubs and lodges, movies, theaters, dance halls, and poolrooms. . . .

To some extent, this "American standard" simply reflected the tendency of families with higher incomes to have larger outlays for recreation and the likelihood that recent immigrants were on the lowest rungs of the economic ladder. For many immigrants, however, participation in urban recreation was part of the broader experience of Americanization. Even though immigrants tended to segregate themselves by national origin, the forms of amusement in tenement districts crossed ethnic lines: saloons, lodges, social, dances, and excursions were common in all working-class neighborhoods.

Forged in an urban society, these American amusements offered a novel conception of leisure to the newly arrived immigrant—the idea of segmenting and organizing leisure into a distinct sphere of activity. David Blaustein, the head of the East Side's Educational Alliance, suggested the differences between the Old World and the New:

> Now to-day the immigrant becomes bewildered when he first comes here to America. As a further illustration, take organized amusement. I call it organized amusement, the way we have picnics, balls, assemblies. The people who come here mostly from eastern Europe are not accustomed to such life. If they have any amusement or gathering it is a birthday party, it is a wedding party, and a funeral; it always centers around the family. But this large scale of amusement, taking out people on excursions by the thousand—when he comes here he becomes bewildered.

For the immigrant, traditional celebrations and everyday pleasures now took place in an unfamiliar context. On the lower East Side, weddings that had once been family affairs were held in rented halls, with dances and entertainment after the marriage ceremony. . . .

A vibrant mixture of Americanized working-class, commercial, and Old World forms of leisure could be found in most immigrant neighborhoods, offering myriad options for pleasure-seekers—and complicating the picture of sex-segregated recreation drawn here. Nevertheless, working-class men of whatever background enjoyed greater opportunities for leisure than their wives. The patterns of men's work, their rights to spending money, and their role in the political and economic life of working-class communities allowed them access to a public world of pleasure and relaxation. In addition, the association of "Americanism" with commercialized recreation and consumption may have heightened the sexual division of leisure in these years. Bevans found that American-born men spent the smallest percentage of their leisure hours with the family than any of the immigrant groups he studied. Women's participation in public and commercial forms of leisure were narrowly defined, their activities located instead in the home, streets, parks, and churches.

Questions for Discussion

1. According to the author, the social life of most immigrant working-class families was segregated by gender. What impact do you think this had on the cohesion of immigrant families?
2. Studies done at the time suggested that men who worked the longest hours for the least pay were most likely to frequent saloons. Why?
3. The saloon was more than a place to drink and socialize. What other roles did it play in the lives of immigrant workingmen? On balance, do you think the saloon had a positive or negative impact on these men and their families?

4. How did Old World and New World leisure and recreation differ, and what impact did that have on the "Americanization" of immigrants?
5. Immigrants are often portrayed as confused and intimidated by their New World surroundings. Based on the picture drawn here of their social, family, and fraternal lives, did they impress you as confused or intimated by their experience of America?

For Further Reading

Gunther Barth, *City People: The Rise of Modern City Culture in Nineteenth Century America* (1980); Paul Boyer, *Urban Masses and Moral Order in America, 1820–1920* (1978); Edwin G. Burrows and Mike Wallace, *Gotham: A History of New York City to 1898* (2000); Dominick Cavallo, *Muscles and Morals: Organized Playgrounds and Urban Reform, 1880–1920* (1981); Howard Chudacoff, *Children at Play: An American History* (2007); Miriam Cohen, *Workshop to Office: Two Generations of Italian Women in New York City, 1900–1950* (1993); Roger Daniels, *Coming to America: A History of Immigration and Ethnicity in America* (2002); Perry Duis, *The Saloon: Public Drinking in Chicago and Boston, 1880–1920* (1983); Foster Rhea Dulles, *A History of Recreation: America Learns to Play* (1965); Edward Robb Ellis, *The Epic of New York City: A Narrative History* (2004); Lewis A. Erenberg, *Steppin' Out: New York Nightlife and the Transformation of American Culture, 1890–1930* (1981); Robert Ernst, *Immigrant Life in New York City, 1825–1863* (1994); Elizabeth Ewen, *Immigrant Women in the Land of Dollars: Life and Culture on the Lower East Side, 1890–1925* (1985); Susan A. Glenn, *Daughters of the Shtetl: Life and Labor in the Immigrant Generation* (1990); Herbert Gutman, *Work, Culture, and Society in Industrializing America* (1977); Kenneth T. Jackson, *Empire City: New York Through the Centuries* (2005); John Kasson, *Amusing the Million: Coney Island at the Turn of the Century* (1978); Lary May, *Screening Out the Past: The Birth of Mass Culture and the Motion Picture Industry* (1980); David Nasaw, *Children of the City: At Work and at Play* (1985); Kathy Peiss, *Cheap Amusements: Working Women and Leisure in Turn-of-the-Century New York* (1986); Roy Rosenzweig, *Eight Hours for What We Will: Workers and Leisure in an Industrializing City: 1877–1919* (1983); Thomas J. Schlereth, *Victorian America: Transformations in Everyday Life, 1876–1915* (1991); Ronald Takaki, *A Larger Meaning: A History of Our Diversity* (1998); Leslie Woodcock Tentler, *Wage-Earning Women: Industrial Work and Family Life in the United States, 1900–1930* (1979).

Flappers, the "New Woman," and Changing Morality in the 1920s

Gerald Leinwand

Many things Americans today take for granted about the economy, gender, and popular culture were either introduced in or came into their own during the 1920s: electronic media and modern advertising techniques, such as marketing research (the forerunner of focus groups); fan magazines and obsessions with celebrity and fame; "talking" Hollywood movies; the popularity of makeup for women (for the first time, "respectable" women used lipstick and rouge); widespread use of birth control; a peer-oriented youth culture; dating—and cars with enclosed roofs that helped make dating a private affair; electric home appliances; the broad impact of African American culture on the entire nation's sensibility, especially through the Harlem Renaissance (there was a reason F. Scott Fitzgerald dubbed the Twenties the "Jazz Age"); by the end of the decade disc recordings replaced phonograph cylinders as the most popular medium for listening to recorded music, including the defiantly powerful blues of African American artists Bessie Smith and Ma Rainey; and the list goes on. In a way, modern America was created during the "Roaring Twenties."

For example, the 1920s was the first time that the *perception* of the country as a place of widespread prosperity and the purchase of consumer goods on credit became defining qualities of American economic life. It was, by far, the most prosperous decade in the country's history to that point. After a slump in 1920 and 1921, manufacturing output increased by more than

In the top illustration, the artist Charles Dana Gibson depicts respectable women enjoying a moment of leisure in a rural setting around 1900. In the bottom photo, two flappers dance the Charleston near the Capitol during the 1920s. What do the illustrations tell you about changing perceptions of women during the early years of the twentieth century?

two-thirds through the end of the decade. Labor productivity rose a stunning 43 percent. Consumer goods poured out of factories because the purchasing power of Americans increased significantly: the average salaries of nonagricultural workers increased by about 30 percent during the decade.

In addition, many retailers allowed customers to purchase goods through installment buying plans. For instance, more than two-thirds of new automobiles sold in the 1920s were bought on credit. Installment purchases played a role in the explosion of automobile sales in the decade (in 1915 there were 2.4 million cars on the road; ten years later there were more than 20 million). Department stores extended credit for the purchase of clothing and electronic appliances. By 1929, with about 60 percent of residences wired for electricity, new gadgets and electronic media began to pervade the American home. More than 40 percent of homes with electricity had radios, and electronic technology made irons, phonographs, vacuum cleaners, and washing machines increasingly common. The "wiring" of the American home, and American lives, had begun.

There were other changes in American homes as well, especially in relationships between women and men. The Twenties was not only the first decade in which all women could vote (though most black women, like most black men, were kept out of voting booths). It was also a time of transition in the history of gender roles. In the next essay, Gerald Leinwand describes the dramatic changes in gender roles and attitudes toward sexuality in the Twenties. It is important to keep in mind that these changes were both real enough to cause alarm in many quarters and fragile enough to fall far short of a full-blown feminist movement. That did not occur until forty years later.

What was real by the 1920s was a major shift in attitudes toward female sexuality. According to surveys taken at the time, female virginity before marriage was on the wane. More than 90 percent of women born before 1890 claimed to be virgins when they married. That number dropped to 74 percent for those born between 1890 and 1899 and to 51 percent of women born between 1900 and 1909. It plunged to 32 percent of those born after 1910. It was not only the small number of young women called "flappers" who were having "fun" in the Twenties (the word "flapper" was a reference to young birds that "flap" their wings when learning to fly). It appears that many young women were putting an end to the traditional "double standard" by joining men who engaged in premarital sex. It should be noted, however, that most women who had premarital sex in the 1920s did so with men they assumed were going to marry them.

Once married, many women, especially those in the middle and upper classes, expected to enjoy greater equality with their husbands. Generalizations about what actually happens within families are always dangerous, but it appears that patriarchy was dealt a major blow in the 1920s, though far from a fatal one. "Companionate" marriage, in which the couple expected to be friends as well as lovers, within a mutually rewarding, emotionally gratifying "partnership," became the marital ideal. How real was this?

It is hard to say—as one wife of the time put it, "When he gets home at night, he just settles down with the paper and his cigar and the radio and just rests."

But the idea that marriage should be sexually and emotionally gratifying for *both* partners was pervasive enough to help cause a rise in the rate of divorce. The more people expect from marriage, the more likely they will be disappointed and possibly end the relationship. Beginning in the late nineteenth century, the United States had the highest divorce rate in the world (it still does). In the Twenties it reached an all-time high to that point: one in seven marriages ended in divorce. In major metropolitan areas, it was much higher in the 1920s: one in four San Francisco marriages ended in divorce, one of five in Los Angeles.

These changes in gender roles and expectations, along with others discussed in the essay, were important. But they did not alter the economic relations between women and men (for instance, the retail credit programs mentioned earlier were usually extended only to the husband); nor did they lead to increased numbers of women in the major professions. Most women in middle-class jobs were nurses and teachers, just as they had been in the nineteenth century. And there were actually fewer female physicians and dentists in 1929 than there were in 1899.

Just as changes in gender roles in the 1920s can be exaggerated, so can the decade's prosperity. As noted earlier, it was the most prosperous decade to that point in American history. But farm families—more than 25 percent of the population—did not share it. Annual per capita farm income plummeted in the Twenties, and by 1929 it was only $273—about 40 percent of the national average. Income was unequally distributed in the rest of the economy as well. The top 0.1 percent of households earned as much as the bottom 42 percent. Put another way, in 1929 Henry Ford had an income of $14 million; the average personal income of Americans that year was $750. It has been estimated that by 1929, an income of about $2,000 was needed for a family of five to purchase the basic necessities of life. In that year, 71 percent of families had an income of $2,500 or less, with 42 percent of them at $1,500 or less.

It was, then, a decade of sharp contrasts and ambiguities, as Gerald Leinwand makes clear in his discussion of the "New Woman" of the 1920s.

Source: Gerald Leinwand, *1927: High Tide of the Twenties* (New York: Four Walls Eight Windows, 2001), pp. 172–190. Reprinted by permission of Basic Books, a member of Perseus Books Group.

In the 1890s the stereotypical young woman representing the ideal of femininity in the Gilded Age, was the large-breasted, well-rounded, somewhat plumpish but tightly corseted Gibson Girl as satirized for *Life*, a humorous weekly magazine, by Charles Dana Gibson. The Gibson Girl's hair was piled high on a patricianly small head; a slim neck and broad shoulders allowing vast expanses of décolletage, the carriage of a West Point cadet. She preferred an elaborate evening gown or the newly popular shirtwaist tucked into a straight skirt, the belted waistband of which showed her exquisitely small waist. The clothing of the Gibson Girl conveyed the message that her husband could support her well and so she did not have to work outside the home. The Gibson Girl's fashionable clothing testified to her husband's ability to support her. "For the Gibson Girl, grooming itself was her profession; to be her husband's prized possession was her career."

The Gibson Girl took her cues in fashion and values from European royalty. She was the embodiment of women as bearers of children, makers of homes, devoted, affectionate, but obedient wives. She was taught to please men rather than herself. The ideal she embodied included innocence, dependence, helplessness, selflessness, goodness, and devotion to others. But these values encouraged ignorance of life's realities and downgraded the merits of education. Even in matters of childbearing and rearing, the Gibson Girl was aware of what was expected of her, but had little guidance in how to succeed at it. . . . The Gibson Girl was solid, stable, a refuge in a storm; in short, the Gibson girl was unflappable.

Unlike the Gibson Girl, the flapper was radiant, energetic, volatile, voluble, brazen. The Gibson Girl evoked the traditional moral code in America. That is, sex was in the background and women were subservient to the appetites of men and only reluctantly partook of sexual intercourse. The flapper flaunted her interest in sex and implied, at least, that she was available for sex for pleasure as well as for procreation.

What "modern" women sought to achieve was the abandonment of the double standard. If higher education was available to men, similar levels of education should be available to women. If men could choose careers in business and/or the professions, equal opportunities should be open to women. If men were free to stray sexually without criticism, women felt that such opportunity should be theirs as well.

The well dressed flapper no longer took her cues from European royalty. Instead, she looked to Hollywood movie stars. The flapper wore a tightly fitting felt cloche hat, two strings of beads, flesh colored hose rolled below the knees, bangles on her wrists, and unbuckled galoshes. She hid her breasts but wore kiss-proof lipstick as did Clara Bow in the 1927 movie "It."

Most symbolically, perhaps, was that the hemline of women's skirts rose from the ankle (1919) to above the knee (1927) "and was rightly taken as the index of the revolutionary change in morals and manners that accompanied and followed the war.". . .

Critics warned that when skirts rose above the knee and stockings were rolled below it, more naked flesh was immodestly revealed than at any time in history. The Young Women's Christian Association circulated a booklet called "Modesty Appeal" and urged women to dress more decorously. Fashion writers insisted that women had gone too far and should lower their skirts during the very next fashion season. Legislative bodies in Utah and Virginia sought to impose limits on hemlines and necklines but to no avail. Of these changes Carmel Snow, the fashion editor of *Vogue*, wrote "Nobody ever again will think of clothes as designed for a creature who sits—she must walk about doing things. . . . [E]fficiency, simplicity, unity—these make for chic. And chic is the one thing sought by the modern woman when she thinks about clothes."

As skirts were shortened, so too did women jettison encumbering petticoats and corsets. A survey in Milwaukee in 1927 of thirteen hundred working girls showed that fewer than seventy wore corsets. Silk or rayon stockings became almost universal and in hot and humid weather many women wore no stockings at all. Dress sleeves were shortened and in some cases vanished altogether.

Hair was worn short and long tresses were out. The "boyish bob" became the vogue and the barbershop, still a bastion for an all male environment, fell to women who found the barber more efficient than the hair stylist.

Seventy-three percent of women in the United States over eighteen years of age used perfume; 90 percent face powder; 73 percent toilet water; 50 percent rouge. In 1927, 7,000 kinds of cosmetics were on the market. The perfume and cosmetics industries, including lipsticks, talcum powder, hair tonics, and hair dyes, had grown six times what it was in 1917. "Fortunes were made in mud baths . . . in patent hair removers, in magic lotions to make the eyelashes long and sweeping, in soaps that claimed to nourish the skin, in hair dyes that restored the natural color, in patent nostrums for 'reducing' and in all the other half-fraudulent traps of the advertisers for the beauty seeker."

As eroticism shifted from the breasts (Gibson Girl) to the limbs (Flapper), the latter's costume also heralded a shift from women as wives and homemakers to competitors of men in business. Flappers' fashion made it possible for women to move around in the world of business, albeit at the lower rungs, as secretaries, stenographers, and telephone operators. The dress and grooming of the flapper not only enhanced sexuality but was efficient for work in an office and for businesslike activities with male and female peers. Black and beige were the preferred colors for the flapper as emerging businesswoman as well as coquette. The flapper, in short, wanted it all.

Some women began smoking in public. They "reached for a Lucky instead of a sweet!" and unhesitatingly entered speakeasies and consumed illicit alcohol. While data are hard to come by, researchers found that women born later than the turn of the century were twice as likely to have lost their virginity before they were married than women of the previous generation. College coeds generally made due with heavy breathing from necking and petting but a few went "all the way." Extra marital sex also became more common. Possibly because of the relatively ready availability of sex from otherwise respectable women, a great many brothels lost their customers, as did street-walking prostitutes.

"I've kissed dozens of men," declared one of F. Scott Fitzgerald's heroines. "I suppose I'll kiss dozens more." Innocent, perhaps, by today's standards, the intent of the declaration was to shock the older generation—and shock it did. Petting in the back seats of enclosed automobiles, dating without a chaperone, dancing the latest craze, the Charleston, drinking illegal whiskey, defying adult authority and the traditions of the Judeo-Christian faiths, making heroes of hoodlums: the affluent youth of America, is not the immigrant poor, at least for a time succeeded in rewriting the rules of behavior and decorum. One writer, describing conditions in 1927, had this to say: "What a gulf separates even two generations! Mothers and daughters often understand each other's viewpoints so little that it seems as though they [aren't] speaking the same language." He goes on to note: "Changes are occurring throughout our whole social system. The education of youth in school and college changes from year to year. Religion is no longer the unchanging rock of ages. The family is becoming smaller. Young people are marrying earlier and getting divorces more frequently. Restaurants and hotels are increasing rapidly in number, and apartments are becoming smaller. More and more women are working for pay outside the home. And most perplexing seems to be our changing morality itself, for the detailed application of moral codes gives very uncertain advice on the new problems of conduct."

From her abode in Paris, Gertrude Stein described the gifted young writers of her day as the "Lost Generation." Before long, her description was applied to the flapper era more generally. Perhaps Stein overstated the case, but the dominant mood in America appeared to be not so much that tomorrow would take care of itself but instead—who cares? The theme was best exemplified by Edna St. Vincent Millay:

My candle burns at both ends;
It will not last the night;
But, ah, my foes, and, oh, my friends—
It gives a lovely light.

Not only were women emancipated from the conventional morality, they were emancipated from the kitchen as well. A visit to an urban American home would have found a small, compact rather than roomy kitchen that was often so central to the rural home. An electric refrigerator took the place of the cool cellar. Nor was it necessary to store large amounts of food, since convenience stores were growing in number, in location, and in the variety of food in small quantities that could be bought.

In 1912, only 16 percent of Americans lived in dwellings provided with electric light. By 1927, 63 percent had electric lights. Household appliances were growing so numerous that 80 percent of the electrically wired homes had electric irons, 37 percent had vacuum cleaners, and more than 25 percent had clothes washers, fans, or toasters. . . .

The era of the flapper, though not her influence, was short-lived. By 1927, the flapper as an American female type was on the way out.

THE NEW WOMAN: FLAPPER NO MORE

The new woman of 1927 was neither feminist nor flapper but was indebted to both. The flapper opened wide the window of opportunity by attacking the double standard in American morality. She saw nothing wrong with smoking a cigarette, visiting a speakeasy for a drink of illegal spirits, or interpreting Freud as to allowing her to enjoy the pleasure of sex. For the most part the flapper was a product of the growing urban environment in which most Americans lived.

The new woman recognizes that the flapper is but a stereotype described by F. Scott Fitzgerald as "lovely and expensive and about nineteen," but is not entirely prepared to flaunt convention. The new woman admires the feminist for her courage but is uncomfortable with her zealotry. She honors the feminist for fighting her battle but believes the worst of the battle is over and that, therefore, it is not necessary to bear a grudge against men and that it is no longer necessary to throw hand grenades. The new woman concedes that a husband and children are necessary to the average woman's fullest development but believes with equal vigor that a career does not preclude motherhood. The new woman seeks happiness within marriage but without the stifling limitations customarily placed upon her. She expects marriage to be a monogamous partnership of equals in which both she and her husband shun promiscuity.

Advertisements in such magazines as the *Ladies Home Journal* for 1927 began to appeal to the new woman. "You think I'm a flapper but I can keep house," announced an ad for S.O.S., that "magic cleaner" of pots and pans. The advertisement continued, "If we get married, I'll keep house better than mother does hers. But I'm not going to turn into a slave. You men! You think drudgery is a sign of good housekeeping." The new woman never had to fear "dishpan hands" if she just used Lux soap. A "clean dazzling smile," Colgate noted, was women's "social weapon." Products for feminine hygiene, for undergarments, for hosiery, boldly appealed to the new woman.

Prominent women were called on to endorse products of various kinds. In the December 1927 issue of the *Ladies Home Journal*, Eleanor Roosevelt, whose husband, Franklin, was about to run for governor of New York State, endorsed the Simmons Beautyrest mattress. "The perfect gift," she called it. . . .

Although women had won the right to vote in 1920 when the Nineteenth Amendment was adopted, by the election of 1928 they did not vote with the discipline and in the numbers required to make them a formidable political factor. Yet political life was beginning to beckon. By 1928, seven women were in Congress, 119 had been elected in 1928 as state representatives, and twelve were state senators. . . .

Despite these achievements, feminists, having won the franchise, now sought to have an equal rights amendment added to the Constitution. Edna Kenton, after describing the pomp and dignity accorded to newly elected Governor Miriam A. Ferguson, the first woman governor of Texas, pointed out that a month before Ferguson had to petition the District Court of Bell County, Texas, to remove the disqualifications that might arise from her status as a married woman. According to Texas law, she first had to get her husband's permission to petition the court to have those disqualifications removed. Failure to proceed in this way might have invalidated such contracts that the governor might have signed on behalf of Texas, since a married woman in Texas was "but a living shadow, not of herself, but her husband—and, like a shadow, incapable of contracting or otherwise acting on her own responsibility."

What was true in Texas was likewise true in other states of the nation. In Virginia and Rhode Island the father was the sole natural guardian of minor children with primary right to custody, control of their education, religion, and general welfare. In Alabama the father had preference as guardian of the child's property, and, in New York and Michigan, the father was entitled to services and earnings of a minor child. The father's consent alone was sufficient to authorize the apprenticing of a child in Colorado, and the father alone was entitled to damages for the wrongful death of a minor child in the District of Columbia. In Massachusetts the father had first right to sue for damages for the seduction of a daughter, and the father had the right to will away the child from the mother in Georgia and Maryland. In the majority of states the services of the wife in the home belonged to the husband. Thus, the right to vote did not also confer on married women equal rights with their husbands.

On December 2, 1923, the National Women's Party proposed to the judiciary committees of both houses of Congress a constitutional amendment which read, "Men and women shall have equal rights throughout the United States and every place subject to its jurisdiction." On July 13, 1927, a delegation from the National Women's Party arrived at the summer White House in Rapid City, South Dakota, to enlist the support of President Calvin Coolidge for the Equal Rights Amendment.

But many "new women" were opposed to the Equal Rights Amendment. The League of Women Voters felt that such a blanket amendment to the Constitution would be "self-defeating and much of the protective legislation adopted on women's behalf would be withdrawn." What would happen to the minimum wage for women, to the statutory eight-hour day for women, or to the guarantee of one day of rest? What would happen to protections afforded working, pregnant women, and what of the penalties for rape? Some women feared the proposed Equal Rights Amendment would require a wife to support an incompetent husband. That kind of equality was not desired by all women. . . .

For professional women, prejudice and opportunity existed side by side. In law, prejudice in employment persisted, as most people preferred to seek legal advice from men. In medicine, discrimination against women was flagrant. In higher education, of 4,700 full professorships, women held but four percent and served mainly in lower instructional ranks at lower salaries than men in the same rank. . . .

If newspaper headlines are any yardstick, the emergence of the "new woman" continued to be viewed apprehensively by many Americans, women as well as men: [the following were from *The New York Times* at various dates in 1927]

"End of Monogamy Seen in Feminism . . ."

"Women Inferior, Asserts Mussolini . . ."

"Modern Life Lessens Sex Fixity [i.e., gender identity] . . ."

"See Peril to Race in Birth Control . . ."

MARGARET SANGER AND THE BIRTH CONTROL MOVEMENT

Birth control, a term coined by Margaret Sanger, while widely practiced by affluent and educated Americans, was still neither generally known nor practiced by the impoverished. Catholic priests continued to thunder against birth control and the faithful were often torn between what they viewed as their obligation to their church and the physical demands of the body. It was Margaret Sanger's mission to extend knowledge of birth control to the many and by the time she died she had largely succeeded.

Margaret Sanger (1883–1966) was the sixth of eleven children born in Corning, New York, to Michael Hennessy Higgins, a rather rebellious, red-headed Irish sculptor. Margaret was seventeen when her mother, exhausted by poverty and excessive child-bearing, died. Despite the fact that the burden of caring for her siblings fell on [Margaret], with family encouragement she became a nurse. In the hospitals in which she served she learned that the greatest plague afflicting women was giving birth to far too many children. She saw firsthand what repeated child-bearing did to the health of still comparatively young women, and the impact of having more children than they could possibly support on the quality of family life. In her *Autobiography* she wrote, "In the hospital I found that seventy-five percent of the diseases of men and women are the result of ignorance of their sex functions. So great was the ignorance of women and girls I met concerning their own bodies that I decided to specialize in women's diseases and took up gynecological and obstetrical nursing. A few years of this work brought me to the shocking discovery—that the knowledge of the ways of controlling birth was accessible to the women of wealth while the working women were deliberately kept in ignorance of this knowledge."

Margaret Higgins married William Sanger, an architect, and had three children. The family moved in a circle of radical intellectuals inclined toward socialism and anarchism. Among the influential leaders of this group were Eugene Debs, Ida Tarbell, Lincoln Steffens, and "Big Bill" Hayward of the International Workers of the World [also known as Wobblies]. It was Hayward who suggested that Margaret go to France where birth control was widely acknowledged and equally widely practiced. In France, Margaret Sanger studied methods of birth control while her husband studied painting. By 1914, she felt she had learned all that she needed to in France and, leaving her husband behind, she returned with her children to the United States. . . .

She became editor of the *Woman Rebel*, a journal devoted to left-wing causes, but she also used the journal as a means of disseminating important information about birth control. It was at this juncture that she ran headlong into her nemesis, Anthony Comstock (1844–1915), a crusader against vice, pornography, gambling, and obscene materials. He was instrumental in securing the passage of postal laws prohibiting obscene materials sent through the mail. Information about birth control was viewed as obscene and so could neither be sent through the mails or otherwise distributed. As the secretary of the New York Society for the Suppression of Vice, Comstock's harassment of Margaret Sanger continued unabated until his death in 1915. Yet, his legacy of opposition to the dissemination of birth control materials remained formidable throughout her pioneering years.

Sanger opened America's first birth control clinic at 46 Amboy Street, an immigrant neighborhood in Brooklyn, New York. In her *Autobiography* she wrote: "The morning of October 16, 1916—crisp but sunny and bright after days of rain—I opened the doors of the first birth control clinic in America." But would the women come? It was not long before she found out. "Halfway to the corner they were standing in line, at least one hundred and fifty, some shawled, some hatless, their red hands clasping the cold, chapped, smaller ones of their children."

Sanger's fight for reproductive rights for women had only just begun. The New York City police department's vice squad, a unit accustomed to raiding gambling dens and brothels, soon raided her clinic. Sanger was arrested for the first of nine times during the course of her crusade for birth control. But despite imprisonment, opposition from organized medicine, religion, and the press, and even ridicule from those she was trying to help, Sanger would not be deterred. In 1921, Margaret Sanger founded the American Birth Control League [the precursor of Planned Parenthood Federation of America, founded in 1942]. . . .

By 1927, when birth control had developed enough momentum, Margaret Sanger organized the first World Population Conference in Geneva. The conference brought together for the first time doctors and social scientists who were concerned with worldwide population. In her preface to the *Proceedings of the World Population Conference,* Sanger wrote: "It has long been my desire to have the population question discussed from an international scientific standpoint, and it is with a feeling of some satisfaction that I am at last able to present to the public so complete and comprehensive a volume on this great question."

Yet among the participants of the conference Margaret Sanger was a prophet without honor. The august scientists present did not relish having their names associated with a woman, much less a politically radical woman, and worse still, a woman whose scientific credentials could not match their own. (She was, after all, only a nurse!) Conference Chairman Sir Bernard Mallet, under pressure from these scholars, agreed to remove the names of "all the workers" [i.e., those considered nonprofessionals] including that of Margaret Sanger, from the program. . . .

"Margaret Sanger," wrote her friend Mable Dodge Luhan, "was the first person I ever knew who was an openly ardent propagandist for the joys of the flesh." Mrs. Luhan wrote that to Margaret Sanger maturity meant "enjoying it (sex) with a conscious attainment of its possibilities." By removing the fear of pregnancy, women could attain at least the same level of enjoyment through sexual intercourse as their male partners. In her book *Woman and the New Race,* Sanger wrote that women should break out of their repressive mentality and welcome sex as "the greatest possible expression and fulfillment of their desires. This is one of the great functions of contraceptives." Despite noteworthy advances in the birth control movement made in 1927, respectability, however, continued to elude Sanger as she could find little enduring support from the medical establishment, the eugenics movement or the feminist movement. . . .

Although birth control was widely practiced among the well-to-do and educated, it was not a subject many liked to talk about. Magazines often refused to take articles on the subject and radio was even more adamant in keeping public discussion of contraception off the air. Feminist groups likewise were reluctant to be associated with the birth control movement even as their members practiced it. Thus, the National Women's Party in its 1927 platform refused to include a plank endorsing birth control for fear of splitting its membership and alienating supporters.

Ambivalence about what they were doing was widespread even among those who regularly resorted to contraceptives. On the one hand, they justified resorting to birth control as an important means of insuring the health of women and as a means of rearing fewer but better cared-for children. In the aftermath of World War I, it was taken as an axiom that if global population could be controlled, an important cause of war would be eliminated. But if married couples could engage in sexual intercourse without the responsibility of caring for children nine months later, what then would keep such marriages on a moral course? What would prevent the non-married from coupling promiscuously and what would that mean for the morality of Americans? What would happen to the American family?

Charlotte Perkins Gilman, for example, in an essay written for the *North American Review,* worried that widespread use of contraceptives would lead to "a degree of sex indulgence without parallel in nature." Yet, she acknowledged that physicians were slowly accepting contraception as they see at first hand what the exhaustion of childbearing can do to the health of women. She acknowledged that economists liked birth control as a means of bringing population growth in line with available food supply. Eugenicists, she pointed out, likewise saw value in birth control as a means of bringing about a higher standard of offspring and a better quality of life for them. She concludes her essay: "Perhaps since birth is women's business it is right that she have some voice in discussing its control. Mrs. Sanger's appeal for the overburdened mother is a just one; it is enough to warrant prompt action, to justify birth control; but there is more to be considered." What more is to be considered? How should a woman square her "duty to have children" with her right to decide "when, where and how many" to have? She conceded that the answer to this question "is not plain to most of us." She worried that "popular knowledge of preventive methods" would, in a "sex crazy" nation, lead to selfishness and indulgence. . . .

Questions for Discussion

1. How did the "Gibson Girl" of the 1890s differ from the "flapper" of the 1920s? How did the flapper's fashions and lifestyle reflect a shift in relations between women and men?
2. Who was the "New Woman"? How did she differ from both flappers and feminists? According to the author, why would most "New Women" oppose the Equal Rights Amendment?
3. According to Margaret Sanger, how would birth control improve the lives of women and children? How would it improve American society? Do you agree with her?
4. Why did many Americans, even those who practiced birth control, worry about its consequences?

For Further Reading

Frederick Allen, *Only Yesterday: An Informal History of the 1920s* (2000); Lionel Bascom, ed., *A Renaissance in Harlem: Voices of an American Community* (1999); Dorothy M. Brown, *Setting a Course: American Women in the 1920s* (1987); Stephanie Coontz, *Marriage, A History* (2006); Angela Davis, *Blues Legacies and Black Feminism* (1999); John D'Emilio and Estelle B. Freedman, *Intimate Matters: A History of Sexuality in America* (1988); Ann Douglas, *Terrible Honesty: Mongrel Manhattan in the 1920s* (1995); Kathleen Drowne and Patrick Huber, *The 1920s* (2004); Lynn Dumenil, *The Modern Temper: American Culture and Society in the 1920s* (1995); Nicholas Evans, *Writing Jazz: Race, Nationalism, and Modern Culture in the 1920s* (2000); Paula Fass, *The Damned and the Beautiful: Youth in the 1920s* (1979); Peter G. Filene, *Him/Her/Self: Gender Identities in Modern America* (1998); David J. Goldberg and Stanley L. Kutler, *Discontented Americans: The United States in the 1920s* (1999); David E. Kyvig, *Daily Life in the United States, 1920–1930* (2002); Angela Latham, *Posing a Threat: Flappers, Chorus Girls, and Other Brazen Performers of the American 1920s* (2000); Ellie Laubner, *Fashions of the 1920s* (2000); David Levering Lewis, *When Harlem Was in Vogue* (1981); Nathan Miller, *New World Coming: The 1920s and the Making of Modern America* (2004); Kathy Peiss, *Hope in a Jar: The Making of America's Beauty Culture* (1999); Chip Rhodes, *Structures of the Jazz Age: Mass Culture, Progressive Education and Racial Discourse in American Modernism* (1998); David Shannon, *Between the Wars: America, 1919–1941* (1979); Susan Strasser, *Satisfaction Guaranteed: The Making of the American Mass Market* (1989); Gary D. Wintz, *The Harlem Renaissance* (2003); Joshua Zeitz, *Flapper: A Madcap History of Sex, Style, and the Women Who Made America Modern* (2007).

8

The Ku Klux Klan Combats the "New Morality" of the 1920s

Nancy MacLean

Some Americans eagerly embraced the new morality of the Jazz Age. Others just as eagerly rejected it. Historians have often interpreted this as a conflict between an "old" and a "new" America. The old one consisted of white, mostly Anglo-Saxon Protestants who lived in rural, small-town communities, especially in the South. These people cherished traditional values: the "old-time religion," the male-dominated family, and children who obeyed their parents. The new United States was brewing in ethnically and racially diverse northern cities. It was bursting with daring new ideas about everything from fashion to personal freedom.

There is much to be said for looking at the divisions of the 1920s in this way. But it does not tell the whole story.

For instance, it was a politically conservative decade, and the scope of that conservatism was national, not regional. In the aftermath of World War I, the federal and state governments organized a campaign to suppress radical political groups. This was a response to a wave of strikes across the county in 1919, including one by police in Boston and a series of unsolved bombings that the authorities claimed were carried out by radicals. The federal government rounded up more than 4,000 individuals suspected of being radicals, aliens, or both. About 600 were deported. None of those arrested or deported were charged with crimes or tried by a jury of their peers, much less convicted of anything—except possibly being radicals and

Women of the Ku Klux Klan march near the Capitol in 1928. What role did concerns about the morality of women play in the rise of the second Ku Klux Klan?

aliens. In addition, twenty-eight states passed laws making it illegal to display red flags. The New York State legislature passed a bill making it a crime to join Marxist organizations; that same body refused to seat five socialists legally elected to the legislature by New York City voters.

To some extent, fears of radicalism were tied to animosities toward immigrants. This was especially true of newcomers who hailed from southern and eastern Europe, especially Catholics and Jews, as well as Asians. In 1924 Congress passed the widely supported National Origins Act. The law included a quota system designed to restrict the number of Catholics and Jews entering the country and to eliminate those from Asia entirely. For example, the annual quota from Great Britain was 65,957. But from Catholic Italy it was limited to 5,802, while eastern European areas (the main source of Jewish immigration) such as Russia and Poland were restricted to 2,712 and 6,524, respectively. Asians were banned altogether. When he signed the bill into law, President Calvin Coolidge said, "America must be kept American." Quotas designed to limit immigration of specific groups remained in effect until 1965.

A conservative political climate dominated the entire nation in the Twenties. Three Republicans were elected president. And the Supreme Court routinely struck down legislation opposed by business interests.

These included minimum wage laws and attempts to bolster the power and membership of labor unions. The anti-union tactics of corporations, the courts, and legislatures were successful. In 1920, labor unions had about 5 million members; in 1929, they had fewer than 3 million.

Cultural conservatism may have been more prominent in the South and other rural areas of the country, but like political conservatism, it was present in every part of the country. For instance, Prohibition—the banning of the manufacture and sale of beverages containing more than one-half of 1 percent of alcohol by the Eighteenth Amendment in 1919—was favored by large numbers of rural people. But it was also supported by many urban Progressive reformers—who believed saloons (a favorite haunt of urban political machines) and alcohol were dangerous to both the political system and the family. In 1915, *all* forty-eight states had "local option" laws—laws allowing local governments to ban the sale of alcohol. Without question, however, there were significant numbers of rural Protestants who viewed Prohibition as a way to strike a blow against Catholics, Jews, and the "immoral" city. Also, at times states enacted "liberal" measures as a way of achieving reactionary or racist goals. For example, in the 1930s states in the Deep South were the first to take Margaret Sanger's advice and provide state funding for contraceptives and family planning—as a means of limiting the birthrate among African American families.

One attempt to promote traditional values that was mostly rural and southern was religious fundamentalism. The term *fundamentalism* first came into common use around 1920, and it is important to keep in mind that it reflected a struggle between two groups within the Protestant camp. Fundamentalists believed in biblical literalism, the notion that the Bible was not only divinely inspired but the literal word of God. They were at odds with "modernist" Protestants, who tried to reconcile the Bible with scientific theories like Darwinian evolution.

In the 1920s, the most spectacular confrontation between the two Protestant camps was the Scopes Trial in 1925—known around the world as the "Monkey Trial." In January 1925, the Tennessee legislature passed a law making it a crime for public schools to "teach any theory that denies the story of the divine creation of man as taught in the Bible." The law was designed to prevent teaching of the theory of evolution in public schools. It was similar in intent to laws already passed during the 1920s in the southern states of Kentucky, Florida, Texas, and North Carolina. Shortly after Tennessee passed its law, Mississippi and Arkansas also banned the teaching of evolution in their public schools.

Two things stand out about the controversy over evolution in the 1920s. One is that it was a peculiarly American controversy: English and other European evangelical and fundamentalist Protestants have never created an anti-evolution crusade. The other is that the struggle against the teaching of evolution endured in the United States long after the 1920s. As late as the 1950s, more than one-half of biology textbooks used in American high schools did not mention the word *evolution*. In 1999, knowledge of evolutionary theory was not part of statewide education standards in Illinois, Kentucky, Tennessee, Mississippi, Arkansas, and Georgia.

In the early years of the 1920s, the Ku Klux Klan captured the loyalties of millions of Americans who were disturbed by everything the "new" America represented: from the birth control movement and the rise of the "new woman" to scientific challenges to biblical authority and the presence of Jews, Catholics, and political radicals in the country. The original Ku Klux Klan appeared in the South after the Civil War and was largely disbanded by the late nineteenth century. The new KKK was organized in 1915. While the southern KKK focused on terrorizing African Americans, it also developed large followings among those in other parts of the country who despised Jews, Catholics, and radicals. The new KKK was popular in midwestern states like Indiana and far western ones like Oregon.

In the next essay, Nancy MacLean describes the attitudes and behavior of the Klan in Georgia. According to MacLean, KKK members feared that changing gender and sexual roles undermined male authority, the Bible, and the family.

Source: Nancy MacLean, *Behind the Mask of Chivalry: The Making of the Second Ku Klux Klan* (New York: Oxford University Press, 1994), pp. 99–100, 111–124.

As a site of debauchery, the Imperial Palace of the [Georgia] Klan rivaled some of the motion picture sets its representatives so habitually rebuked. The national chaplain of the Klan, Caleb Ridley, a well-known Atlanta minister and Prohibitionist, was arrested in 1923 for driving while intoxicated. Imperial Wizard [William] Simmons, according to numerous people in a position to know, drank heavily, relished pornography, and regularly patronized prostitutes. His assistants E.Y. Clarke and Mary Elizabeth Tyler, the masterminds of the Klan's growth after 1920, were once arrested together, inebriated and in the flesh, during a tryst in a hotel. The list could go on. The unsavory conduct of the highest leadership helped cause its overthrow and replacement in 1922—and cost their movement much of its following over the decade. The hypocrisy of the order's national officials is more than ironic, however. It underscores, in a circuitous way, their Machiavellian appreciation of the appeal of morality campaigns for the people they hoped to attract. And, indeed, rarely did local chapters suffer such scandals. To rank-and-file members, the Klan's professed commitment to purity meant a great deal.

The Klan in fact staked its bid for power on its value as a tool for restoring "traditional" values. Purity campaigns became the core of recruitment drives in localities around the country. A former Klan organizer reported in 1924 that officers from the Imperial Palace instructed local Klans, once organized, to "clean up their towns." One of the Klan's oaths of citizenship thus bound the member "to correct evils in my community, particularly vices tending to the destruction of the home, family, childhood and woman-hood." Klaverns around the country boasted that their efforts had arrested the drift toward immorality: "whole communities that seemed traveling fast on the road to hell suddenly have turned toward Heaven." Clearly, national officials thought these clean-ups an excellent way to prove the value of the Klan to its constituency. They were right. Across the country, the Klan ingratiated itself with solid middle-class white citizens on the basis of its unrivaled commitment to community moral "clean-ups."

The demand for purity served several ends. Its immediate object was to subdue internal threats to family discipline: from men who failed to act their parts, from children who repudiated the Spartan tastes of their parents, and from wives who sought to renegotiate the marriage compact. Yet the movement's emphasis on moral purity was more than a strategy to boost enrollments and bolster parental authority and male dominance. Respectability was also a prime marker of status for the lower-middle-class men who joined the Klan in such numbers. Their moral standards were the visible sign of their distance from, and purported superiority to, both the working class and the elite. Taking a stand for the old-time virtues was thus also a means of building internal cohesion and collective confidence among the white Protestant petite bourgeoisie the Klan hoped to mobilize.

A postwar moral panic paved the way for the growth of the Klan in Clarke County. It was not the first time local residents had worried about alcohol, gambling, and prostitution; agitation over such issues had a long history in Athens [Georgia] as elsewhere in the nation. But when such affronts accompanied economic disaster and social strife, and when pre-marital sex joined the list of transgressions, the mixture proved volatile. Experimentation in marriage or morals, explained one Klan-recommended writer on the family, was particularly risky "in this age of unrest and discontent and instability." The editor of the *Athens Daily Banner* summarized the common diagnosis in 1921: "The tendency of the times toward disorder and crime and revolution and unrest" had a taproot: "disregard for authority both parental and governmental." "Bolshevism and socialism and all the radical isms rampant" were the harvest of lenient parenting. The return of the state's authority would "have to start in the home"; parents must "compel obedience and respect."

What both writers . . . had in common was a conviction that ordered, hierarchical families undergirded ordered, hierarchical society, and a perception that the behavior of contemporary young people, women in particular, endangered both. Unnerved by postwar unrest, they looked to the family to provide a model of stability and authority for the rest of society. In "purifying" domestic life, they would rid the wider world of its evils.

Evangelical ministers first sounded the alarm in Athens. In a 1920 sermon, the Reverend W.F. Dick of the Athens Free Methodist Church denounced "the evils of our day" abundant in Clarke County. Dick flayed "the public dance hall . . . the pool room, the card table and other kinds of sin practiced in Athens." Many adults, locally and nationwide, shared his anxiety about the implications of the dance mania" for the sexual mores of youth, particularly girls. The coupling of dances with other alleged sins illustrated how hostility toward youthful sexuality merged with a more sweeping urge to control subordinates.

Pool halls, for example, affronted the very premises of the Protestant work ethic. "The pool room," explained a representative of the Georgia Anti-Poolroom League in 1922, "diverts man power" from economic development and family support. It encouraged general moral laxity, particularly in young men" "idleness . . . dissipation . . . intoxicants . . . profanity . . . lascivious stories . . . and the love of chance.". . .

The Klan first sallied into public view in Athens in 1921 as the war on vice gained momentum. In that year, bootleggers mocked the elitist pretensions of the local guardians of morality in so doing confirmed their fears about the correlation between alcohol and rebellion. When the mayor warned bootleggers to quit their trade or leave town, they responded with a "defiant letter" of their own. In it could be heard echoes of the labor revolt that had recently swept the nation. Banding together as "Bootlegger's Union Local No. 13," the writers defended the "small pint man." They served notice to the Athens press that "a bootlegger is making his money as honest as some of these nice honest-to-goodness people, who are always kicking at what the other fellow is doing." And they vowed to continue selling to anyone who wanted to buy their wares. . . .

In late March of 1924, in the midst of a statewide recruitment campaign, the Klan renewed agitation over the "exceedingly deplorable" state of local morality. As evidence, it cited bootleggers who sold their wares on the courthouse square and "a corps of [prostitutes] who prey constantly on the young college students." In order to put its own stamp on the issues, the Klan pointed in particular to the operation of two pool rooms a stone's throw from the university. Patronized by "the vermin and dregs of society," they were "harbors of vice and corruption." They also had Italian owners, as the Klan was at pains to point out. The order's publicist and his colleagues argued that in order to right the moral climate, "the Semitic influence in Athens must be checked," and the leverage of Catholic and Jewish voters— the alleged "ring" to which the Klan attributed all ideas or values contrary to its own—"broken by an organization just as powerful.". . .

The Athens purity crusade may have been unique in its particulars, yet it emerged from ideas and fears that local [Ku Klux Klan] members shared with their counterparts elsewhere in the United States. The Klan promoted moral "clean-ups" to exorcise dangers to the ordered homes it believed a stable and powerful nation depended on. Unless the country realized that "its life depends upon a moral 'clean-up,'" as one [Klan] official put it, it was "doomed to inevitable destruction."

The rationale for these endeavors came from the conviction, common to both evangelical Protestantism and republicanism, that immorality would erode family commitments, demoralize the citizenry, and undermine the state. Imperial Wizard [Hiram Wesley] Evans associated the idea of freedom as license with the Old World: such libertinism endangered not only its practitioners "but the social structure." Since the United States government was of, by, and for the people, he reasoned, the state had the right—indeed the obligation—to patrol the "moral standards" of the populace. The reason it had to do so was straightforward. "Our young," [Klansman] Samuel Saloman explained, are apt pupils." "Moral teachings they may receive in well-regulated homes will avail but little if they see such teachings constantly set at naught" in the outside world.

Klansmen feared the waning of parental power. Modern "children rule the roost," deplored Klan author E.F. Stanton. "Lack of control of parents over their children," another writer alleged, had led to the "most deplorable results," prostitution among them. Some Klansmen worried about how the unprecedented leisure enjoyed by young people would affect their characters. Others found the values of youth scandalous. "Pleasure has become the god of the young people of America," remarked one Georgia Klansman, "and a very unwholesome and lascivious pleasure it is." Still others found the peer culture of youth impertinent. Kate Yarborough, the wife of Athens Klansman Scott Yarborough, later complained that "my children calls me old-fashioned, 'cause I don't try to dress like they do, and talk proper.". . .

While young people's attitudes and work habits caused concern, their sexuality appeared by far the greatest threat. Imperial Wizard Evans adduced as one of the Klan's primary motives "the more breakdown that has been going on for two decades." It had gone so far, he said, that "those who maintained the old standards did so only in the face of constant ridicule." The order excoriated a range of expressions of youthful sexuality: suggestive fashions for girls, "petting parties," and "parking" in cars. More generally, Klansmen declared that they were "implacably opposed to all the amatory and erotic tendencies of modern degeneracy." The Klan pitted itself against those who would follow "the fleshly propensities which are all selfish and sensual and which produce anarchy."

Klansmen found particularly insidious the commercial entertainments contemporary youth flocked to. "Degrading, depraving or disgusting" movies [Klan newspaper], the *Kourier* charged, were "undermining morals." Not only films, Imperial Wizard [William] Simmons maintained, but also jazz music and "filthy fiction" were "polluting" society. Contemporary young people were being "submerged," according to another leader, "in a sea of sensuality and sewage." The profusion of such pollution metaphors was an index of Klansmen's desire to buttress the older chain of command in relations between parents and children.

Indeed, the Klan expected family members, especially women and children, to subordinate their individual aspirations to the needs of the corporate unit. The hierarchy of power in the home was offered as a model for other institutions in society. One Klan-recommended author used the untrammeled sway of the head of the family as an example business firms should replicate. Another explained that the merit of the ancient Roman citizen was that "in obeying his father he learned to obey the state."

The order's discussions of divorce made evident some of the threats to such obedience. [The Klan publication] the *Searchlight* attributed the soaring divorce rate to the selfishness of modern partners. It condemned those who approached marriage not with a sense of the "duty they owe to their children and society," but instead with an eye to their own fulfillment. Such individualism threatened the foundations of the home and with it "the social and economic structure of the nation.". . .

Klan tracts and speakers dwelt far less on men's behavior than on women's. This was in part because male roles were changing less than female roles, and in part because Klansmen were more interested in controlling others than in self-scrutiny. Nevertheless, they expounded a particular model of masculinity. Klansmen expected men to marry, to provide for their families, and to exercise control over their wives and children. "God intended," affirmed one Klan minister, "that every man should possess insofar as possible, his own home and rule his own household."

Rule over one's woman was mandated by another staple of the Klan's conception of masculinity: "honor"; or, as it was sometimes called, "chivalry." Honor dictated a commitment to protect the virtue of "American" women. Historically, honor in fact rested on a man's ability to control the sexuality of his female relations. Their "purity" was the complement to his "honor"; hence Klansmen's insistence on the "chastity of women." Yet it seemed that young women no longer shared these "high ideals." The job of Klansmen, then, said Imperial Kludd [chaplain] Caleb Ridley of Atlanta, was "to make it easier for women to be right and do right." Similarly, an Athens Klan lecturer spoke of "fathers' duties to their daughters" as essential aspect of the order's commitment to "protection of the home and the chastity of our womanhood.". . .

The focus on young women illustrated how parents' authority over children was of a piece with that of men over women in the world the Klan sought to defend. Many of the Klansmen's less self-conscious pronouncements expressed resentment of female self-assertion. "We pity the man," taunted the Klan press, "who permits the loss of manhood through fear of [his] wife." Similarly, the author of *Christ and Other Klansmen* censured "women [who] blaspheme God by disobeying their husbands." Other writers upbraided "the gadabout mother" and the wife "who cares more for the unhealthy activities of social duties" than for her obligations to her husband. As the reference to health suggests, Klansmen tried to naturalize gender hierarchy. American women already *were* emancipated; change should go no further. Feminists should cease complaining about such "pretended wrongs" as the burdens of housework. "God or nature" dictated women's roles, not men and society, so nothing could change them.

Having options outside the household might lead women to deviate from their natural functions. That, according to the Klan, was childbearing and childrearing. The entry of women into the labor force and politics, Klan leader E.Y. Clark stated, could thus pose "a real danger unless there is some strong organization constantly preaching that women's place is in the home." "Citizenship for our young American women," explained Imperial Wizard Simmons, "includes the essential duty of motherhood," just as for men it included breadwinning. Only one or two children would not do, moreover. The Klan felt it necessary, said the Imperial Wizard, to "insist upon 2, 3, 4, and sometimes 5 or 6 children." Women who rejected childbearing "as a burden" needed a "socializing education." "If society is to live," [Klansman Samuel] Saloman explained, women must "cheerfully" accept their familial duties. The Klan was therefore, as one speaker put it, "violently opposed to birth control."

Although hostile to sexual emancipation, the Klan was not an outright foe of all women's equality. The order's commitment to moral uplift in fact led it to support rights for white Protestant women. "Subjugated women," the *Searchlight* explained, "means subjugated morals." Hence "the Klan believes," as one of its statements of principle read, "in the equality of the sexes without hesitation." Klansmen recognized that women could no longer be confined to the household; rather, they must work with their menfolk to achieve common political and social goals. The order even asserted on occasion that some of the world's problems resulted from the exclusion of women from power. In short, Klansmen were not hidebound conservatives; grudgingly or not, they accommodated the desires of their female counterparts for expanded roles.

Indeed, the Klan championed suffrage for Protestant white women. As did many others, Klansmen viewed female suffrage as the best defense for Prohibition. Two Klan-associated politicians in Georgia, W.D. Upshaw and W.J. Harris, the former a past president of the Anti-Saloon League, became the first men in the state to vote for the Nineteenth Amendment. An Athens Klan leader and city alderman, W.R. Tindall, beat even the League of Women Voters to the fray when he attacked a 1924 plan to levy a special tax on women voters "as unfair, unjust and contrary to our principles of government." The Klan also counted on women's votes to thwart [Roman Catholic] Al Smith's bid for the presidency in 1928; after his defeat, the order paid tribute to "the Protestant Women of America."

Just as it endorsed women's votes, so the Klan respected the activism of like-minded women. Throughout the United States, it frequently praised the work of the WCTU [Women's Christian Temperance Union] and helped its chapters with particular projects. The Klan even adopted a take-off on the female temperance motto "For God, Home, and Native Land." In turn, the WTCU in many places backed the Klan's moral reform work. . . .

Nevertheless, recognition of women by Klansmen was always shot through with ambivalence. . . . However much Klansmen might try to cooperate with women who shared their social goals, female initiative set them on edge; the undertow of patriarchal prerogative impeded full solidarity. This undertow was most obvious in Klansmen's relations with the Women of the Ku Klux Klan (WKKK).

Established by the Imperial Palace in June of 1923, the WKKK was announced as "a Protestant Women's Organization which is for, by, and of women." Yet the reality was murkier. Leaders of the men's Klan maintained ultimate control over the women's Klan, a control symbolized by their ability to appoint wives to office in the WKKK. Male Klan propagandists also tended to describe Klanswomen as the "mothers, wives, and daughters" of Klansmen, despite the fact that many were not related to male Klansmen, and to portray the WKKK as "auxiliary" despite its claims to independence. These ambiguities hint at the tensions in gender relations that the Klan had hoped to submerge: both the women's desire for control over their own affairs and the men's reluctance to surrender any real power.

Similar troubles surfaced when Klansmen attacked other groups in women's names. As in local practice, so in ideology: the Klan used respectability as a weapon, a tool to differentiate its own constituents from those it would direct their passions against. Sexual politics figured prominently in the Klan's efforts to stir anti-communism and anti-Catholicism, for example. Klansmen's recitations of the sexual subversion practiced by Communists and Catholics aimed to convince their audiences of the essential "otherness" of the groups at issue, to dehumanize them so as to loosen inhibitions against aggression. Yet these disquisitions revealed more of the speakers' won attitudes toward women than they realized.

Communists came in for the lion's share of attack. Klansmen warned that communism would destroy the family as their constituency understood it. The argument was most amply developed in Samuel Saloman's *Red War on the Family*. Saloman's work was typical of the Klan's anti-communism: rife with exaggerated and absurd charges, it nonetheless had a rational core. That core was an assumption the Klan wholeheartedly agreed with: that the hierarchical family was the basis and guarantor of ordered society. Saloman's central charge against socialism flowed from this. In recasting marriage and morality, it would destroy civilization, as had similar experiments in ancient Greece and Rome. "Monogamic [monogamous] marriage" without easy recourse to divorce, Saloman insisted, was "the sheet anchor of our civilization"; whoever opposed it "must be regarded as a foe." If conventional marriage and its safeguards weakened, gender roles would also erode as "men became more effeminate and women more masculine." The blurring of these boundaries would result in chaos and moral decay.

Like the Klan, Saloman couched his argument in the chivalric tradition. He reminded men of their obligation to shelter women from danger. Yet, behind the pretense of care, lurked a sense of personal loss for the men who posed as women's Galahads. To shock male readers resentful at the loss of their gender privileges, Saloman quoted a tract asserting that, in socialist society, women "will be entirely independent" economically, socially, and in intimate relationships. Horrified, he cited communists' commitment to making housework and child-care no longer the responsibility of individual women but of the whole society. This theme of the loss of women's private services was echoed in the Klan press; in Russia, complained another writer, "the young and the old are cared for by all the people impersonally."

The Klan's anti-radicalism, in fact, exposed how the mask of chivalry concealed an unwillingness to surrender proprietary rights to women. Saloman's primary charge against socialists was that they advocated the "muck of free love." One clue to the nature of the threat is that virtually all such passages focused on the liberation of *women's* sexuality. Indeed, Saloman complained that the philosophy of free love was "running wild among the enlightened and emancipated and sex-conscious women of America and Europe." He could see no goal in the emancipation of woman but allowing her "to devote herself to free and unrestrained love." Saloman simply could not imagine women as autonomous individuals making their own choices. Rather, their release from being the "property" of one man could only result in their becoming the property of all. Unions based on mutual attraction and commitment, free from state sponsorship, could mean only "the morality of the brothel." The liberation of women would thus reduce her to a "harlot," a "clandestine prostitute." Why? The "community [ownership] of property necessarily and logically involves the community of women."

This equation exhibited starkly the way gender infused class and class, gender in Klan thought. As [Karl] Marx and [Frederick] Engels once pointed out, the specter of the "community of women" could only make sense to men who saw women as property. In other words, it only had meaning for those who understood their control over their wives and daughters to be integral to their own class status, as it was in the republican tradition adapted by the Klan. Denying men of other classes access to Klansmen's "own" women was therefore necessary to police class borders. Klansmen thus interpreted workers' revolution as a challenge to their dominion over the women of their group. "Underdogs would not satisfy their cravings of centuries," Saloman warned, in their effort to break the bourgeois male's monopoly on "luscious womanhood."

If communism held the worst dangers to domestic order, Catholicism came in a close second. Here, too, the purported deviants were charged with violating the natural order of relations between the sexes. But here the immediate targets were priests and nuns. The core of the Klan's case against them was that their abstention from heterosexual marriage and reproduction necessarily led to unnatural, antisocial perversions. . . .

Whereas Klansmen criticized socialist society for giving men too little authority over women, they accused priests of having too much. Priests usurped powers that rightfully belonged to male household heads. Associated as it was with folk memories of aristocratic men sexually exploiting the female relatives of their male subordinates, this allegation resonated with the general case made against the Catholic church for monarchical pretensions. Evans abhorred the "galling subjection" of the Catholic feudal societies of Europe wherein "no man save the king truly owned anything; no property nor children, nor wife, nor life that could not be taken from him at the whim of every superior." A wife and children were thus among the pieces of property a man had a right to control; the horror of Catholicism was its alleged interference with this control. Klansmen's principal complaints centered on two phenomena . . . "the confessional" and "the corruption of the priesthood."

Attacks on the practice of confession were virtually transparent defenses of male dominance in domestic life. The Klan's case had been laid out by [Georgia politician and Klan member] Tom Watson in the 1910s. He charged that confession allowed a priest to act as the "confidante of another man's wife," to whom she divulged the couple's "inmost secrets . . . all that is sacred between her husband and herself." The information priests would obtain included "sexual procedures and techniques with her husband, extramarital activities, masturbation, homosexuality, and unnatural fornication." This violation of the husband's privacy, Watson warned, would "rot out the heart" of the nation. That it was the husband's privacy, not the couple's, that was at issue was evident in the subtitle borne by another anti-confessional tract in the Klan's arsenal: *An Eye-Opener for Husbands, Fathers, and Brothers.*

The sexual power attributed implicitly to priests in the critique of the confessional was made explicit in discussions of nuns. In *What Goes on in Nunneries,* Tom Watson had defined convents as places where "bachelor priests keep unmarried women under lock and key, and whose children are killed." Elsewhere Watson described the nun's obligations as those of "the temple girl." Portraying the convent as a "securely locked seraglio," he invoked the sexual exploitation of lower-class women in the harems of the East. The Klan took up this theme. Georgia Klan leader and *Searchlight* editor J.O. Wood won election to the General Assembly on a platform calling for more rigid inspection of convents.

Klansmen were more ambivalent about nuns than about priests. They generally imputed to nuns a perverse hyper-sexuality. Yet, as in the complaints about the confessional, the charges assumed nuns to be the passive victims of priests, who exploited their social power to gain sexual access. [Klanswoman] Alma White, for example, condemned priests for exercising "tyranny over helpless victims behind convent walls." Houses of the Good Shepherd [Catholic orphanages], according to the *Searchlight*, were no more than "slave pens" that promoted "the debauchery of Southern orphan girls." The common denominator in such allegations was an inability to come to terms with women who removed themselves for the institution of marriage. Klansmen simply refused to believe that women might choose to be free from husbands and children; hence their insistence that women in Catholic institutions were held against their will.

Questions for Discussion

1. According to the author, the fear of "moral disorder" played a vital role in the Ku Klux Klan's popularity in the 1920s. Do you agree? What evidence does she use to support this view? What sort of immoral behavior most concerned the KKK? Which social classes were most likely to respond to these fears?
2. How did the KKK view the family and its role in society? According to the Klan, what were the major sources of danger to the survival of the family? Why did Klan members view political radicalism as harmful to the family?
3. How did the KKK view gender roles within the family? In society? Did the Klan support women's right to vote? Why? Did the KKK want all women to vote?
4. How do you account for the popularity of the Klan during the 1920s? What issue do you think was most important in attracting people to the Klan?

For Further Reading

Kenneth Ackerman, *Young J. Edgar: Hoover, the Red Scare, and the Assault on Civil Liberties* (2007); Edward Behr, *Prohibition: Thirteen Years That Changed America* (1997); Kathleen Blee, *Women of the Klan: Racism and Gender in the 1920s* (1992); David Chalmers, *Hooded Americanism: The History of the Ku Klux Klan* (1987); Chris Finan, *From the Palmer Raids to the Patriot Act: A History of the Fight for Free Speech in America* (2008); Ann Hagedorn, *Savage Peace: Hope and Fear in America, 1919* (2008); David Horowitz, *Inside the Klavern: The Secret History of a Ku Klux Klan in the 1920s* (1999); Kenneth T. Jackson, *The Ku Klux Klan in the City, 1915–1930* (1992); Edward J. Larson, *Trial and Error: The American Controversy over Creation and Evolution* (2003), *Summer for the Gods: The Scopes Trial and America's Continuing Debate over Science and Evolution* (1998); Shawn Lay, ed., *The Invisible Empire in the West: Toward a New Historical Appraisal of the Ku Klux Klan in the 1920s* (2003); Michael Lerner, *Dry Manhattan: Prohibition in New York City* (2007); Nancy MacLean, *Behind the Mask of Chivalry: The Making of the Second Ku Klux Klan* (1995); Leonard Moore, *Citizen Klansmen: The Ku Klux Klan in Indiana, 1921–1928* (1997); Jeffrey Moran, *The Scopes Trial: A Brief History with Documents* (2002); Michael Newton, *The Invisible Empire: The Ku Klux Klan in Florida* (2001); Thomas Pegram, *Battling Demon Rum: The Struggle for a Dry America, 1800–1933* (1999); Wyn Graig Wade, *The Fiery Cross: The Ku Klux Klan in America* (1998).

9

The Great Depression in the City

The Housewives' Meat Strike of 1935

Annelise Orleck

The Great Depression was the longest economic collapse in American history. It began with the "crash" in Wall Street stock values on October 29, 1929, and lasted until the onset of American involvement in World War II, in 1941. For more than a decade it looked as though the American version of capitalism was threatened, especially its "free market" aversion to government regulation of the economy. And it seemed that a new vision of government was evolving: many hoped government would insure the basic economic security of all Americans. Neither of these things happened, but for twelve tumultuous years, Americans experienced a "depression" whose impact was as psychological as it was economic, and whose cruelty scarred everyone in its path. Most of the following essay deals with the Depression's impact on industry and cities—the impact on farms is described in Chapter 10.

Numbers tell some of the story. By 1932, the worst year of the Depression, more than 13 million workers were unemployed, about 25 percent of the workforce. That was only part of the employment picture. Millions who did not lose their jobs had their hours and wages reduced. On average, workers earned 40 percent less in 1932 than in 1929. The picture is still not complete: hundreds of thousands worked but did not get paid for extended periods of time. This was especially true of municipal employees like teachers, police, and firefighters, as hundreds of cities flirted with or experienced bankruptcy in the 1930s. For example, Chicago schoolteachers worked but did not receive a dime in wages from November 1932 to March 1933.

Unemployed, homeless men occupy a New York City "Hooverville." In the center is an undecorated Christmas tree. Was it fair to blame President Hoover for the plight of these men?

It is likely that as much as 40 percent of the industrial and agricultural workforce was unemployed or underemployed during the Great Depression. Put another way, in a population of about 120 million, up to 60 million people experienced poverty and severe deprivation during the 1930s.

Many small businesses closed, and most major corporations cut production. The value of stocks traded on the New York Stock Exchange, which more than doubled in the late 1920s, plunged to 15 percent of their value by 1932. By that year, national income was down by more than 50 percent, as was manufacturing, which employed the majority of nonfarm workers. Banks closed by the thousands: between 1929 and 1931, about 5,000 of the country's 25,000 banks shut their doors. Tens of thousands of depositors lost their savings.

Unemployment and falling wages were only part of the statistical story. Many families, unable to meet payments on their mortgages, lost their homes. In 1930, there were 150,000 foreclosures, and another 200,000 the following year. By 1933, 1,000 families lost their homes *each day*, and more than one-half of the country's mortgages were in foreclosure. Most Americans at the time rented rather than owned their homes or apartments. Evictions for failing to pay rent were epidemic. For instance, in each month of 1930, 12,000 New York City families were forced from their apartments. Most of them had nowhere else to go, and their furniture and other belongings were placed on sidewalks. In 1932, which included one of the coldest winters recorded to that point, there were 37,000 evictions in New York *every month*.

But statistics cannot capture what it was like to live through the heart-break of those years. People starved to death—and not because of food shortages. There was a surplus of food, but many could not afford it. As the Depression deepened in the early 1930s, President Herbert Hoover more than once proclaimed that no one had starved. But they had, though how many will never be known. In 1933, the New York City Children's Welfare Bureau estimated that at least 150,000 children in that city suffered from mal-nutrition; the Bureau noted that in many African American homes, there was "no food at all." In 1932, thirteen unidentified bodies in the Boston morgue had symptoms of starvation. The following year in Albany, New York a ten-year-old girl collapsed and died of starvation while seated at her desk in school; across the country in San Francisco a four-year-old boy died from starvation after his family was denied public assistance because they were Mexican. A final example (among many) comes from testimony before Congress in 1932 by officials from Philadelphia. They described a pregnant woman and her children whose only nutrition for eleven days, except for two meals, consisted of stale bread.

Under these circumstances it was difficult for families to stay together. Many unraveled under the stresses of unemployment, hunger, and evictions. By 1932 at least 2 million homeless, jobless people roamed the country. Many were married men who, for years, had been the "breadwinners" in their fam-ilies. Ashamed of their inability to fulfill their primary male gender role, they abandoned their families and rode the rails from state to state. Or they lived as "hobos" in the makeshift shantytowns of splintered wood, bent metal, and broken dreams called "Hoovervilles," in mock honor of the president of the United States. Among these rootless wanderers, there were up to a quarter million young people, most of them boys in their teens whose families could not support them. Women and girls were among the homeless as well. On September 20, 1931, *The New York Times* reported that "several hundred homeless, unemployed women sleep nightly in Chicago's parks."

The impact of the Depression on families went beyond hunger, home-lessness, and abandonment. Some couples stayed in unhappy marriages because they could not afford a divorce. From 1929 to 1932, the divorce rate dropped by 25 percent. Other couples, who would have liked to marry, could not because they lacked jobs and money—the marriage rate plunged by more than 20 percent in those years. The birthrate decreased for the same reasons throughout the 1930s.

Of course, not everyone suffered during the Great Depression. Millions kept their jobs and their homes. But some suffered more than others. African Americans living in cities were economically marginal even in the prosperous 1920s. For them, the Depression made a bad situation worse. In New York's Harlem and Chicago's Southside, the two largest black communities in the North, two-thirds of workers were unemployed. Mexican Americans were targeted by angry whites, who wanted to reserve jobs for "real" Americans. More than 400,000 workers were sent back to Mexico, most against their will, some of them "real" American citizens. Finally, industrial workers of all ethnic backgrounds were hit hard because their wages did not increase enough during the 1920s. By the end of the decade, they could not buy the consumer goods they produced in factories. Their families lived from paycheck to paycheck, they were in debt to install-ment buying plans, and most had not a dime in savings. A few weeks without a paycheck meant disaster.

During the earliest and worst years of the Depression, from 1929 through 1932, there were no government safety nets to tide people over. Programs designed to provide a modicum of economic security—such as unemployment insurance, Social Security, the Federal Deposit Insurance Corporation, Fannie Mae (the Federal National Mortgage Association), and Aid to Families with Dependent Children—were created by Franklin D. Roosevelt's New Deal. But even the New Deal failed to end the Depression.

Protests over these conditions were common throughout the 1930s. In the next essay, Annelise Orleck describes protests by housewives over the high price of meat. Protesting the price of food might seem appropriate gen-der behavior for housewives. But Orleck's article makes it clear that these women understood how the economic system worked: they were convinced that as citizens, as well as women and wives, they had the right to protest against and change that system.

Source: Annelise Orleck, "'We Are That Mythical Thing Called the Public': Militant Housewives during the Great Depression," *Feminist Studies* 19, no. 1 (Spring 1993), 147–172.

Between 1926 and 1933 housewives' self-help groups sprang up across the United States. In cities surrounded by accessible growing areas (such as Dayton, Ohio; Richmond, Virginia; and Seattle, Washington), housewives and their husbands created highly developed barter networks. Unemployed workers, mostly male, exchanged skills such as carpentry, plumbing, barber-ing, and electrical wiring. Women—some workers' wives, others unem-ployed workers themselves—organized exchanges of clothing and food. These organizations grew out of small-scale gardening collectives created by housewives during the late 1920s to feed their communities.

In Seattle, unemployed families organized quickly in the aftermath of the 1929 stock market crash; but then this was an unusually organized city, described by a local paper in 1937 as "the most unionized city in the country." In 1919, Seattle had been the first city in the United States to hold a general strike. During the 1920s, Seattle's labor unions again broke new ground by calling on working-class women and men to organize as consumers. When the Depression hit, Seattle's vast subsistence network [in which farm and city wives organized bartering to exchange timber and fish from western Washington for fruits and vegetables from the eastern portion of the state] was described in the national press as a model of self-sufficiency, "a republic of the penniless," in the words of the *Atlantic*. By 1931–32, 40,000 Seattle women and men had joined an exchange in which the men farmed, fished, and cut leftover timber from cleared land, while the women gathered food, fuel, and clothing. The women also ran commissaries where members could shop with scrip for household essentials. By 1934, an estimated 80,000 people statewide belonged to exchanges that allowed them to acquire food, clothing, and shelter without any money changing hands.

In larger cities like New York, Chicago, Philadelphia, and Detroit, self-help groups also sprang up during the early years of the Depression, but housewives there had little chance of making direct contact with farmers. Rather than establishing food exchanges, they created neighborhood councils that used boycotts and demonstrations to combat rising food prices. And, rather than rehabilitating abandoned buildings for occupation by the homeless, as the unemployed did in Seattle, housewives in larger cities battled with police to prevent evictions of families unable to pay their rents.

Tenant and consumer councils took hold in neighborhoods where housewives had organized rent strikes and meat boycotts in 1902, 1904, 1907, 1908, and 1917. They organized in the same way as earlier housewife activists had done—primarily through door-to-door canvassing. Boycotts were sustained in the latter period, as in the earlier one, with picket lines and street-corner meetings. Even their angry outbursts echoed the earlier housewives' uprisings: meat was destroyed with kerosene or taken off trucks and thrown to the ground. Flour was spilled in the streets, and milk ran in the gutters.

But although its links to earlier housewives' and labor union struggles are important, the 1930s' housewives' revolt was far more widespread and sustained, encompassing a far wider range of ethnic and racial groups than any tenant or consumer uprising before it. The earlier outbursts were limited to East Coast Jewish immigrant communities, but the housewives' uprising of the 1930s was nationwide and involved rural as well as urban women. It drew Polish and native-born housewives in Detroit, Finnish and Scandinavian women in Washington State, and Scandinavian farm wives in Minnesota. Jewish and Black housewives were particularly militant in New York, Cleveland, Chicago, Los Angeles, and San Francisco.

The 1930s' housewives' movement can also be distinguished from earlier housewives' actions by the sophistication and longevity of the organizations it generated. Depression-era housewives moved quickly from self-help to lobbying state capitals and Washington, D.C. Leaders like the "diminutive but fiery" Mary Zuk of Detroit displayed considerable skill in their use of radio and print media. Their demands of government—regulation of staple food prices; establishment of publicly owned farmer-consumer cooperatives—reflected a complex understanding of the marketplace and the potential uses of the government bureaucracy.

Leaders of these groups also demonstrated considerable sophistication about forming alliances. Shortly after [Franklin] Roosevelt was elected president, hostilities between Communist and non-Communist women in the labor movement was temporarily set aside. AFL [American Federation of Labor]-affiliated women's auxiliaries and CP [Communist Party]-affiliated women's neighborhood councils worked together to organize consumer protests and lobby for regulation of food and housing costs. This happened in 1933, well before the CP initiated its Popular Front policy urging members to join with "progressive" non-Communist groups and well before the Congress of Industrial Organizations extended its hand to Communists to rejoin the labor movement.

This rapprochement highlighted the desperation that gripped so many working-class communities during the Depression. Although anti-Communist charges were leveled against housewife organizers throughout the Depression, such accusations did not dampen the enthusiasm of rank-and-file council members. To many non-Communists in the movement, the question of who was Communist and who wasn't did not seem terribly relevant at a time when millions faced hunger and homelessness. Detroit housewife leader Catherine Mudra responded this way to charges of Communist involvement in the Detroit meat strike of 1935: "There may be some Communists among us. There are a lot of Republicans and Democrats too. We do not ask the politics of those who join. . . . All we want is to get prices down to where we can feed our families.". . .

Depression-era organizing against high food prices reached its peak during the summer of 1935. Working-class women activists from Communist and non-Communist organizations convened two regional conferences the previous winter, one for the East Coast, another for the Midwest, to coordinate protests against the sales tax and high cost of living. Representatives from AFL women's union auxiliaries, parents' associations, church groups, farm women's and Black women's groups attended. By that summer, they had laid plans for the most ambitious women's consumer protest to that time.

It began when the Chicago Committee against the High Cost of Living, headed by Dina Ginsberg, organized massive street meetings near the stockyards to let the meat packers know how unhappy they were with rising meat prices. New York housewives in the UCWCW [the United Council of Working Class Women] quickly raised the ante by organizing a citywide strike against butcher shops.

On May 22 women in Jewish and Black neighborhoods around New York City formed picket lines. In Harlem, according to historian Mark Naison, the meat strike "produced an unprecedented display of coordinated protest by black working-class women." The strike lasted four weeks. More than 4,500 butcher shops were closed down by housewives' picket lines. Scores of women and men around the city were arrested. The New York State Retail Meat Dealers Association threatened to hold Mayor Fiorello

LaGuardia responsible for damage to their business as a result of the strike. The mayor, in an attempt to resolve the strike, asked federal officials to study the possibilities for reducing retail meat prices.

[Rose Nelson] Raynes, citywide coordinator of the meat strike, describes what happened next.

> It was successful to a point where we were warned that the gang-sters were going to get us. . . . We decided to call the whole thing off but first we organized a mass picket line in front of the whole-sale meat distributors. . . . About three, four hundred women came on the picket line. It was supposed to be a final action. But instead of it being the wind-up it became a beginning.

Housewives across the United States promptly joined in. Ten thousand Los Angeles housewives, members of the Joint Council of Women's Auxiliaries, declared a meat strike on June 8th that so completely shut down retail meat sales in the city that butchers cut prices by the next day. In Philadelphia, Chicago, Boston, Paterson, St. Louis, and Kansas City, newly formed housewives' councils echoed the cry of the New York strike: "Stop Buying Meat Until Prices Come Down!"

On June 15, a delegation of housewives from across the country descended on Washington, D.C., demanding that the Department of Agriculture enforce lower meat prices. Clara Lemlich Shavelson described the delegation's meeting with Secretary of Agriculture Henry Wallace. "The meat packers and the Department of Agriculture in Washington tried to make the strikers' delegation believe that the farmer and the drought are to blame for the high price of food. But the delegation would not fall for this. They knew the truth."

The Polish housewives of Hamtramck, Michigan, a suburb of Detroit, did not believe Wallace's explanation either. A month after the end of the New York strike, thirty-two-year-old Mary Zuk addressed a mass demon-stration of housewives gathered on the streets of Hamtramck to demand an immediate reduction in meat prices. When the reduction did not come by that evening, Zuk announced a meat boycott to begin the following day.

On July 27, 1935, Polish and Black housewives began to picket Hamtramck butcher shops, carrying signs demanding a 20 percent price cut throughout the city and an end to price gouging in Black neighborhoods. When men, taunted by onlookers who accused them of being "scared of a few women," attempted to cross the lines, they were "seized by the pickets . . . their faces slapped, their hair pulled and their packages confiscated. . . . A few were knocked down and trampled." That night Hamtramck butchers reported unhappily that the boycott had been 95 percent effective.

Within a matter of days the meat boycott spread to other parts of Detroit, as housewives in several different ethnic communities hailed the onset of a "general strike against the cost of living." Jewish women picketed kosher butcher shops in downtown Detroit neighborhoods. Protestant women in outlying regions such as Lincoln Park and River Rouge declined to picket or march but instead set up card tables on streetcorners to solicit no-meat pledges from passing housewives.

Housewives also sought government intervention. Detroit housewives stormed the city council demanding that it set a ceiling on meat prices in the metropolitan area. "What we can afford to buy isn't fit for a human to eat," Joanna Dinkfeld told the council. "And we can't afford very much of that." Warning the council and the state government that they had better act, Myrtle Hoaglund announced that she was forming a statewide housewives' organization. "We feel that we should have united action," she said. "We think the movement of protest against present meat prices can be spread throughout the state and the nation." As evidence, she showed the city council bags of letters she had received from housewives around the country, asking how to go about organizing consumer boycotts.

Throughout August the meat strikers made front page news in Detroit and received close attention in major New York and Chicago dailies. The women staged mass marches through the streets of Detroit, stormed meat-packing plants, overturned and emptied meat trucks, and poured kerosene on thousands of pounds of meat stored in warehouses. When these actions resulted in the arrest of several Detroit women, hundreds of boycotters marched on the city jails, demanding the release of their friends. Two hours after her arrest, Hattie Krewik, forty-five years old and a mother of five, emerged from her cell unrepentant. A roar went up from the crowd as she immediately began to tell, in Polish, her tale of mistreatment at the hands of police. By the end of the first week in August, retail butchers in Detroit were pleading with the governor to send in state troops to protect their meat.

Although without a doubt the butchers suffered as a result of this boycott, the strikers in Detroit, like the strikers in New York, frequently reiterated that the strike was not aimed at retail butchers or at farmers. It was aimed, in Clara Shavelson's works, at the "meat packer millionaires." To prove that, in the second week of August, a delegation of Detroit housewives traveled to Chicago where they hooked up with their Chicago counterparts for a march on the Union stockyards.

Meeting them at the gates, Armour & Company president R.H. Cabell attempted to mollify the women. "Meat packers," he told them, "are not the arbiters of process, merely the agencies through which economic laws operate." The sudden rise in prices, he explained, was the fault of the Agricultural Adjustment Administration which had recently imposed a processing tax on pork.

"Fine," Mary Zuk responded. The housewives would return to Washington for another meeting with agricultural secretary Wallace. On August 19, 1935, Zuk and her committee of five housewives marched into Wallace's office and demanded that he end the processing tax, impose a 20 percent cut on meat prices, and order prompt prosecution of profiteering meat packers. Wallace, perhaps sensing how this would be played in the press, tried to evict reporters from the room, warning that he would not speak to the women if they remained. Zuk did not blink. She replied: "Our people want to know what we say and they want to know what *you* say so the press people are going to stay." The reporters stayed and had a grand time the next day reporting on Wallace's unexplained departure from the room in the middle of the meeting. "Secretary Wallace Beats Retreat from Five Housewives," the *Chicago Daily Tribune* blared. *Newsweek* reported it this way:

> The lanky Iowan [Wallace] looked down into Mrs. Zuk's deep-sunken eyes and gulped his Adam's apple.

> MRS. ZUK: Doesn't the government want us to live? Everything in Detroit has gone up except wages.

> Wallace fled.

In the aftermath of Zuk's visit to Washington, *Newsweek* reported housewives' demonstrations against the high price of meat in Indianapolis, Denver, and Miami. The *New York Times* reported violent housewives' attacks on meat warehouses in Chicago and in Shenandoah and Frackville, Pennsylvania. And Mary Zuk, the "strong-jawed 100 lb. mother of the meat strike," became a national figure. The Detroit post office announced that it was receiving letters from all over the country addressed only to "Mrs. Zuk—Detroit."

Although boycotts and strikes continued to be used as a tool in the housewives' struggle for lower prices, the movement became more focused on electoral politics as the decade wore on. Both Shavelson and Zuk used the prominence they'd gained through housewife activism to run for elected office. Shavelson ran for New York State Assembly in 1933 and 1938 as a "real mother fighting to maintain an American standard of living for her own family as well as for other families." She did not win but she fared far better than the rest of the CP [Communist Party] ticket.

Zuk ran a successful campaign for the Hamtramck City Council in April of 1936. Although the Hearst-owned paper warned that her election would be a victory for those who advocate "the break-up of the family," Zuk was swept into office by her fellow housewives. She won on a platform calling for the city council to reduce rents, food process, and utility costs in Hamtramck. After her election she told reporters that she was proof that "a mother can organize and still take care of her family."

In some ways what the Hearst papers sensed was really happening. Zuk's campaign represented an express politicization of motherhood and the family. On Mother's Day, 1936, seven hundred Zuk supporters rallied outside the city council to demand public funding for a women's healthcare clinic, childcare centers, playgrounds, and teen centers in Hamtramck. They also called for an end to evictions and construction of more public housing in their city. The government owed this to mothers, the demonstrators told reporters.

Two years earlier, in Washington State, the Women's Committee of the Washington Commonwealth Federation (WCF) had successfully elected three of its members to the state senate—Mary Farquharson, a professor's wife; and Marie Keene and Katherine Malstrom, the wives of loggers. Their campaign had been built around a Production-for-Use initiative to prohibit the destruction of food as a way of propping up prices. Such waste, they said, was an outrage to poor mothers in the state, who had been fighting the practice since the beginning of the Depression. The ballot measure also proposed a state distribution system for produce so that farmers could get a fair price and workers' families could buy food directly from farmers. Led by Katherine Smith and Elizabeth Harper, committee members collected 70,000 signatures to put the measure on the 1936 ballot.

The Production-for-Use initiative failed by a narrow margin but it made national news as columnists across the country speculated on the impact it might have on the U.S. economic system. Other WCF campaigns were more successful, however. The most important of these was the campaign to create publicly owned utilities in Washington State. Washington voters were the only ones to approve state ownership of utilities, but voters in localities across the country endorsed the creation of city and county utility companies during the 1930s. . . .

The unique alliance that created a nationwide housewives' uprising during the 1930s and 1940s would not reemerge, but it laid the groundwork for later consumer and tenant organizing. Housewives' militance politicized consumer issues nationwide. "Never before has there been such a wave of enthusiasm to do something for the consumer," *The Nation* wrote in 1937. Americans have gained "a consumer consciousness," the magazine concluded, as a direct result of the housewives' strikes in New York, Detroit, and other cities. The uprising of working-class housewives also broadened the terms of the class struggle, forcing male union leaders to admit that "the roles of producer and consumer are intimately related."

Housewives' groups alleviated the worst effects of the Depression in many working-class communities by bringing down food prices; rent and utility costs; preventing evictions; and spurring the construction of more public housing, schools, and parks. By the end of World War II, housewives' activism had forced the government to play a regulatory role in food and housing costs. Militant direct action and sustained lobbying put pressure on local and federal politicians to investigate profiteering on staple goods. The meat strikes of 1935 and of 1948 through 1951 resulted in congressional hearings on the structure of the meat industry and in nationwide reductions in prices. The intense anti-eviction struggles led by urban housewives and their years of lobbying for public housing helped to convince New York City and other localities to pass rent-control laws. They also increased support in Congress for federally funded public housing.

Perhaps an equally important legacy of housewives' activism was its impact on the consciousness of the women who participated. "It was an education for the women," Brooklyn activist Dorothy Moser recalls, "that they could not have gotten any other way." Immigrant women, poor native white women, and Black women learned to write and speak effectively, to lobby in state capitals and in Washington, D.C., to challenge men in positions of power, and sometimes to question the power relations in their own homes.

By organizing as consumers, working-class housewives not only demonstrated a keen understanding of their place in local and national economic structures, they also shattered the notion that because homemakers consume rather than produce, they are inherently more passive than their wage-earning husbands. The very act of organizing defied traditional notions of proper behavior for wives and mothers—and organizers were often called upon to explain their actions.

Union husbands supported and sometimes . . . even instigated their wives' community organizing. However, that organizing created logistical problems—namely who was going to watch the children and who was going to cook dinner? Some women managed to do it all. Others could not. Complaining of anarchy in the home, some union husbands ordered their wives to stop marching and return to the kitchen. In November 1934, *Working Women* magazine offered a hamper of canned goods to any woman who could answer the plaint of a housewife whose husband had ordered her to quit her women's council.

First prize went to a Bronx housewife who called on husbands and wives to share childcare as "they share their bread. Perhaps two evenings a week father should go, and two evenings, mother." The same woman noted that struggle keeps a woman "young physically and mentally" and that she shouldn't give it up for anything. Second prize went to a Pennsylvania miner's wife who agreed with that sentiment. "There can't be a revolution without women. . . . No one could convince me to drop out. Rather than leave the Party I would leave him." And an honorable mention went to a Texas farm woman who warned, "If we allow men to tell us what we can and cannot do we will never get our freedom." The prize-winning essays suggest that, like many women reformers before them, Depression-era housewife activists became interested in knocking down the walls that defined behavioral norms for women only after they had personally run up against them.

In defending their right to participate in a struggle that did not ideologically challenge the traditional sexual division of labor, many working-class housewives developed a new sense of pride in their abilities and a taste for political involvement. These women never came to think of themselves as feminists. They did, however, begin to see themselves as legitimate political and economic actors. During this period, poor wives and mothers left their homes in order to preserve them. In so doing, whether they intended to or not, they politicized the home, the family, and motherhood in important and unprecedented ways.

Questions for Discussion

1. In what ways did the political activism of housewives reinforce traditional gender roles? In what days did it challenge them?
2. What demands did the housewife-activists make? How did their demands differ if they lived in cities or rural areas?
3. The author suggests that dire conditions caused by the Great Depression created a sense of unity among housewives from different, and sometimes hostile, ethnic and racial groups. Did you find her argument convincing?
4. What were the major tactics used by housewives to achieve their goals? Did they work during the Depression? According to the author, what were their long-term consequences?
5. In your opinion, if economic difficulties similar to those in the 1930s were to happen today, would there be protests like those described by Orleck?

For Further Reading

Ann Banks, *First Person America* (1980); Caroline Bird, *The Invisible Scar* (1966); Julia Kirk Blackwelder, *Women of the Depression: Caste and Culture in San Antonio, 1929–1939* (1984); Michael Bordo, Claudia Goldin, and Eugene White, eds., *The Defining Moment: The Great Depression and the American Economy in the Twentieth Century* (1998); Alan Brinkley, *The End of Reform: New Deal Liberalism in Recession and War* (1996), *Voices of Protest: Huey Long, Father Coughlin and the Great Depression* (1983); Lizabeth Cohen, *Making a New Deal: Industrial Workers in Chicago, 1919–1939* (1990); Todd DePastino, *Citizen Hobo* (2005); Sarah Jane Deutsch, *From Ballots to Breadlines: American Women, 1920–1940* (1994); Ronald Edsforth, *The New Deal: America's Response to the Great Depression* (2000); John Kenneth Galbraith, *The Great Crash* (1997); Alonzo Hamby, *For the Survival of Democracy* (2004); David M. Kennedy, *Freedom from Fear: The American People in Depression and War, 1929–1945* (1999); William Leuchtenburg, *Franklin D. Roosevelt and the New Deal* (1963); Kristie Lindenmeyer, *The Greatest Generation Grows Up: American Childhood in the 1930s* (2005); Robert A. McElvaine, *The Great Depression: America 1929–1941* (1984), *The Depression and New Deal: A History in Documents* (2000), ed., *Down and Out in the Great Depression: Letters from the "Forgotten Man"* (1983); George McJimsy, *The Presidency of Franklin D. Roosevelt* (2000); Gerald D. Nash, *The Crucial Era: The Great Depression and World War II, 1929–1945* (1992); Annelise Orleck, *Common Sense and a Little Fire: Women and Working Class Politics in the United States, 1900–1965* (1995); Eric Rauchway, *The Great Depression and the New Deal* (2008); Vicki Ruiz, *Cannery Women, Cannery Lives: Mexican Women, Unionization, and the California Food Processing Industry, 1930–1950* (1987); Arthur M. Schlesinger Jr., *The Age of Roosevelt*, 3 vols. (1957–1960); Amity Shales, *The Forgotten Man: A New History of the Great Depression* (2008); Gene Smiley, *Rethinking the Great Depression* (2002); Bernard Sternsher, *Women of Valor: The Struggle Against the Great Depression as Told in Their Own Life Stories* (1999); Patricia Sullivan, *Days of Hope: Race and Democracy in the New Deal Era* (1996); Joe William Trotter Jr., *From Raw Deal to a New Deal? African Americans, 1929–1945* (1996); Errol Lincoln Uys, *Riding the Rails: Teenagers on the Move During the Great Depression* (2003); Winifred Wandersee, *Women's Work and Family Values, 1920–1940* (1981); Susan Ware, *Beyond Suffrage: Women in the New Deal* (1981), *Holding Their Own: Women in the 1930s* (1982).

10

The Great Depression on the Farm

The Dust Bowl

Timothy Egan

As bad as things were in cities during the Great Depression, they were worse in rural areas. The incomes of most family farmers, including tenants and sharecroppers, were already depressed in the 1920s. During and immediately following World War I, prices for wheat, corn, cotton, and other crops were at all-time highs, bolstered by exports to a Europe devastated by war. But with the war over and immigration curtailed, in the early 1920s prices for most farm commodities began a decade-long decline. Unlike manufacturers, who cut back on production in hard times, the more farm income sank, the more crops farmers planted. That led to surpluses, glutted markets, lower prices, and even less farm income. The wages of industrial workers rose steadily during the Twenties; those of farmers, who were about 30 percent of the national workforce, declined. By 1929, the average per capita income of nonagricultural workers was four times that of agricultural laborers. Between 1929 and 1932, farm income dropped by more than two-thirds.

Disparities in income were not the only differences between rural and city dwellers. City residents increasingly enjoyed the benefits of new technologies, educational opportunities, and modern medicine. On the eve of the Great Depression, most city residences had electricity; by contrast, only one in ten farmhouses had electricity or indoor plumbing. Inadequate funding for education in many rural areas led to illiteracy rates more than double those in cities. Nearly 20 million rural residents lacked access to a hospital,

Dry dust buries a truck and other farm machinery in South Dakota in the 1930s. What were the main reasons for the environmental disaster known as the Dust Bowl?

a doctor, or a nurse. Controllable diseases like hookworm and malaria ravaged young and old.

The situation was especially dire in the South, where sharecropping and tenant farming led to massive poverty and ruthless exploitation of the powerless. Lorena Hickok, a journalist who toured rural America on behalf of the Roosevelt administration in 1934, reported finding "half-starved Whites and Blacks" in Georgia. They had "less to eat than my dog gets at home," she wrote, "for the privilege of living in huts that are infinitely less comfortable than his kennel."

Black Americans living in the South were treated as though slavery had not been abolished. For black sharecroppers and tenants, in many ways it had not. A telling example of their condition was revealed by an early New Deal program designed to increase the income of farmers: the Agricultural Adjustment Act (AAA) of 1933. The basic idea behind AAA was to lower farm production, thereby decreasing the supply of crops and raising the prices farmers received for them. Toward this end, the AAA paid farmers not to plant a portion of their fields. In 1933, administrators in the Department of Agriculture proposed giving direct payments to all farmers, whether they owned the land or not. That included southern black tenants and sharecroppers.

The response by a white landowner, who happened to be United States Senator Ellison Smith of South Carolina, opens a window on white attitudes toward the independence of black people living in the South. Senator Smith told a Department of Agriculture administrator: "Young fella, you can't do this to my niggers, paying checks to them. They don't know what to do with the money. The money should come to me. I'll take care of them. They're mine." The money came exclusively to Senator Smith—and to the other white landowners.

In the next essay, Timothy Egan describes another somber episode of farm life during the Great Depression: the human and environmental disaster known as the Dust Bowl. The Dust Bowl was a huge, flat portion of the Southern Plains that included parts of Texas, Oklahoma, Kansas, New Mexico, and Colorado. This largely arid region was suited to livestock grazing, not farming. In effect, this was how the original settlers of the southern Great Plains—Native Americans—carved a living from an inhospitable land. They followed buffalo herds that ate the hundreds of species of short grasses covering the Plains; the roots of the grasses sank into the arid earth and bonded the topsoil together. Droughts, prairie fires, extraordinary extremes of temperature, hailstorms, snowstorms, windstorms—these acts of nature regularly bombarded the Southern Plains. But as long as the grasses and their roots held the soil in place, both the animals and humans who lived there survived.

This changed as hundreds of thousands of land-hungry farmers, enticed by the Homestead Act of 1862 and the Enlarged Homestead Act of 1909, pushed Indians off the land, destroyed the buffalo herds, and proceeded to plant crops on land meant for grass. They carved up millions of acres and pulled up the grass, first with horse-drawn plows and later with fuel-driven tractors. In the process, they tore away the roots that held the ground in place. They planted corn, wheat, and sugar beets; when prices for those commodities went down, they planted more. They sliced up an environment meant for something else in the reckless pursuit of the Jeffersonian agrarian myth of family self-sufficiency, personal independence, abundance, and profit.

In 1931, the drought came—and stayed for the remainder of the 1930s. A reduction in rainfall (from a norm of eighteen inches per year to ten or eleven inches) was accompanied by temperatures that reached well over 100 degrees and lasted for weeks at a time. Crops dried up and died, while the rootless soil cracked. When the winds came, they lifted the earth skyward, creating the dust storms that consistently pounded the region for years. Dust went everywhere, got into everything, and knew no borders. For example, on May 9, 1934, a storm that began on the Plains traveled east, carrying more than 300 million tons of soil through the air. It blew through New York City, dropping dust everywhere, and kept going, moving hundreds of miles into the Atlantic Ocean, where it landed on ships.

As Timothy Egan points out, the drought was an act of nature. But the destruction of the soil, the dust storms, and the Dust Bowl were products of human greed and a reckless disregard for the natural environment. In the aftermath of the drought and the dust storms, tens of thousands of families were forced to leave their homes. Many wandered the countryside, refugees in their own country. John Steinbeck's 1939 novel, *The Grapes of Wrath*, is a classic portrayal of their plight.

Timothy Egan's essay is a concrete example of how private lives and public issues are connected. Egan describes the Plains ecosystem and why it was not meant for farming. He also tells the story of a poor family of homesteaders who came to the Southern Plains in 1914. They struggled at first, prospered during World War I, struggled again in the 1920s, and then confronted the relentless dust storms during the Great Depression. On the surface, farming the Great Plains was a result of personal decisions made by thousands of families who decided to settle on and profit from cheap land. But those decisions had public consequences, including the destruction of a natural environment that, in turn, devastated the lives of those same thousands of families in the 1930s.

Source: Excerpts from *The Worst Hard Time: The Untold Story of Those Who Survived the Great American Dust Bowl* by Timothy Egan. Copyright © 2005 by Timothy Egan. Used by permission of Houghton Mifflin Harcourt Publishing Company. All rights reserved.

The name *Oklahoma* is a combination of two Choctaw words—*okla*, which means "people," and *humma*, the word for "red." The red people lost the land in real estate stampedes that produced instant towns—Oklahoma City, Norman, and Guthrie among them. But the great land rushes never made it to the Panhandle [a strip of land on the Texas-Oklahoma border]. No Man's Land [the far western end of Oklahoma Panhandle] was settled, finally, when there was no other land left to take.

It was a hard place to love; a tableau for mischief and sudden death from the sky or up from the ground. Hazel Lucas, a daring little girl with straw-colored hair, first saw the grasslands near the end of a family journey to claim a homestead. Hazel got up on the tips of her toes in the horse-drawn wagon to stare into an abyss of beige. It was as empty as the back end of a day, a wilderness of flat. The family clawed a hole in the side of the prairie just south of Boise City. It was not the promised land that Hazel had imagined, but it had possibility. She was thrilled to be at the beginning of a grand adventure, the first wave of humans to try to mate with this land. She also felt scared because it was so foreign. The lure was price, her daddy said. This land was the only bargain left in America. . . . Here it was free, though there was not much left to claim. By 1910, almost two hundred million acres nationwide had been patented by homesteaders, more than half of it in the Great Plains. Hazel missed trees. She wanted just one sturdy elm with a branch strong enough to hold a swing. And she didn't want to live in a hole in the ground, with the snakes and tarantulas, and sleeping so near to the stink of burning cow manure. Nor did she want to live in a sod house. . . .

Hazel's family arrived in No Man's Land in 1914, the peak year for homesteads in the twentieth century—53,000 claims made throughout the Great Plains. Every man a landlord! . . . The federal government was so anxious to settle No Man's Land that they offered free train rides to pilgrims looking to prove up a piece of dry land. . . . The slogan was "Health, Wealth, and Opportunity." Hazel's father, William Carlyle, known as Carlie, built a dugout in 1915 for his family and started plowing grass on his half-section, a patch of sandy loam. The home was twenty-two feet long by fourteen feet wide—308 square feet for a family of seven. . . .

In trying to come to terms with a strange land, perhaps the biggest fear was fire. The combination of wind, heat, lightning, and combustible grass was nature's perfect recipe for fire. One day the grass could look sweet and green, spread across the face of No Man's Land. Another day it would be a roaring flank of smoke and flame, marching toward the dugout. Hazel Lucas was petrified of prairie fires, and for good reason. A few years before the family arrived, a lightning bolt lit up a field in New Mexico, igniting a fire that swept across the High Plains of Texas and Oklahoma. It burned everything in its wake for two hundred miles. . . .

The Lucas family stayed through the fires, floods, and the peculiar social life because the land was starting to pay. Not as grassland for cattle, but as crop-producing dirt. Carlie dug up part of his half-section using a horse-drawn plow and planted it in wheat and corn. The Great War, starting in 1914, meant a fortune was about to be made in the most denigrated part of America, all of the dry-land wheat belt. Turn the ground, Lucas was advised, as fast as you can. . . .

[N]o group of people took a more dramatic leap in lifestyle or prosperity, in such a short time, than wheat farmers on the Great Plains. In less than ten years, they went from subsistence living to small business-class wealth, from working a few hard acres with horses and hand tools to being masters of wheat estates, directing harvests with wondrous new machines, at a profit margin in some cases that was ten times the cost of production. In 1910, the price of wheat stood at eighty cents a bushel, good enough for anyone who had outwitted a few dry years to make enough money to get through another year and even put something away. Five years later, with world grain supplies pinched by the Great War, the price had more than doubled. Farmers increased production by 50 percent. When the Turkish navy blocked the Dardenelles, they did a favor for dry wheat farmers that no one could have imagined. Europe had relied on Russian for export wheat. With Russian shipments blocked [by the Turkish navy], the United States stepped in, and issued a proclamation to the plains: plant more wheat to win the war. And for the first time, the government guaranteed the price, at two dollars a bushel, through the war, backed by the wartime food administrator, a multi-millionaire public servant named Herbert Hoover. Wheat was no longer a staple of a small family farmer but a commodity with a price guarantee and a global market.

When he first came to No Man's Land, Carlie Lucas had hoped to make just enough from his half-section to feed his family. But within a few years of arriving, he was part of the great frenzy to turn over ground a get as much wheat out as possible to sell abroad. If he could produce fifteen bushels an acre on his half-section that meant 4,800 bushels at harvest. It cost him about thirty-five cents per bushel to grow. At a selling price of two dollars a bushel, his profit was nearly eight thousand dollars a year. In 1917, this was a fortune. . . . People had been farming since Biblical times, and never had any nation set out to produce so much grain on ground that suggested otherwise. If farmers on the High Plains were laying the foundation for a time bomb that would shatter the natural world, any voices that implied such a thing were muted.

What had been an anchored infinity of grassland just a generation earlier became a patchwork of broken land. In 1917, about forty-five million acres of wheat were harvested nationwide. In 1919, over seventy-five million acres were put into production—up nearly 70 percent. And the expansion would continue in the decade after the war, even as there was no need for it. It was one of the occasional episodes in human history when fortunes were said to go only one way. . . .

The Stock Market crashed on October 29, 1929, a Tuesday, the most disastrous session on Wall Street to date in a month of turmoil. . . . Over the next three weeks, the market lost 40 percent of its value, more than thirty-five billion dollars in shareholder equity—money enough to float a hemisphere of nations. The entire American federal budget was barely three billion dollars. . . .

[W]hile prairie families may not have owned stock, they did own wheat, and it was starting to follow the course of the equities market. On Wall Street, people put 10 percent down to borrow against the future growth of a stock; in Kansas a dry-land wheat farmer did the same thing—gambling on grain. . . .

[T]he Lucas family was getting ready to start the first harvest of their winter wheat, a June cutting, when the sky darkened and rumbled. Carlie Lucas had died, suddenly, leaving the farm to his widow, Dee, and her five children. She had help from her late husband's brother, C.C., and two young sons, now stout. Her daughter, Hazel Lucas, had married Charlie Shaw and headed off for Cincinnati. With the prices down and loans to repay for all the new farm machinery, the Lucases needed this crop. Maybe, if the wheat came in right, Dee Lucas could get shoes for the kids and bring something special into the house that Carlie had built next to the old dugout. Electricity was not an option. In town, there was a picture show with a piano player accompanying the screen narrative, and diners were lit up, as were some houses. But in the rest of No Man's Land, the juice had yet to arrive. Nobody had washing machines, vacuum cleaners, or incandescent light bulbs. . . .

A June storm is always troublesome, carrying the currents of systems confused by the cold of late spring and the heat of early summer. The most severe hailstorms on the High Plains are in May and June. When the two systems struggled—humid east, dry west—it usually meant friction, strong wind, and clattering. A glance at the sky and here it was, the roll of the squall line. Dee Lucas ordered her children to the root cellar. The hail fell fast, pounding hard, the big ice stones bouncing when they hit, though some exploded on impact. It got louder. The hail balls were as big as grapefruits. They smashed north-facing windows. It sounded like a stampede of horses over the field. When Dee Lucas emerged from the cellar, she saw that the wheat field was flattened, covered with ice balls. Hail sometimes fell bigger; in Kansas a storm dropped ice that measured six inches in diameter, big enough to knock a person cold or cause a concussion. Anything above a marble in size could be ruinous, breaking windows, cracking or denting cars and houses. C.C. Lucas looked out: the damage stretched all the way to his eighty acres of wheat as well. Nothing was spared; all the grain lay squashed on the ground. . . . The grain crop was lost—a year's work gone in five minutes. Dee Lucas tried to hold back tears; her eyes clouded and they came quick, in a torrent. C.C. Lucas started to cry as well. Sure they were next year people— you had to make our peace with the Panhandle—but that didn't make it easier. Anybody who lived in No Man's Land for long knew about nature's capricious power. . . .

At the start of 1930, wheat sold for one-eighth of the price from ten years earlier. At forty cents a bushel, the price would barely cover costs, let alone service a bank note. Across the plains, there was only one way out, a last gasp: plant more wheat. Farmers tore up what grass was left, furiously ripping out sod on the hopes they could hit a crop when the price came back. . . .

"No one has yet starved," said President Hoover, trying to calm people at year's end. He spoke too soon. A few months later people rioted in Arkansas, demanding food for their children. Then it happened closer to home. A mob stormed a grocery store in Oklahoma City, after the mayor had rejected their petition for food. Rioting over food: how could this be? Here was all this grain, food enough to feed half the world, sitting in piles at the train station, going to waste. Something was out of balance. Productivity surged, while wages fell and jobs disappeared. That left too much of everything—food, clothes, cars—and too few people to buy it. At one point, the going rate for corn was listed at minus three cents a bushel.

Hazel [Lucas Shaw, who with her husband had returned to Oklahoma] heard about a job opening the next year, 1930, at the New Hope School outside Boise City.

"What salary would you like?" the clerk asked her.

Hazel had been thinking about this for some time and was ready with her answer: "One hundred per month."

The clerk frowned. "Is something wrong?" Hazel said. "If you can't pay a hundred, I would accept ninety."

"We can't pay you anything," said the clerk.

"Nothing?"

"But we still want to hire you. We need another teacher."

"You can't pay anything?"

The New Hope School was broke. Farmers were drowning in debt and had stopped paying taxes. Without taxes, the school could not pay teacher salaries. But they still wanted Hazel. They offered to pay her a warrant, a paper that could be cashed in later for ten dollars.

She accepted the job and the warrant. But when Hazel took the first of her paper promises to the bank she was turned away. John Johnson's bank refused to cash them. There was simply no way to expect that tax receipts would ever make the school solvent. As each month of the school year passed, Hazel realized that the New Hope School would not be paying a teacher for some time. She worked that year without pay. . . .

On September 14, 1930, a windstorm kicked up dust out of southwest Kansas and tumbled toward Oklahoma. By the time the storm cut a swath through the Texas Panhandle, it looked unlike anything ever seen before on the High Plains. People called the government to find out what was up with this dirty swirling thing in the sky. The weather bureau people in Lubbock didn't know what to make of it or how to define it. Wasn't a sandstorm. . . . And it wasn't a hailstorm, though it certainly brought with it a dark, threatening sky, the kind of formation you would get with a roof-buster. The strange thing about it, the weather bureau observers said, was that it rolled, like a mobile hill of crud, and it was black. When it tumbled through, it carried static electricity, enough to short out a car. And it hurt, like a swipe of coarse-grained sandpaper on the face. The first black duster was a curiosity, nothing else. The weather bureau observers wrote it up and put it in a drawer. . . .

The tractors had done what no hailstorm, no blizzard, no tornado, no drought, no epic siege of frost, no prairie fire, nothing in the natural history of the southern plains had ever done. They had removed the native prairie grass, a web of perennial species evolved over twenty thousand years or more, so completely that by the end of 1931 it was a different land—thirty-three million acres stripped bare in the southern plains.

And what came from that transformed land—the biggest crop of all time—was shunned, met with the lowest prices ever. . . .

Subsistence farming may have kept people alive, but it did nothing for the land, which was going fallow section by section. At the end of 1931, the Agricultural College of Oklahoma did a survey of all the land that had been torn up in their state during the wheat bonanza. They were astonished by what they found: of sixteen million acres in cultivation in the state, thirteen million were seriously eroded. And this was before the drought had calcified most of the ground. The erosion was due to a pair of perennial weather conditions on the plains: wind and brief, powerful rain or hailstorms. But it was a third element—something new to the entire ecosystem—that was really to blame, the college agriculture experts reported: neglect. Farmers had taken their machines to the fields and produced the biggest wheat crops in history, transforming the great grasslands into a vast medium for turning out a global commodity. And then they ditched it. . . .

When the native sod of the Great Plains was in place, it did not matter if people looked twice at a piece of ground. Wind blew twenty, thirty, forty miles an hour, as always. Droughts came and went. Prairie fires, many of them started deliberately by Indians or cowboys trying to scare nesters off, took a great gulp of grass in a few days. Hailstorms pounded on the land. Blue northers [storms originating in Canada] froze it so hard it was like broken glass to walk on. Through all the seasonal tempests, man was inconsequential. As long as the weave of grass was stitched to the land, the prairie would flourish in dry years and wet. The grass could look brown and dead, but beneath the surface, the roots held the soil in place; it was alive and dormant. The short grass, buffalo and blue grama [a species of grass], had evolved as the perfect fit for the sandy loam of the arid zone. It could hold moisture a foot or more below ground level even during summer droughts, when hot winds robbed the surface of all water-bearing life. In turn, the grass nurtured pin-tailed grouse, prairie chickens, cranes, jackrabbits, snakes, and other creatures that got their water from foraging on the native turf. Through the driest years, the web of life held. When a farmer tore out the sod and then walked away, leaving the land naked, however, that barren patch posed a threat to neighbors. It could not revert to grass, because the roots were gone. It was empty, dead, and transient. . . . What was happening to the land in the early 1930s was nearly unnoticed at first. Still, it was a different world, off balance, and ill. So when the winds blew in the winter of 1932, they picked up the soil with little resistance and sent it skyward. . . .

The land would die an easy death. Fields were bare, scraped to hard-pan in places, heaving in others. The skies carried soil from state to state. With no appreciable rain for two years, even deep wells were gasping to draw from the natural underground reservoir. One late winter day in 1933, a battalion of heavy clouds massed over No Man's Land. At midday, the sun disappeared. Lights were turned on in town in order to see. The clouds dumped layers of dust, one wave after the other. . . .

Hazel Lucas Shaw watched the dust seep through the thinnest cracks in the walls of their rental house, spread over the china, into the bedroom, onto the sheets. When she woke in the morning, the only clean part of her pillow was the outline of her head. She taped all the windows and round the outer edge of doors, but the dust always found a way in. She learned never to set a dinner plate out until ready to eat, to cook with pots covered, to leave no standing water out for long or it would turn to mud. She had decided to give up the teaching job that paid worthless scrip and to try and start a family. . . .

The temperature fell more than seventy degrees in less than twenty-four hours one February day in 1933. It reached fourteen below zero in Boise

City and still the dust blew in with the arctic chill. Hazel tried everything to stay warm and keep the house clean. Dust dominated life. Driving from Boise City to Dalhart, a journey of barely fifty miles, was like a trip out on the open seas in a small boat. The road was fine in parts, rutted and hard, but a few miles later it disappeared under waves of drifting dust. Unable to see more than a car length ahead, the Shaws followed telephone poles to get from one town to the next. . . .

The High Plains lay in ruins. From Kansas, through No Man's Land, up into Colorado, over in Union County, New Mexico, and south into the Llano Estacado of Texas, the soil blew up from the ground or rained down from above. There was no color to the land, no crops, in what was the worst growing season anyone had seen. Some farmers had grown spindles of dwarfed wheat and corn, but it was not worth the effort to harvest it. The same Texas Panhandle that had produced six million bushels of wheat just two years ago now gave up just a few truckloads of grain. In one county, 90 percent of the chickens died; the dust had got into their systems, choking them or clogging their digestive tracks. Milk cows went dry. Cattle starved or dropped dead from what veterinarians called "dust fever. . . ."

One night just before dinner, after clearing the floor, the dining table, the lampshades, and the kitchen counter of their daily dust at her home in Boise City, Hazel Shaw put on her white gloves and smiled. She had an announcement for her husband. "I'm pregnant.". . .

Hazel gave birth . . . April 7, 1934. They named her Ruth Nell. She was plump and seemed healthy, but the doctor was concerned about taking her outside. The air was not safe for a baby. He ordered Hazel to stay in the hospital for at least ten more days and remarked that the young family might want to consider moving out of No Man's Land. Others were buttoning up their homes and getting out before the dust ruined them. But the Lucas family had planted themselves on this far edge of the Oklahoma Panhandle at a time when there wasn't even a land office for nesters. They were among the first homesteaders. What would it mean for the pioneers to leave? And if they moved, it was not just the uncertainty of where to go and what to do but also the feeling that they would never again own something. It was a big step down from working on your own quarter-section to being adrift, with strangers staring at you like just another piece of Okie trash, saying you should be deported. . . .

She started to cough that winter, a baby's ragged hiccup, and it never stopped. Though Hazel Shaw had sealed the windows and doors and draped an extra layer of wet sheets over the openings, the dust still found Ruth Nell in her crib. It was oily and black some mornings, covering the baby's face. Her lips were frothed and mudded, her eyes red. She cried and coughed, cried and coughed. Hazel lubricated her tiny nostrils with Vaseline and tried to keep a mask over her face, but the baby coughed or spit it off. A doctor took tests, listened to the hurried heart. Ruth Nell was diagnosed with whooping cough. You should probably leave, for the life of your baby, the doctor advised.

South forty miles in Texhoma, Loumiza Lucas was tucked under quilt layers inside the family home. The matriarch of the Lucas clan, Hazel's grandma, was coughing hard, just like the baby. Loumiza was eighty years old, a widow for twenty-one years, with nine children, forty grandchildren, thirty great-grandchildren. There was yet no Social Security.

"It's hard to be old and not have anything," a widowed North Dakota farmer's wife wrote the president in 1934, in a letter that was typical in its pleading tone. "I have always been poor and have always worked hard, so now I am not able to do any more. I am all worn out but am able to be around and I thank God that I have no pains."

Loumiza was in pain. The dust filtered into her home like a toxic vapor. She stopped eating. She grew weaker. Every time she brought her teeth together she tasted grit. Her bedroom was a refuge but not a pleasant one. It was a dusty hole in a homestead. She could not be moved because the risk of travel exposed her to the wind-borne sand. . . . The windows were sealed so tightly that light from her beloved land was completely blocked. It did not matter: she hated what No Man's Land had become. It was better to remember it as it was when she came into this country, arriving by covered wagon to Texhoma, and north to a half-section of their own, her and Jimmy, in the free kingdom of No Man's Land. . . .

Two days after Ruth Nell's first birthday, Hazel and her husband decided to flee, breaking her family apart for the health of the baby, as the doctor had recommended. They had to get out now or risk the baby's life. This year, 1935, had been one duster after the other and April showed no sign of letup, no rain in the forecast, four years into the drought. At the end of March, black blizzards had fallen for twelve straight days. During one of these storms, the wind was clocked at forty miles an hour or better—for a hundred hours. . . .

Hazel hurried along her plan to get Ruth Nell out of Boise City. She arranged to stay with her in-laws in Enid, Oklahoma, well to the east. But just as they were ready to depart, a tornado touched down not far from Enid, the black funnel dancing around the edges of the very place where Ruth Nell was to find her refuge. It was a gruesome thing, ripping through homes, throwing roofs to the sky. Now what—stay or go? Hazel and Charles felt they had no choice but to go. . . .

Sheriff Barrick said the roads out of town were blocked by huge drifts [of wind-blown sand]. The CCC [Civilian Conservation Corps] crews would no sooner dig out one drift than another would appear, covering a quarter-mile section of road. A caravan of Boise City residents who had tried to leave earlier in the week with all their belongings loaded into their jalopies were pinned down at the edge of town, and they were forced to return. The volume of dirt that had been thrown to the skies was extraordinary. A professor at Kansas State College estimated that if a line of trucks ninety-six miles long hauled ten full loads a day, it would take a year to transport the dirt that had blown from one side of Kansas to the other—a total of forty-six million truckloads. Better days were not in the forecast.

Hazel made it south to Texhoma, where she and Ruth Nell could ride the train to the eastern part of the state. If the baby could take in some clean air for a few weeks, living with her grandparents, she might shake this horrid cough. The journey to Enid was not easy. A few weeks earlier, a train full of CCC workers slid off the dust-covered tracks and rolled, killing several young men. Hazel's train sputtered its way east, stopping frequently so the crews could shovel sand from the tracks. Hazel tried to stay positive, but it looked awful outside: all of the Oklahoma Panhandle blowing and dead, no life of any form in the fields, no spring planting, no farmers on the roads. By the time mother and daughter made it to Enid, the baby's cough was no better. Her little stomach must have been in acute pain from the hacking, and she might have fractured a rib from coughing. . . . The doctors tried to clean out her lungs by suctioning some of the gunk, but the baby would not settle. . . . The doctors confirmed Hazel's fears—Ruth Nell had dust pneumonia. She was moved into a section of the hospital in Enid that nurses called the "dust ward." The baby's temperature held above 103. She could not hold down milk from a bottle; it came back up as spit and grime. The doctor's wrapped the baby's midsection in gauze and loose-fitting tape, as a way to hold in place the fractured ribs and diminish the pain in the stomach muscle. . . .

"You must come," Hazel phoned her husband from the hospital in Enid. "Come now. Ruth Nell looks terrible. I'm so afraid.". . .

By the time Charles made it to St. Mary's Hospital, he was covered in dirt, his face black. He went to the dust ward. Hazel was crying. Ruth Nell had died an hour earlier. . . .

Back in No Man's Land, Hazel's Grandma Lou stopped coughing. She had been running a fever for several days and could not hold down food. "How's the baby?" She asked. "How is Ruth Nell? Any word?"

Her son had not heard. Loumiza turned away and closed her eyes. She would not see the homestead green again, would not see any more of the starving land. She slipped under layers of quilt and took her last breath, dying within hours after her youngest great-grandchild fell. The family decided to stage a double funeral for baby Ruth Nell and the Lucas family patriarch. They would hold the ceremony at the church in Boise City, then proceed out of town to a family plot for burial on Sunday, April 14, 1935.

Questions for Discussion

1. The author mentions food riots in Oklahoma. They happened in other rural areas as well. In the previous chapter we read about housewives' meat boycotts in cities. Were there connections between the two events? Were they caused by shortages of meat and farm produce? What insights do these issues give you about the causes of the Great Depression?

2. Historically, Americans tended to romanticize rural, small-town life while being suspicious of city life. In your view, was this justified? What strikes you as the

most significant differences between the daily lives of farm families and city families at this time?

3. Prior to the Great Depression, American farmers increased production when prices for their commodities sank. But manufacturers did the opposite. How do you account for the difference?

4. Farming on land meant for grazing is an example of seeking profit while ignoring the consequences for the environment. Is this right? Can you think of issues today concerning the economy and the environment that parallel those of the 1930s?

For Further Reading

David Conrad, *The Forgotten Farmers: The Story of Sharecroppers in the New Deal* (1982); Timothy Egan, *The Worst Hard Time: The Untold Story of Those Who Survived the Great American Dust Bowl* (2006); Bruce Gardner, *American Agriculture in the Twentieth Century: How It Flourished and What It Cost* (2007); James N. Gregory, *American Exodus: The Dust Bowl Migration and Okie Culture in California* (1989); Donald Grubbs, *Cry from the Cotton: The Southern Tenant Farmers Union and the New Deal* (1999); Caroline Henderson, *Letters from the Dust Bowl* (2004); Dwight Hoover, *A Good Day's Work: An Iowa Farm Family in the Great Depression* (2007); R. Douglas Hurt, *Problems of Plenty: The American Farmer in the Twentieth Century* (2003); David M. Kennedy, *Freedom from Fear: The American People in Depression and War, 1929–1945* (1999); Howard Kester, *Revolt Among the Sharecroppers* (1997); David Kyvig, *Daily Life in the United States, 1920–1940* (2002); Ann Marie Low, *Dust Bowl Diary* (1984); Van Perkins, *Crisis in Agriculture: The Agricultural Adjustment Administration and the New Deal* (1969); Amity Shales, *The Forgotten Man: A New History of the Great Depression* (2007); John Steinbeck, *The Grapes of Wrath* (1939); Frank Stallings, *Black Sunday: The Great Dust Storm of April 14, 1935* (2001); Lawrence Svobida, *Farming the Dust Bowl* (1986); Stewart Tolnay, *The Bottom Rung: African American Family Life on Southern Farms* (1998); Donald Worster, *The Southern Plains in the 1930s* (1979).

CHAPTER

11

Rosie the Riveter Gets Married

Women during World War II

Elaine Tyler May

World War II ended the Great Depression. Within months of the December 7, 1941, Japanese attack on Pearl Harbor, the United States government embarked on unprecedented levels of spending and centralized economic planning. The federal government took charge of the economy, shifting the nation's manufacturing focus from consumer products like cars to wartime goods like tanks. The results were full employment, good wages, huge profits, and creation of the greatest war machine in history. In defense plants scattered around the country, an array of war materials rolled off assembly lines in astonishing quantities. During the war, Americans produced 88,000 tanks, 634,000 jeeps, 300,000 aircraft, 2 million trucks, 1,500 naval ships, 6.5 million rifles—and 40 billion bullets to load them with.

The war mobilized the American population as well as the country's industrial resources. It launched one of the great migrations in the nation's history. Americans have always moved in quest of opportunity. In the nineteenth century, tens of thousands of farm families moved from east to west in search of cheap, fertile land; in the twentieth century, millions of African Americans moved from south to north, seeking both economic opportunity and freedom. The early 1940s was no different. By the millions Americans pulled up stakes and moved to San Diego, San Francisco, Detroit, Seattle, Pittsburgh, and other cities where defense work offered higher wages than most blue-collar workers ever dreamed of earning. In a population

How does this cartoon express the ambivalence of Americans toward married women who worked during World War II?

of 130 million, about 15 million changed their county of residence during the war years; 8 million of them moved permanently to different states. An additional 16 million served in the armed forces.

The mobilization of the population not only helped win the war. It sowed changes in society that ultimately altered the prospects of entire groups of Americans. For example, when the war began, about 75 percent of African Americans still lived in the South, one-third of them in desperate straits as sharecroppers. Nationwide, 90 percent of black families had incomes below the federal poverty level. There were no federal laws against lynching and other acts of violence toward African Americans. And, like much of the rest of society, the armed forces either practiced racial segregation (the army and navy) or did not allow blacks to serve at all (the marines and air corps).

The war did not put an end to these situations, but it made a start from which there was no turning back. For example, with war on the horizon in 1941, African American leaders urged President Franklin D. Roosevelt to force companies doing defense work not to discriminate against blacks in hiring or wages. When Roosevelt refused, A. Philip Randolph, head of the all-black Brotherhood of Sleeping Car Porters, threatened to organize tens of thousands of African Americans for a march on Washington to protest the situation.

Shortly before the march was scheduled to take place, Roosevelt caved in. He issued an executive order forbidding discrimination in defense industries because of "race, creed, color, or national origin." It was the first act by an American president to combat racial injustice since the Emancipation Proclamation of 1863. During the war, more than 700,000 African Americans left the South to take advantage of Roosevelt's order. Harsh conditions would continue to haunt black people for decades after the war. The armed forces remained segregated until 1948, less than 10 percent of southern blacks could vote in 1950, and the Civil Rights movement did not get under way until the mid-1950s. But the war signaled that a change was in the air.

It did for women as well, although as Elaine Tyler May points out in the next essay, in ways that were contradictory. There was something to the legend of "Rosie the Riveter." With so many in the armed forces (including 350,000 women serving in noncombatant roles), the country faced a dire labor shortage. Government, business, magazines, and popular songs urged women to put on working clothes and do their part for victory. The popular song "Rosie the Riveter" claimed Rosie was protecting her Marine boyfriend Charlie by "working overtime on the riveting machine." Few if any women riveted, but by the millions they welded, drove tractors, worked on assembly lines, and did clerical work. By 1943, women were about 10 percent of the workforce in defense plants, with 500,000 working in aircraft industries and 250,000 in shipbuilding yards. They worked alongside men and made a major contribution toward winning the war.

More women worked in these years than ever before in the nation's history. But there were not as many "Rosies" as one might think. About 19 million women worked during the war. By 1944, 36 percent of women were on the job. This was only about 3.5 million more women than would normally have been in the workforce. And it was only a small increase in the number of married women who worked. Before the war in 1940, 9 percent of married women with children worked; in 1944, 12 percent of them were on the job. Most of them were married women with older children.

Nevertheless, this situation made many people, including most women, uncomfortable. They believed a woman's proper place was in the home, especially if she was married with children. They agreed the wartime labor shortage made it necessary to recruit women for jobs normally reserved for men; but they also believed most women should leave those jobs and return to their domestic roles once the war was over. A telling metaphor for these attitudes was the "lunchbox" issue at defense plants. If a women worker carried her lunch in a metal box, like men, she would be "called out" by her male colleagues. A metal lunchbox symbolized permanence. They wanted women workers to bring their lunch in paper bags, which were disposable—like women's grip on those jobs.

In the next essay, Elaine Tyler May portrays these contradictory views of women, work, domesticity, and gender during World War II. May shows that the war emergency created opportunities for women to move beyond traditional gender roles regarding sexuality, marriage, work, and childrearing. But she also discusses attitudes and trends during the war that pointed toward a revival of the Victorian gender values that would dominate American society and family life after the war.

Source: Elaine Tyler May, "Rosie the Riveter Gets Married: American Women During World War II," in Lewis A. Erenberg and Susan E. Hirsch (eds.), *The War in American Culture: Society and Consciousness during World War II* (Chicago: University of Chicago Press, 1996), Chapter 5, pp. 128–141.

> *Chicago was just humming, no matter where I went. The bars were jammed, and unless you were an absolute dog, you could pick up anyone you wanted to. There were servicemen of all varieties roaming the streets all the time. There was never, never a shortage of young, healthy bucks. We never thought of getting tired. Two, three hours of sleep was normal. I'd go down to the office every morning half dead, but with a smile on my face, and report for work. There was another girl there who was having a ball too, and we took turns going into the back room and taking a nap on the floor behind a desk.*
>
> —YOUNG WORKING WOMAN DURING WORLD WAR II

As the epigraph suggests, World War II opened up all kinds of opportunities for women. New possibilities for work, play and sexual adventure were everywhere. Yet women also faced hardships as fathers, sons, and husbands left for war, families relocated, and disruption became the norm. Taken together, all the changes, challenges, and difficulties of wartime had a lasting impact on the lives of American women. But at the time, long-term effects were not on people's minds. The question was how to respond to the emergency.

Emergency was nothing new to the young adults coming of age at the time of World War II. They had been reared on the trials and hardships of the depression. When war broke out they faced a new emergency calling for strength and sacrifice. Although the war brought an end to the depression, as prosperity returned it ushered in new challenges for women and men. Traditional domestic roles were thrown into disarray, and even the disruption took new forms. In wartime the stigma attached to employment for married women evaporated. Women not only were tolerated in the paid labor force, they were actively recruited to take "men's jobs" as a patriotic duty, to keep the war economy booming while the men went off to fight. Men were called to war, where their role as soldiers took precedence over their role as breadwinners. Families coped with new realities as men vanished to foreign shores to ward off the enemy, leaving women to fend for themselves.

These readjustments, challenging traditional gender roles and domestic norms, held the potential for long-term changes in public as well as private life. The war emergency opened the way for a restructuring of the economy along gender-neutral lines, bringing an end to sex segregation in the workplace. In addition, wartime dislocation might have led to postponement of marriage and childbearing, continuing the demographic trends of the thirties toward fewer and later marriages. But these possibilities did not materialize. In spite of the many gains women made during the war and their struggles to hold onto those gains, opportunities for them dried up in postwar America. Ironically, the experiences of wartime ultimately reaffirmed a domestic ideal of breadwinner, homemaker, and children. At a time when domesticity faced its greatest challenge, young men and women turned to marriage and childbearing in unexpected numbers.

Let us first look at what some historians consider to be the most substantial change of the 1940s: the entry of unprecedented numbers of female workers into the paid labor force. As a result of the combined incentives of patriotism and good wages, women began streaming into jobs, many for the first time. The fastest-growing group in the workforce was married women, who took jobs during the war in record numbers. In a booming economy responding to the needs of the war effort, the stigma attached to employed wives evaporated.

Yet this entry of women into the paid labor force was not as far reaching as it appeared on the surface. When we look closely at who these women were and what they did—particularly when we consider long-term possibilities— their opportunities appear much more limited. In the first place, at the beginning of the 1940s women entered jobs with tremendous disadvantages. In 1939 the median annual income for women was $568, compared with $962 for men, and for black women it was a mere $246. By 1940 women constituted only 9.4 percent of union members, although they made up 25 percent of the operatives. Women had few levers for improving their working conditions. Considering the strong sentiment that had prevailed in the 1930s against women's holding jobs at all, it is not surprising that even feminist organizations fighting job discrimination stressed women's need to work over their right to employment—a strategy that underscored women's responsibility to their families as their primary concern.

Moreover, when we examine the statistics closely, we find that young married women, those most likely to have small children at home, made the smallest gains in employment during the 1940s—even less than prewar predictions. The reason is demographically as well as culturally interesting. Since single women had provided the largest proportion of the paid female labor force before the war, the demands of production during the forties quickly exhausted the supply. Few young single women were available, for the war almost immediately brought a drop in the marriage age and a rise in the birthrate. Because of these developments, young women who might previously have been expected to work for a few years were marrying and having children instead. Young married women with children were encouraged to stay home. . . .

The removal of these young women from the labor market opened the way for older married women—those without young children at home—to enter the paid labor force. These women were the fastest-growing group among the employed, a trend that would continue after the war. Between 1940 and 1945, the female labor force grew by over 50 percent. The proportion of women employed rose from 28 to 37 percent, and women made up 36 percent of the civilian workforce. Three-fourths of these new female employees were married. By the end of the war fully 25 percent of all married women were employed—a huge gain from 15 percent at the end of the 1930s.

Not everyone was comfortable with this development, however. A writer in *Fortune* magazine lamented: "There are practically no unmarried women left to draw upon. This leaves, as the next potential source of industrial workers, the housewives. We are a kindly, somewhat sentimental people with strong, ingrained ideas about what women should or should not do. Many thoughtful citizens are seriously disturbed over the wisdom of bringing married women into the factories."

In spite of their visibility, women still remained in a fairly small number of occupations. For all the publicity surrounding "Rosie the Riveter," few women took jobs that were previously held exclusively by men, and most of those jobs ended at the conclusion of the war. These developments are typical of a pattern that began during the war and continued during the postwar years: numerical expansion of opportunities flowing into a limited range of occupations. Although more and more women were welcomed into the paid labor force, most of them still ended up in low-paying, sex-segregated jobs.

Women did not accept this situation passively. They recognized their value and fought for better wages and working conditions. The activism of women working at the California Sanitary Canning Company provides one dramatic example. Energetic labor organizers like Luisa Moreno and Dorothy Ray Healy built a powerful union of largely Mexican and Mexican American women who were able to achieve a wage increase and recognition of their union. . . .

One reason for the wartime success of these women was the strength of their numbers. Women composed 75 percent of all workers in the California canneries. Because they were in the majority, their segregation from male employees allowed them to develop a female work culture in the plants. In other industries where men were in the majority, the segregation of women was a disadvantage. Automobile manufacturing, for example, remained male dominated. Before the war, women accounted for only 10 percent of all autoworkers, and they were concentrated in relatively few jobs. After an initial shutdown, the industry retooled for war production. When the plant reopened in 1942, male workers were in short supply and women were hired in unprecedented numbers. By the end of 1943 one-fourth of the industry's workers were female.

Throughout the war, however, the automobile industry kept women in certain jobs and men in others. The boundaries continued to shift as new definitions of "women's work" were required, but the sex-segregated labor force remained. Despite the dramatic upswing in women's workforce participation, the unions had no fully developed class consciousness that would include women in their concerns, nor was there a strong feminist movement to assert women's needs. As a result, gender division of labor survived the war.

In spite of women's dramatic contributions to the war effort, they were not able to achieve equal pay or working conditions. . . . Instead of equal rights women got "protective" legislation, but those laws did not protect them from ill treatment on the job. Sexual harassment was rampant. One female war worker complained:

> At times it gets to be a pain in the neck when the man who is supposed to show you work stops showing it to you because you have nicely but firmly asked him to keep his hands on his own knees; or when you have refused a date with someone and ever since then he has done everything in his power to make your work more difficult. Somehow we'll have to make them understand that we are not very much interested in their strapping virility. That the display of their physique and the lure of their prowess leaves us cold. That although they have certainly convinced us that they are men and we are women, we'd rather get on with our work.

In spite of such difficulties women took advantage of every opportunity the war offered. Almira Bondelid was a housewife when her husband left for overseas, but she did not sit home and wait for his return: "I decided to stay in San Diego and went to work in a dime store. That was a terrible place to work, and as soon as I could I got a job at Convair [war production plant]. I worked in the tool department as a draftsman, and by the time I left there two years later I was designing long drill jigs for parts of the wing and a hull of B-24s."

Unfortunately for women like Almira Bondelid, highly skilled, well-paid jobs like the one she finally secured were not likely to last once the war ended. Even before the end was in sight, married women were encouraged to return to their domestic duties when the conflict was over. In addition, single women were expected to relinquish their jobs and find husbands. Although the war offered single women many new opportunities, they also encountered hostility to their newly acquired freedom.

There is no question that wartime offered women new chances to participate in public life and to enjoy a certain amount of sexual freedom, as the epigraph to this chapter suggests. But at the same time, during the wartime emergency, single women were often seen as a threat to stable family life and to the moral fiber of the nation at war. As single women poured into the labor force along with their married sisters, there were fears that they might not be willing to settle down to family life once the emergency ended. Perhaps these anxieties arose because, unlike the 1930s, the war years brought a noticeable number of women out of their homes and traditionally sex-segregated jobs into occupations previously reserved for men. In addition, the war removed men from the home front, demonstrating that women could manage quite well without them. Single women now became targets of campaigns urging them back into their domestic roles, campaigns that continued after the war.

Along with their new economic endeavors, the perceived or potential sexual activity of single women also became a cause for alarm. A typical wartime pamphlet warned: "The war in general has given women new status, new recognition. Women are 'coming into their own' in this war. Yet it is essential that women avoid arrogance and retain their femininity in the face of their new status. In her new independence she must not lose her humanness as a woman. She may be the woman of the moment, but she must watch her moments." This theme echoed through the proscriptive literature written during the war. One textbook explained why women had to watch their moments so carefully: "The greater social freedom of women has more or less inevitably led to a greater degree of sexual laxity, a freedom which strikes at the heart of family stability. When women work, earn, and spend as much as men do, they are going to ask for equal rights with men. But the right to behave like a man meant [sic] also the right to misbehave as he does. The decay of established moralities came about as a by-product." In this remarkable passage, the authors state as a scientific fact their opinion that social freedom and employment for women cause "sexual laxity," moral decay, and the destruction of the family.

Women were urged to stay "pure" for the soon to be returning veterans, and men were told to avoid contact with single women for fear of catching venereal diseases. As [historian] Allan Brandt has shown, wartime purity crusades marked a revision of the germ theory: germs were not responsible for spreading disease, "promiscuous" women were. Widely distributed posters warned soldiers that even the angelic "girl next door" might carry disease. "She may look clean, but . . ." read the caption next to one picture of everybody's sweetheart. Wartime ushered in a preoccupation with all forms of non-marital sexuality that had been dormant since the Progressive Era. It ranged from concern about prostitution and "promiscuous" women to fierce campaigns against homosexuals and other "deviants" in military and civilian life.

These campaigns were not fully effective, however. Young women found tremendous new chances to pursue sexual relationships and forge communities during the war. More young women moved into the city and away from neighborhood and parental supervision. Many now earned their own money and took charge of their own leisure time and behavior. For some young heterosexual women experiencing this new independence, men in uniform held special appeal. "When I was sixteen," recalled a college student a few years later, "I let a sailor pick me up and go all the way with me. I had intercourse with him partly because he had a strong personal appeal for me, but mainly because I had a feeling of high adventure and because I wanted to please a member of the armed forces." With so many girls in this adventurous spirit, one teenage boy described wartime as "a real sex paradise. The plant and the town were just full of working girls on the make. Where I was, a male war worker became the center of loose morality."

Lesbians found similar opportunities, especially in the military. Phyllis Abry quit her job as a lab technician to join the WACS [Woman's Army Corps] because she "wanted to be with all those women." Homosexuality was not allowed in the military, of course, but lesbians were not easily identified. "I remember being very nervous about them asking me if I had any homosexual feelings or attitudes," she recalled. "I just smiled and was sweet and feminine."

The military establishment was not fully prepared for the impact of large numbers of women, and it took pains to promote a "feminine" image of female recruits. The entry of women into the armed forces during the war marked a major change from the past. They were recruited into every part of military service except combat. As Oveta Culp Hobby, director of the Women's Auxiliary Army Corp, proclaimed, women "are carrying on the glorious tradition of American womanhood. They are making history! This is a war which recognized no distinctions between men and women." To the female Americans she hoped to recruit, she said, "This is YOUR war." Women of "excellent character" who could pass an intelligence test could enlist, provided they had no children under fourteen. The WAVES [Women Accepted for Voluntary Emergency Service] accepted healthy women with no dependents under eighteen if they were unmarried. A WAVE who married could remain in the service as long as she had finished basic training and her husband was not in the service. The birth of a child brought an "honorable discharge."

At first glance it appears as though the armed forces offered dramatic new opportunities for women to shed their domestic roles. Yet on closer examination it is clear that the war emergency gave these endeavors a temporary quality while making it impossible to combine jobs in the service with family life. In addition, every effort was made to dispel prevailing notions that military work would make women "masculine" or ruin their moral character. The military presented the image of the female recruit as very "feminine" as well as domestically inclined. A guidebook for women in the armed services and war industries, for example, included a photograph of a young WAVE with a caption that described her as "pretty as her picture in the trim uniform that enlisted U.S. Navy WAVES will wear in winter.". . . Women were needed for their "delicate hands" and "precision work at which women are so adept," and in hospitals where "there is a need in a man for comfort and attention that only a woman can fill.". . .

These publicity measures met with only partial success amid public sentiment suspicious of women in non-traditional roles. In fact, rumors about the supposedly promiscuous sexual behavior and scandalous drunkenness of female recruits were so widespread that the armed forces had to refute the charges publicly. One result was the institutionalizing of the double standard in the military: men were routinely supplied with contraceptives (mainly to prevent the spread of venereal disease), but women were denied access to birth control devices. In addition, in the rare cases when sexual transgressions were discovered, women were punished more severely than men. Lesbianism was another reality of wartime that the military took pains to suppress. The public image they hoped to promote was the military woman whose postwar career would be as a housewife and mother. . . .

At the same time that women's nontraditional war work was given a domestic aura, their tasks within the home gained new patriotic purpose. Millions of women did volunteer work during the war, and much of it involved traditional skills such as canning, saving fats, and making household goods last longer. Much as homemakers in the depression recognized the importance of their domestic skills for the survival of their families during the economic emergency, so the homemakers of the war years saw their work as contributing to the success of the war emergency.

Wartime, then, encouraged women to enter the workforce and contribute to the war effort, but not at the expense of their domestic duties. As a result, the potential for a restructuring of the paid labor force that would dismantle the sex-segregated pattern of employment never materialized. In spite of all the changes wrought by the war, in the long run work for women remained limited to certain occupations, with low pay and the expectation of short duration. Traditional marriage, complete with economic dependence on the male breadwinner, was still the norm. It was, in fact, one of the primary reasons given for fighting the war.

Popular culture was filled with many such messages. One example was produced under the sponsorship of the Office of Facts and Figures. It was a series of programs aired on all major radio networks in 1942 in an effort to mobilize support for the war. One highly acclaimed segment, "To the Young," included this exhortation:

YOUNG MALE VOICE: "That's one of the things this war's about."

YOUNG FEMALE VOICE: "About us?"

YOUNG MALE VOICE: "About all young people like us. About love and gettin' hitched, and havin' a home and some kids, and breathin' fresh air out in the suburbs, about livin' an' workin' decent, like free people."

Demographic patterns during the 1940s show that Americans conformed to this expectation. Women may well have entered war production, but they did not give up on reproduction. The war brought a dramatic reversal in patterns of family formation that had characterized the 1930s. Whereas the depression was marked by later marriages and declining marriage rates and birthrates, the trends toward younger marriages and an increasing birthrate normally associated with the postwar era were well under way during the war years. Over one million more families were formed between 1940 and 1943 than would have been expected during normal times. And as soon as Americans entered the war, the birthrate began to climb. Between 1940 and 1945 it jumped from 19.4 to 24.5 per 1,000 population. The marriage rate also accelerated, spurred in part by the possibility of draft deferment for married men in the early war years, and in part by the imminence of departure for foreign shores. We find, then, the curious pattern of widespread disruption in domestic life accompanied by a surge into marriage and parenthood.

We find these same patterns in popular entertainment. Whereas the most popular motion picture of the 1930s was *Gone with the Wind*, a story of survival during hard times focused on a shrewd and tough woman whose domestic life ends up in shambles, the top box office hit of the 1940s was quite different. The 1943 war propaganda film *This Is the Army*, starring Ronald Reagan, was the most successful movie of the decade. In this film the men are center stage as they finish the job their fathers began during World War I. The plot revolves around the efforts of the central character's sweetheart to persuade her reluctant soldier to marry her. Finally she succeeds, and they wed just before the hero leaves to fight on foreign shores. As he marches off with his buddies, she remains at home, providing the vision of what the men are fighting for.

Off the screen as well, images of celebrities shifted. For men, the brave soldier eager to return to hearth and home provided the ideal masculine type. Film heroes, like all able-bodied male Americans, were expected to pull their weight in the war effort. Men who got deferments were resented—all men were urged to do their military duty. It is interesting that the "he-man" was the most popular male image during the 1930s, when the economic depression threatened to undercut the strong and independent male. During the war, however, men had plenty of chances to prove their masculinity in traditionally manly ways. The soldier was the prototypical he-man, after all. Now we find women paying homage to men's gentler qualities. In an item titled "What Should a Girl Expect from a Man?" female stars stressed such qualities as "kindness and tact," "keeping his temper," and "courtesy, consideration and sweetness." Instead of references to the tough guy, women now mentioned "manners, fidelity, companionship."

For women we also find a new image portrayed by female stars. Rather than continuing the trend of the 1930s toward more autonomous women as role models, which might be expected in the wartime situation, female celebrities were suddenly featured predominantly as wives and mothers. [Hollywood actress] Ann Sothern, in a 1944 article titled "What Kind of Woman Will Your Man Come Home To?" urged women to fit their lives to their men's. She told her readers to take an interest in their husbands' interests.

> What he is doing, what we're fighting for, what will come afterward. Your plans for your life together afterward are important. We began planning our house together—our "perfect house." Then we began to think about the nursery and that became the most important room in the house-to-be, the most important thing in our plans for the future and it made us feel our sense of responsibility to that future. When he comes back it may take a few years for him "to find himself"—it's [your] job—not his—to see that the changes in both of [you] do not affect the fundamental bonds between [you]. I won't bother to remind you of the obvious, to keep your appearance—to preserve for him the essence of the girl he fell in love with, the girl he longs to come back to. I know that a lot of men are dreaming of coming back not only to those girls who waved good-bye to them. They are dreaming of coming back to the mothers of their children! . . .

Along with the wifely focus of the 1940s came a move away from flamboyant sexuality, as exhibited by stars of the 1930s like Mae West, toward a more prudent respectability. Young starlets were featured who lived quiet, simple lives with their parents, shunning the fast life of Hollywood. Bette Davis, noted for her strong-minded independence in the 1930s, proclaimed in 1941 that men and women were equals today in business, politics, and sports—they are as brave, intelligent and daring collectively as are men. But it's still "a man's world in spite of the fact that girls have pretty much invaded it." And because it is a man's world, women must protect the most precious thing they have: their reputations. For modern women still want what grandma wanted: "a great love, a happy home, a peaceful old age." Do not be afraid to be termed a "prude," said Davis, "Good sports are dated every night of the week—prudes are saved for special dates. Good sports get plenty of rings on the telephone, but prudes get them on the finger. Men take good sports out—they take prudes home—yes, right home to Mother and Dad and all the neighbors."

In keeping with such expressions of enthusiasm for marriage and the family, even men's sexual fantasies were often publicly constructed around images of conjugal bliss. The walls of barracks were decorated with pinups of women in alluring poses reminding the men why they were fighting. Movie star Betty Grable was the most popular pinup, not because she was the most sexy and glamorous, but because she had a rather wholesome look. Grable came to represent the girl back home, and the "American way of life" that inspired the men to fight. As one soldier wrote in a letter to Grable: "There we were out in those damn dirty trenches. Machine guns firing. Bombs dropping all around us. We would be exhausted, frightened, confused and sometimes hopeless about our situation. When suddenly someone would pull your picture out of his wallet. Or we'd see a decal of you on a plane and then we'd know what we were fighting for.". . .

Most soldiers would go home . . . and propel the marriage rates and birthrates to new heights. For women, the opportunities that had opened in public life during the war shrank with the return to peace. The War Manpower Commission assumed that "the separation of women from industry should flow in an orderly plan." Frederick Crawford, head of the National Association of Manufacturers, found a point of agreement with his usual adversaries, the [labor] union leaders, when he said, "From a humanitarian point of view, too many women should not stay in the labor force. The home is the basic American institution." Many women rejected this idea. As one argued, "War jobs have uncovered unsuspected abilities in American women. Why lose all these abilities because of a belief that 'a woman's place is in the home'? For some it is, for others not." But her words would be drowned in a sea of voices calling on women to prepare to assume their places in the kitchens and bedrooms of returning servicemen.

By the time young adults emerged from the depression and the war, they had been sobered by years of emergency that propelled them toward a vision of "normalcy" focused on traditional family life. The war had extended the state of crisis that characterized the depression and further disrupted domestic gender roles. Yet when the war ended, gone were the positive role models of independent women who offered a viable alternative to marriage, as the nation turned to a reaffirmation of family value and female subordination. There was no positive vision of marriage resting on economic equality; nor was there any trend in the economy toward gender equality. Rather, men and women alike expected to relinquish their emergency roles and settle into domestic life as breadwinners and homemakers. During as well as after the war, all the major institutions in which Americans lived and worked came to foster this vision of a nation finding its ultimate security in the traditional American home.

Questions for Discussion

1. According to the author, was the "Rosie the Riveter" image of World War II working women accurate? What evidence does the author present to support that image? What evidence is presented to counter it?
2. What percentage of women worked during the war? How many of them were married with children? What does this tell you about opportunities for women during the war?
3. According to the author, the war provided women with greater latitude in matters of sexuality. How did Americans respond to this situation? How did the military regard the sexual behavior of its male and female recruits?
4. In your opinion, on balance, did World War II disrupt or reinforce family life and traditional gender roles? What evidence from the article can you present to support your view?

For Further Reading

Michael C. C. Adams, *The Best War Ever* (1994); Karen Anderson, *Wartime Women: Sex Roles, Family Relations, and the Status of Women during World War II* (1981); Alan Berube, *Coming Out under Fire: The History of Gay Men and Women in World War II* (1990); John Morton Blum, *V Was for Victory: Politics and American Culture During World War II* (1976); Paul Boyer, *By the Bomb's Early Light: American Thought and Culture at the Dawn of the Atomic Age* (1985); D'Ann Campbell, *Women at War with America in the 1940s: Private Lives in the Patriotic Era* (1984); William Chafe, *The Paradox of Change: American Women in the Twentieth Century* (1991); Stephanie Coontz, *The Way We Never Were: American Families and the Nostalgia Trap* (1992); John D'Emilio and Estelle Freedman, *Intimate Matters: A History of American Sexuality* (1988); Susan Hartmann, *The Home Front and Beyond: American Women in the 1940s* (1982); Marilyn Hegarty, *Victory Girls, Khaki-Wackies, Patriotutes: The Regulation of Female Sexuality during World War II* (2007); David M. Kennedy, *Freedom from Fear: The American People in Depression and War, 1929–1945* (1999); Andrew Kersten, *A. Philip Randolph: A Life in the Vanguard* (2006); Alice Kessler-Harris, *Out to Work: A History of Wage-Earning Women in the United States* (1982); David Kryder, *Divided Arsenal: Race and the American State during World War II* (2000); Richard Lingeman, *Don't You Know There's a War Going On? The American Home Front, 1941–1945* (1970); Elaine Tyler May, *Homeward Bound: American Families in the Cold War Era* (1988); Ruth Milkman, *Gender at Work: The Dynamics of Job Segregation by Sex during World War II* (1987); Alan S. Milward, *War, Economy, and Society, 1939–1945* (1979); Steven Mintz and Susan Kellogg, *Domestic Revolutions: A Social History of American Family Life* (1988); Richard Overy, *Why the Allies Won* (1995); Paula Pfeffer, *A. Philip Randolph: Pioneer of the Civil Rights Movement* (1996); Constance Reid, Clara Allen, and Sandra M. Gilbert, *Slacks and Calluses: Our Summer in a Bomber Factory* (2004); Rosalind Rosenberg, *Divided Lives: American Women in the Twentieth Century* (1992); Leila Rupp, *Mobilizing Women for War: German and American Propaganda, 1939–1945* (1978); Studs Terkel, *"The Good War": An Oral History of World War II* (1984); William Tuttle, *Daddy's Gone to War: The Second World War in the Lives of America's Children* (1993); Harold Vatter, *The U.S. Economy in World War II* (1985); Emily Yellin, *Our Mothers' War: American Women at Home and at the Front during World War II* (2004).

Children and Conflict on the Home Front during World War II

William M. Tuttle Jr.

A good deal has been written about World War II being "the good war" fought by the "greatest generation" on behalf of a unified people that made enormous sacrifices to defeat the enemy. Americans did make great sacrifices to defeat the Axis powers. Even though wages were high during the war years, there was rationing of meat, butter, coffee, and many other commodities. To conserve gasoline, which was also rationed, more than 60 percent of the population either walked to work or took public transportation. And most people observed the 35-mile-an-hour speed limit imposed on private vehicles. To conserve metal and fabric required for uniforms and other military needs, Americans went without bobby-pins, nylon stockings, metal zippers, double-breasted suits, and pleats on pants and skirts. In 1941, the government said aluminum needed for defense production was in short supply. Within weeks families donated more than 70,000 tons of pots, pans, and other household goods made from that metal. Defense workers in shipyards offered to work for free on Sundays.

In addition, one of every five families had at least one member in the armed forces. The American portion of the war lasted less than four years—members of the military served an average of three of those years. (By comparison, the Vietnam conflict lasted more than ten years, with combat service time averaging one year.) Of the 16 million Americans in the armed forces during World War II, 400,000 were killed.

Mexican Americans arrested and chained during the 1943 Zoot Suit riots in Los Angeles. Why would clothing worn by young people inspire such violence? Can you think of other examples where fashions worn by the young incited violent reactions?

The idea that Americans selflessly gave of themselves in the quest for victory can be exaggerated. Tens of thousands of men tried to avoid military service, and there was a healthy black market in rationed consumer goods. Without question, however, there was plenty of sacrifice, whether imposed by the government or voluntary.

But was there unity? In the aftermath of Pearl Harbor, did Americans put aside their differences toward the shared goal of winning the war? As William M. Tuttle Jr. notes in the next essay the racial, ethnic, regional, religious, and other differences that historically divided Americans did not disappear during the war. In some ways they intensified.

For example, many whites resented African Americans who obtained good-paying jobs in defense plants. In one factory, white women went on "strike" rather than share bathroom facilities with black women they worked with; in another case, white men resentful over promotions given to African Americans, beat black fellow workers. There were vicious fights between white and black members of the armed forces; a couple of them resulted in the lynching of African American servicemen. And there were major race riots in Detroit, Philadelphia, and other cities as newly arrived blacks and whites, both often from the South, competed for jobs and scarce housing. Pain could be inflicted in ways other than physical abuse. A number of German prisoners of war were brought to the United States during the conflict. Some of the prisoner camps were in the South. Black servicemen watched as segregated restaurants that refused to serve them, fed the white enemy.

As Tuttle points out, the most notorious example of disunity and prejudice during the war was caused by Executive Order 9066, issued by President Roosevelt in 1942. The president's order did not mention Japanese Americans. It simply designated certain "military areas" off-limits and to which "any and all persons may be excluded." In this case, "any and all" meant only Japanese Americans. More than 112,000 of them—mostly citizens, many of them children—were evacuated from their homes on the West Coast and placed in eleven detention camps, mostly in the Southwest.

The assumption behind the evacuation was that Japanese, like other Asians, could never become loyal citizens, even if they were born in the United States. If left free, they would commit espionage on behalf of the Japanese government. No evidence was ever presented to support this claim, and not a single Japanese American was convicted of spying or espionage. Nevertheless, the United States Supreme Court decided the forced evacuation was constitutional. Students were pulled from schools and colleges, breadwinners from their jobs, families from their homes, and owners from their businesses. It was conservatively estimated that Japanese Americans suffered more than $400 million in property losses. In 1948, the government tacitly admitted the injustice done to Japanese Americans during the war: it gave them $37 million in reparations.

Tuttle describes other domestic conflicts during the war, most notably the "zoot suit" riots in Los Angeles in 1943, when young Mexican American men were beaten by rampaging white servicemen. What makes Tuttle's essay unique is his focus on children and young people. Children were both victims and perpetrators of religious, ethnic, and racial prejudice. How, Tuttle asks, do children learn prejudice and hatred? How did young Mexican American and black children living in Los Angeles during the war feel when they read this sign at municipal pools: "Tuesdays reserved for Negroes and Mexicans" (the pools were drained and cleaned once-a-week on Wednesday). What were white children's reactions to that sign? How do the young process "reality" when one day their parents and teachers tell them that Americans are one people, but on the next, those same parents and teachers express prejudice toward Americans of different creeds or colors? And how did all of this play out during the dislocations and anxieties caused by the war?

Source: William M. Tuttle Jr., *Daddy's Gone to War: The Second World War in the Lives of America's Children* (New York: Oxford University Press, 1993), Chapter 10, pp. 162–189.

There was a central contradiction on the American homefront during the Second World War: Amidst enthusiastic national unity there existed deep racial, ethnic, and cultural animosities that occasionally exploded into violence. Although historians have recognized this contradiction in studies of the 1943 race riots and of the government's internment of 112,704 Japanese Americans, they have barely scratched the surface in exposing the fractures that rent the homefront. Buried have been countless stories of the hostility suffered by children because of their race, ethnic heritage, and religious beliefs. Suffering most were America's children of color, but also affected were its Jewish-American children, children of German and Italian descent, Mexican-American children, and children of religious pacifists and nonconformists.

This chapter exposes the persistence of prejudice during the war. The victims were children, but so too were many of the bigots. For these reasons, it is important to understand the influences that fostered hatred and meanness in wartime America. This chapter begins with . . . vignettes that are emblematic of the gap between lofty ideals and ugly realities on the homefront.

Wanda Davis and the Jehovah's Witnesses: Nine-year-old Wanda Davis experienced hurt and dismay in 1943. Her beliefs were those of a Jehovah's Witness. The Witnesses were unpopular, Wanda remembered, because they refused to "worship an emblem of the state" and thus would not salute the flag or pledge their allegiance to it. The Witnesses' enemies were legion: governments throughout the world, including Nazi Germany; Roman Catholic and Protestant clerics; the American Legion and Veterans of Foreign Wars; vigilante mobs; and the police officers who openly sided with mobs assaulting the Witnesses. . . .

In Winnsboro, Texas, in December 1942, O.L. Pillars and a number of Jehovah's Witnesses were handing out magazines when a mob approached. As the Witnesses packed up and began to leave, they noticed that parked in the street was a "sound car," with the local Baptist minister sitting behind the wheel. "He started ranting and raving about how Jehovah's Witnesses would not salute the flag," Pillars recalled. "He told how he would be happy to die for Old Glory, and that anyone not saluting the flag should be run out of town." As soon as Pillars and the others had passed the automobile, "we looked ahead to see another mob coming right toward us." The city marshall intervened by arresting the Witnesses. And that night he permitted lynchers to enter the jail and drag the prisoners outside. "I was taking a terrible beating," Pillars remembered. "Blood was gushing from my nose, face, and mouth." Beaten senseless, then revived by douses of cold water, Pillars would not relent, and every time he refused to salute the 2-by-4 inch flag which the vigilantes had brought with them, they struck him again. Finally they put a hangman's noose around his neck, threw the rope over an extended pipe, and began to pull it taut. "As I was lifted off the ground," Pillars said, "the rope tightened and I lost consciousness." What he did not learn until he woke up later in a hospital bed was that the rope had broken.

Although the Witnesses were known for their refusal to salute the flag, it was the school-age children who suffered the cruelty inflicted by classmates and teachers. In 1943 the Supreme Court reversed an earlier ruling and up-held the Witnesses' position. Writing the majority opinion, Justice Robert H. Jackson compared the flag-salute requirement to the totalitarian practices of America's wartime enemies and asserted "that compulsory unification of opinion achieves only the unanimity of the graveyard."

Teachers did not need the mandate of the Supreme Court, however, to impose their will on nonconforming students. In 1943 Wanda Davis was a third-grader in a two-room schoolhouse in Tulare, California, in the San Joaquin Valley. Each room had four grades with about thirty students, and Wanda was the only one in her room not to salute the flag. Her teacher became angry and threatened her. Salute the flag, she ordered the girl, or she would swat her with the wooden paddle she kept by the side of her desk. Wanda obeyed, but she felt horrible, having betrayed her religion. . . .

Rick Ceaser: Born in 1936, Rick Ceaser lived in Detroit during the Second World War. His father had come from Sicily in 1912; his mother was a second-generation Italian American. Even though his mother was a native-born United States citizen, the federal government ordered her to appear before an official to attest to her loyalty; Rick accompanied her on this mission. They spent "long hours waiting in line to get this done." He remembered that his mother became "very frustrated since she had been born in Detroit, and annoyed by the questions she was being asked. I remember feeling like they thought we were on the side of the Italians, and it scared me."

The Ceasers lived in a Jewish neighborhood, and at school, Rick recalled, "I was always relieved to be taken for a Jew. I remember once when a big Jewish holiday was coming up and my teacher asked all the children who would be absent that day to raise their hands. Only about three or four of us were not Jewish. But when I kept my hand down, the teacher asked me, 'Richard, won't you be celebrating the holiday?' When I told her I wasn't Jewish, she asked me what I was. I told her I was Italian and all the kids *booed!* This was in 1944, I was seven. . . . To avoid further incidents, Ceaser purposely failed the second grade "because," he recalled, "I wanted to get in a class that didn't know me.". . .

Rick Ceaser's homefront experiences were crucial to his childhood development. Living as a member of a disdained group reinforced his intro-version: "I had few friends during that time except for a family of Italians that lived around the block." He remembered that he was proud of his two older brothers who were serving in the armed forces; worried about his parents who fretted constantly about his brothers; "ashamed of being Italian, and afraid the bombs would drop soon. And yet I didn't really know what the war was all about." Rick was not alone in his insecurities. Ethnic children, particularly those of German and Italian descent, felt at risk in their schools and neighborhoods. . . .

Racism and Riots: Newcomers of all kinds often encounter suspicion and hostility. A notable wartime example were the migrants who came from the southern Appalachians to Detroit and other Midwestern cities. Even more despised than the "hillbillies," however, were the African-American migrants. During the war social scientists conducted surveys of racial opinions in the United States. Donovan Senter, who worked for the Bureau of Agricultural Economics of the Department of Agriculture, took a train trip in 1942 from Dallas, Texas, to the Florida panhandle. "Just two ears listening," he reported, but what he heard was "a rising din of racial hatred." Whites expressed anger bordering on rage that African Americans had obtained defense jobs, were receiving decent salaries, and refused any longer to bow to white supremacy: "No nigger should get the money a white man does. . . . We won't tolerate them niggers workin' around a white woman. . . . They get impossible when they get a little money. . . ." One southerner's solution was to draft only black men "and let them get shot before the white men.". . .

It was not surprising, then, that during the war upwards of a million African Americans took a harsh look at their southern surroundings and decided to migrate to the North and West. But to the migrants, the mentality of many white northerners seemed disturbingly similar—and, in its own way, just as ugly and uncompromising. This was evident in 1942 in Detroit. A few miles from Rick Ceaser's apartment house, a federal project to house African-American war workers and their families was under construction. Named for the black abolitionist Sojourner Truth, the project was scheduled for occupancy on Saturday morning, February 28.

Polish Americans in the neighborhood next to the housing project prepared for battle, and violence erupted. At 6 a.m. on moving day, according to an eyewitness, "automobiles with horns blowing drove throughout the Polish section, arousing people to come and defend their rights. The Polish came, by the hundreds. The first Negro [moving] truck to appear was destroyed." Hysteria prevailed: knives flashed, volleys of rocks and stones flew through the air, a shotgun roared, an overturned car was set ablaze. This was a war for territory; motivated by both hatred and desperation, blacks and whites battled each other. But blacks bore the brunt of the injuries. Because of the biased police response, most of the people hospitalized were black, and of the 109 rioters held for trial for carrying concealed weapons or disturbing the peace, only three were white. In the days following the rioting, white people predicted victory. They would be waiting, one man warned, if blacks tried to move in; "the minute it starts, there will be hundreds of people blocking all the streets like there was last time. The police are on our side, too—they don't want to see them get in any more than we do." Outside the project, whites set up a picket line led by three boys aged seven and eight. For his part, a discouraged African-American boy said, "I'm a Jap from now on."

Sixteen months later, in June 1943, massive racial violence erupted in Detroit. In three days, thirty-four people died—twenty-five blacks and nine whites—and over 700 were injured. In the downtown area white rioters, most of them young men, pulled black people off streetcars; they overturned cars driven by blacks, savagely beat the occupants, and set the cars on fire.

Armed with knives and clubs, mobs of between 100 and 400 whites chased individual blacks down streets and up alleys. As one streetcar with a black conductor entered the area of rioting, a drunken white man approached and saw the conductor: "Here's some fresh meat. Fresh meat boys. The conductor's a nigger, c'mon some fresh meat.". . .

Other riots erupted that summer—242 racial battles in forty-seven different cities, including Harlem, Philadelphia, Mobile, Alabama, and Beaumont, Texas. Six African-Americans died in Harlem in August; at least 400 people were injured. But in Los Angeles in 1943, there was a different kind of riot; in that city, mobs of up to 1,000 white soldiers and sailors hunted for zoot-suiters, most of whom were Mexican-American youth. The zoot suit, which was also popular among African Americans in various cities, consisted of a long draped coat, key chain, and "Porkpie hat"; the pants were high waisted, with baggy legs and pegged cuffs; a duck-tailed haircut completed the ensemble. Whites seemed to view this manner of dress not only as a threat but as an insult that needed to be avenged. Thus, the Los Angeles city council responded to the violence not by dispersing the mobs, but by declaring the wearing of a zoot suit to be an act of "vagrancy," which was a misdemeanor justifying arrest. When finally rescued from frenzied mobs, therefore, the bloodied zoot suiters found themselves not in ambulances headed to a hospital, but in paddy wagons on the way to jail.

There was little justice in Los Angeles that summer. A grand jury looking into crime and violence explained that "Mexican youths are motivated to crime by certain biological or 'racial' characteristics." This "would be laughable," lamented educator George L. Sanchez in 1943, "if it were not so tragic, so dangerous, and, worse still, so typical of biased attitudes and misguided thinking which are reflected" throughout the United States.

Diana Bernal: In numerous towns, cities, and farm communities, Mexican-American children worried about their personal safety on the homefront. Since many were very poor, their lives already were precarious: health care was substandard, schools were segregated, and prejudice against Mexican Americans was virulent in the Southwest as other parts of the country. Diana Bernal, a homefront girl in San Antonio, remembered her father's difficulty in getting work; her mind flashed on the sign she had seen frequently during the war: "No Mexicans Hired." She could not "eat in the same restaurants as other people," nor swim in the same pools. Feeling insecure because of their second-class status, some Mexican-American children feared that the hatred unleashed against the nation's enemies might spill over and harm them and their families. "At times," Diana wrote, "I could picture ourselves in a concentration camp. I would question why the Japanese Americans were placed in camps. Are they going to do the same to us because we are Mexican?" Theresa Negrete, a Mexican-American girl living hundreds of miles away in Scottsbluff, Nebraska, also had a fear of internment. Twice during the war, servicemen on leave had "torn up" the Eagle Café, which was owned by a Japanese-American family. "There was so much propaganda against the Japanese that," Theresa confessed, "I did not like them." When I'd see them I would actually stick out my tongue at them. We were told they were killing our boys, and they wouldn't let us forget with songs like 'Remember Pearl Harbor,' " which urged Americans to "remember Pearl Harbor as we did the Alamo!" And Theresa, fearing that "maybe other people were remembering the Alamo when they saw me," worried that after the authorities had rounded up all the Japanese Americans, they would come next for the Mexican Americans.

Executive Order 9066: On February 19, 1942, President Franklin D. Roosevelt took up his pen and signed Executive Order 9066, thus stripping more than 112,000 Japanese Americans on the West Coast of their freedom. Within little more than a month, the Army had taken these men, women, and children from their homes in California, Oregon, and Washington, and locked them behind barbed wire in isolated locations in the Mountain States and the Southwest. Most of the internees were young; more than three-fourths were under twenty-five, and 30,000 were schoolchildren. Moreover, almost 6,000 children were born in the camps. Their numbers—when added to the infusion of 1,037 Japanese Hawaiians and several hundred people of Japanese ancestry from Panama, Peru, and elsewhere—swelled the total to about 120,000, including 77,000 who were United States citizens. The large number of children and youth skewed the population in the camps. And as young adults left the camps for military service or college, the remaining population was increasingly split between children and older people.

Some Japanese-American fathers did not accompany their children to the camps, but these father absences were of a different kind than was usual during the war. "On the very day of my eldest daughter's 11th birthday, February 21, 1942," recalled Masao Takahashi, "I was roused from my sleep very early in the morning. The FBI, along with four Seattle policemen, searched my house, ransacking closets" before taking him away to a detention center run by the Justice Department. He thought he would be released in time to share his daughter's birthday cake later that day. "However, when we were stripped naked and thoroughly inspected, I was shaken. After about a month and a half, my family came to the train station when a group of us were transferred to [the detention center at] Missoula, Montana." Takahashi was "allowed a few minutes to walk to the fence and say goodbye to them. I was at a loss to find comforting words," he remembered with sadness tinged with bitterness forty years later. "Boarding the train, I heard my daughter crying out, 'Papa, Papa.' I can still hear the ring of their crying out in my ears today."

Charges of criminal behavior were never brought against Masao Takahashi; indeed, no Japanese American was convicted of espionage, treason, or sedition. Even the alleged "crime," disloyalty to the United States, was not against the law. The real issue was the racist presumption that the Japanese Americans were part of an enemy race; on that basis, they were rounded up by the Army and put in prison camps. "It was really cruel and harsh," recalled Joseph Y. Kurihara, a veteran of the First World War. "To pack and evacuate in forty-eight hours was an impossibility. Seeing mothers completely bewildered with children crying from want and peddlers taking advantage and offering prices next to robbery made me feel like murdering these people. I could not believe my very eyes what I had seen that day."

One interned mother was Yuri Tateishi. On the day that she and her family were evacuated from Los Angeles, her three-year-old son developed the measles. She covered him up, but a nurse noticed the spots and took him away. All the way to Manzanar, the internment camp in northern California, to which the Tateishis were being taken, "when I thought about how he might wake up and be in a strange place, with strange people, I just really broke down and cried." He stayed at the hospital for three weeks before rejoining his family. Other internees were Mary Tsukamoto, her husband, and five-year-old daughter. After staying in temporary barracks in Fresno, California, until October 1942, the Tsukamotos were taken by train to the re-location camp at Jerome, Arkansas. Upon arrival, Mary Tsukamoto recalled her daughter "cried for a whole week—she cried and cried and cried. She was so upset, because she wanted to go home, she wanted to get away from camp. Adults felt the same way," she admitted, "but we weren't children and so could not dare to cry. I remember I always felt like I was dangling and crying deep inside, and I was hurt.". . .

Anomalies abounded, as did cruelties. Not only were Japanese-American families interned; so too were Japanese orphans, including babies for whom "loyalty" was scarcely an issue. And so were crippled Japanese-American children, who were taken away from their doctors and nurses and relocated along with everybody else. There was also the issue of children of mixed heritage. Some Alaskan Indians who were part Japanese were sent to assembly centers, including children ill with tuberculosis. A religious missionary reported to the Children's Bureau that at an assembly center in northern California, two children aged six and eight were taken from their non-Japanese-American mother and placed in an internment camp with their father, who did not want them. She also wrote about a twelve-year-old boy whose Japanese father had died in Tokyo when the boy was not yet one. The boy's mother, who was Caucasian and a United States citizen, "brought him back [as] a little baby and raised him 100% American." But now "he has been taken from her and put in [a] Japanese Camp—twelve years old, a delicate boy who knew no Japanese people.". . .

The Japanese-American internees were sent to arid and desolate spots. Although the names were evocative—Rivers, Arizona; Heart Mountain, Wyoming; Topaz, Utah; Manzanar, California—the camps themselves were bleak and demoralizing. Still, every morning in the camps' grade schools, these homefront children, imprisoned because of their race, pledged allegiance to the flag—"one nation, indivisible, with liberty and justice for all."

The message of these . . . vignettes is that racism, nativism, and religious bigotry were all examples of homefront prejudice. But at what age did children's racial and ethnic hostility arise? In research done in the 1940s, psychologist Marian Radke Yarrow and her colleagues investigated children's group stereotypes and prejudices. "Local neighborhood patterns and family group memberships," they wrote, "are among the important sub-cultural differences which influence the responses." In a neighborhood marked by tensions between Catholics and Jews, for example, "the children show a heightened awareness of these groups." And the most important influences on children's attitudes are adults' "values and interpretations of the social world.". . .

Also at work during the childhood years are powerful environmental factors. As the child's world expands to include school, other attitudinal influences begin to rival those exerted by parents, siblings, extended family, and neighbors. And children learn prejudice in these new settings. During the Second World War, popular culture was a major influence on children. Another was the school, for it was there that homefront children found not only teachers and books but also peers. . . .

The people most despised in wartime America were the Japanese. The hatred which the homefront children possessed was frightening at times, but perhaps understandable, considering that their anti-Japanese attitudes reflected the parental, cultural, and peer influences that surrounded them. With the Pearl Harbor bombing, many of the homefront children witnessed their parents' hatred. They heard the epithets shouted by their fathers and mothers: "The little slant-eyed bastards," growled one father. "Dirty Japs," "Dirty yellow Japs," and "Little Yellow Bastards" were other denunciations. Some children stood helplessly as their enraged parents smashed to pieces any toys "made in Japan." One homefront girl, a first-grader, had won a race; her prize was a doll made in Japan. But her mother destroyed it. Another homefront girl had a toy piano she "dearly loved"; but her father took it to the basement and "chopped it all to pieces with an ax.". . .

Another homefront mother implanted deep fears in her daughter with warnings about the "yellow peril." The family lived on the Pacific coast, in Eureka, California, and the mother warned that the Japanese might invade. Moreover, she implied that, if they did, they would rape her and the other women: "She asked if I wanted a sister with yellow skin and slanted eyes." Certainly the behavior of adults directly influenced the children. Once, a family relative who was about to go overseas dropped by to say goodbye. A three-year-old boy dressed in a sailor suit asked where he was going. "To whip some big Japs," he replied. "Well, I can whip the little ones," said the boy.

The homefront children saw disturbing examples of anti-Japanese hatred. Signs appeared in restaurant windows: "No Dogs or Japs Allowed." One father referred to dried peaches as "Jap ears." In trying to understand this anti-Japanese hatred, a Japanese-American homefront girl, Tatsuko Anne Tachibana, has discerned a truth that applies to the wartime treatment not only of the Japanese Americans but of other racial and ethnic groups as well. The causes of Japanese-American mistreatment were twofold, she wrote: "racism and fear." "I was very afraid of anyone with slanted eyes," wrote a white homefront girl, and other homefront children admitted they shared this fear. . . .

Although Hitler and Mussolini were powerful emotional symbols of the enemy, the common people of Germany and Italy usually were not. The war against the Japanese was different. It "became a kind of racist fight," a homefront boy remembered, "whites against the yellow race. In Europe it was a little different. You felt that Europeans were good people. They just followed the wrong leaders." Another perceived distinction, explained a homefront girl, was that while the German soldiers were "fathers/ sons/brothers," the Japanese had "sprung into being family-less" and, as a result, were "unspeakably evil, vicious, & sub-human." Thus, all the Japanese were enemies, no matter whether they were leaders like Hirohito or Tojo, kamikaze pilots, jungle soldiers, or even United States citizens of Japanese ancestry. Typifying this perspective was an advertisement for lapel buttons that appeared in *Newsweek* in 1942. The button for the German enemy displayed a picture of Hitler with the words "Wanted for Murder" printed above his head. The button for the Japanese read: "Jap Hunting License—Open Season—No Limit."

"I remember being called a 'Jap' in grade school, which hurt a lot," remembered Tatsuko Anne Tachihana of an incident that occurred before her family was placed in an internment camp. The "Japs" were customarily the wartime enemy on the school playgrounds and in the fields and vacant lots, and children's war fantasies involved dog fights with Japanese Zeroes and dodging Japanese machine-gun fire during imaginary landings on Pacific island beaches. Also, in school, recalled a homefront girl, children drew "cartoons of villainous looking Orientals with knives hidden behind their backs." Indeed, sometimes the victims of anti-Asian prejudice were not even of Japanese ancestry, but were Chinese or Filipino. One homefront boy remembered a Filipino classmate in his grade school in Cleveland: "We would chase him down the street, yelling 'Jap! Dirty Jap!'" Although the image of the Chinese "as our wonderful allies" was highly positive, even if condescending, *Time* magazine deemed it necessary to publish an article on "How to Tell Your Friends from the Japs." After listing differing physical characteristics, most of them specious, *Time* asserted: "Those who know them best often rely on facial expressions to tell them apart: the Chinese expression is likely to be more placid, kindly, open, the Japanese more positive, dogmatic, arrogant.". . .

Not surprisingly, the anti-ethnic sentiments of the war years found their way into homefront children's play. Here is one taunting jump-rope rhyme:

> *Red, white and blue,*
> *Your father is a Jew,*
> *Your mother is Japanese,*
> *And so are you!*

Children mimicked adults in using rhymes to malign other people, especially people of color and Jews. Sometimes Jews or African Americans appeared together in these rhymes, as in this piece of doggerel which circulated during the presidential election campaign of 1944. In it, President Roosevelt addressed his wife Eleanor Roosevelt:

You kiss the niggers,
I'll kiss the Jews;
And we'll stay in the White House
As long as we choose.

Behind the façade of national unity, homefront girls and boys who were [Japanese], black or ethnic suffered insults from neighbors, classmates, and teachers, as well as from the cruel stereotypes that portrayed them in popular culture. In *The Nature of Prejudice,* [psychologist] Gordon Allport described the psychic damage done when other children began to use "linguistic tags"—"nigger," "Jap," "kike"—which were the "symbols of power and rejection." But those children who imbibed the hate of wartime also suffered. The case of Nancy Berner, who was a homefront girl in Indianapolis, was not unusual. She had learned her lessons well at home, in school, watching the newsreels at the local theater, and reading *Life* magazine. "We were taught pure hate from all these," she wrote. "The fear, hate and prejudice I learned took years to overcome."

Questions for Discussion

1. It has often been said that the attack on Pearl Harbor in 1941 unified the country. It's even been said that World War II was one of the last times Americans were a united people. Based on evidence presented in this essay how do you interpret the word "united" in describing the home front?
2. During World War II, America and its allies fought against Japan, Germany, and Italy. Were people on the home front equally hostile toward Americans of German, Japanese, and Italian descent? Describe the differences and similarities in attitudes toward these groups.
3. Mexicans, Jews, and Africans were not enemies during the war. Why, then, were Americans descended from those groups targets of prejudice?
4. Whatever the depth of unity during the war, there is no question that most Americans made sacrifices in those years. In your opinion, would Americans today be equally willing to make those kinds of sacrifices?

For Further Reading

Janet Abu-Lughod, *Race, Space, and Riots in Chicago, New York and Los Angeles* (2007); John Morton Blum, *V Was for Victory: Politics and American Culture during World War II* (1976); Roger Daniels, *Concentration Camps, USA* (1970); Lewis Erenberg and Susan Hirsch, eds., *The War in American Culture: Society and Consciousness during World War II* (1996);

Sandra Gilbert and Lawrence Distasi, *Una Storia Segreta: The Secret History of Italian American Evacuation and Internment during World War II* (2004); Erica Harth, *Last Witnesses: Reflections on the Wartime Internment of Japanese Americans* (2003); David M. Kennedy, *Freedom from Fear: The American People in Depression and War, 1929–1945* (1999); Andrew Kersten, *Race, Jobs, and the War: The FEPC in the Midwest, 1941–46* (2000); Daniel Kryder, *Divided Arsenal: Race and the American State during World War II* (2000); Richard Lingemann, *Don't You Know There's a War Going On? The American Home Front, 1941–1945* (1970); Mauricio Mazon, *The Zoot Suit Riots* (1988); Alan S. Milward, *War, Economy and Society, 1939–1945* (1979); Brenda Moore, *Serving Our Country: Japanese American Women in the Military during World War II* (2003); Eduardo Pagan, *Murder at the Sleepy Lagoon: Zoot Suits, Race, and Riot in Wartime L.A.* (2006); Greg Robinson, *By Order of the President: FDR and the Internment of Japanese Americans* (2003); Ronald Takaki, *Double Victory* (2000); William Tuttle Jr., *Daddy's Gone to War: The Second World War in the Lives of America's Children* (1993); Yoshiko Uchida, *Desert Exile: The Uprooting of a Japanese American Family* (1984); Emily Yellin, *Our Mothers' War: American Women at Home and the Front during World War II* (2004).

The Federal Government's Campaign Against Homosexuals and Other "Sex Offenders" During the McCarthy Era

David K. Johnson

The United States emerged from World War II as the greatest economic and military power in history. It enjoyed a monopoly on nuclear weapons (the Soviet Union did not possess an atomic bomb until 1949). And because it was the only major industrial nation whose territory was not invaded or bombed during the war, its enormous manufacturing base was intact. With Europe's and Japan's industrial capacity destroyed, the United States had no major global economic competitors for years following the war.

That helps account for the astonishing economic boom that lasted from 1945 to 1970. There were periodic ups-and-downs in the economy during that quarter century, and 20 percent of the population lived in poverty. Nonetheless, no people in history enjoyed so much affluence on such a grand scale for so long. By 1950, the United States accounted for more than 50 percent of the world's industrial production. More than 80 percent of the world's automobiles were produced in America, as was 57 percent of its steel, 62 percent of its oil, and 43 percent of its electricity. Americans—about 7 percent of the global population—earned 42 percent of the world's income.

Dwight David Eisenhower, elected president in 1952. How did President Eisenhower justify firing federal employees because of their sexual orientation or other moral "flaws"?

And thanks to New Deal–era progressive taxation and the power of labor unions, at no time before or since in modern American history was income distributed as equitably as during the years 1945 to 1970. Families earning "middle-class" incomes doubled in that time. Middle- and working-class families left their rented apartments in cities for home ownership in the suburbs. Between 1945 and 1960, 19 million families purchased new homes in the suburbs—by the mid-1950s, more than 1,000 families moved each day from city to suburb. And by 1960, for the first time in modern American history, a majority of families owned their homes. A Cape Cod house in New York's Levittown, opened in 1947, cost about $8,500; a family could put down as little as 10 percent on the house and, with a low-interest twenty-five- to thirty-year mortgage (and depending on taxes), have monthly payments of about $60.00.

In addition to home ownership, for the first time most employees enjoyed paid vacations, pension plans, and medical benefits on the job. They purchased new cars with regularity: in 1950 there were 39.3 registered million automobiles; in 1960, there were 73.8. By the mid-1950s, they could load the entire family into the car and enjoy a new concept in dining: the "fast-food" drive-in restaurant pioneered by McDonald's in 1955. With McDonald's hamburgers selling for 15 cents and coffee at 5 cents, a family of four could eat out for about $2.00—in their new car.

These were also the years when the ideal of "family togetherness" was at its peak. After fifteen years of depression and war, American men and women wanted to enjoy the security and stability they associated with family life. In a remarkable reversal of long-standing demographic trends, they married earlier (in the 1950s one-half of the women who married were under twenty), they had more children (during the "baby boom" of 1946 to 1964, more than 76 million children were born), and they divorced less frequently (the divorce rate tumbled from 17.9 percent in 1946 to 9.6 percent in 1953). In a revival of Victorian-era gender values, the ideal family had a breadwinner husband-father and a stay-at-home wife-mother-homemaker.

In economic terms, the "American Dream" had finally become a reality, at least for a majority of white people. Yet the economic boom was accompanied by massive insecurity and fear. Good news on the economic front was frequently accompanied by bad news on the Cold War front. Historians continue to debate the causes of the Cold War confrontation between the United States and the Soviet Union. There is debate as well about the reasons for widespread fears that *within* the country, unknown numbers of American citizens were involved in a communist plot to subvert and ultimately destroy the nation.

The post-war red scare is commonly labeled "McCarthyism" because of the ruthless witch hunt tactics employed by Senator Joseph McCarthy, a Republican from Wisconsin. But fears about the existence of an internal communist conspiracy were widespread. They cannot be blamed on the bullying and lies of a lone senator. Much of the zeal behind the hunt for communists came from conservative Republicans who, for years, had bellowed against what they viewed as the "socialistic" programs of Franklin Roosevelt's New Deal, such as Social Security. To those people, the New Deal and communism were nearly identical. But in the twenty-five years after the war, liberals as well as conservatives, Democrats as well as Republicans, claimed the country was in imminent danger because of the disloyalty of fellow Americans.

For example, J. Howard McGrath, attorney general in the Democratic administration of President Harry Truman, warned in 1948 that communists "are everywhere." They lurked secretly, he claimed, in "factories, offices, butcher shops, on street corners, in private businesses—and each carries in himself the germs of death for society." When not hiding in butcher shops, communists were busy subverting activities synonymous with "Americanism." The Illinois American Legion warned that the state's Girl Scouts were being "infiltrated" by communist propaganda. Moviemaker Walt Disney told a congressional committee that communist cartoonists in Hollywood were trying to get Mickey Mouse to spout the "communist line." Because communism was associated with the color red, the Cincinnati baseball team changed its name for a time from "Reds" to "Redlegs."

Innovations in popular culture, the arts, and even science came under suspicion. Some were convinced the new music called "rock-and-roll" was a communist plot to undermine the moral fiber of the nation's youth. Others believed water infused with fluoride to fight tooth decay (rampant at the time) was part of a "red" conspiracy to destroy the physical fiber of Americans. Citizens in Peoria, Illinois, organized a boycott of the play "Death of a Salesman" because they believed it was "communist dominated."

These and countless other examples of fears about a red menace may seem bizarre. But from the late 1940s well into the 1960s, the red scare undermined civil liberties and cast a shadow of fear and suspicion across the country. Why this was so is puzzling, because few Americans were actually drawn to the Communist party. During the height of the Great Depression in the 1930s, when many believed capitalism was finished, perhaps 200,000 people joined the American Communist party at one time or another. Many were members for a brief time. By the early 1950s, the Communist party was, in effect, declared illegal. More than 100 party officials were jailed, while others had their Social Security and military disability payments stopped. None of these individuals was convicted of an actual crime, other than affiliation with a political party most Americans disliked and considered "foreign." By the mid-1950s, party membership was perhaps 5,000.

But thousands of people suspected of being Communist party members in the past—or of associating with people who were—lost their jobs. They were never convicted (in most cases, never even accused) of spying or espionage. School teachers, college professors, labor union officials, Hollywood actors and screenwriters, as well as government employees were fired. Millions were forced to take "loyalty oaths" or forfeit their jobs; during the 1950s and 1960s, millions of others were spied upon by the FBI, the CIA, and local police "red squads."

At the height of the McCarthy era, from the late 1940s to the late 1950s, anything particular groups did not like came to be viewed as anti-American and part of the communist conspiracy. That could mean ethnic groups like Jews. On the floor of Congress, Representative John Rankin of Mississippi, a Democrat and a member of the House Committee on Un-American Activities, said, "Remember, communism is Yiddish." Others claimed the Civil Rights movement was a communist plot, and Martin Luther King Jr. a communist.

Something else many disliked was homosexuality. In the next essay, David K. Johnson describes the efforts of the Eisenhower administration to "cleanse" the United States government of employees suspected of being homosexual. Officials claimed it was necessary to fire homosexuals because they were "security risks." Even if they were loyal citizens, their sexual orientation supposedly made them susceptible to blackmail; once black-mailed, they might give state secrets to the communist enemy. But sex, not communism, was behind this witch hunt. A United States Senate report on homosexuality in government in 1950 noted that "These perverts will frequently attempt to entice normal individuals to engage in perverted practices. . . . One homosexual can pollute a Government office."

Of course, at this time homosexuality was, in effect, illegal. Every state had laws against "sodomy," and police vice squads frequently raided bars that catered to lesbians and gay men. In New York City, San Francisco, and Philadelphia, newspapers often printed the names of men and women arrested in these raids. Because the vast majority of homosexuals at the time were "in the closet" and had no legal protections, this could result in loss of a job. Or such exposure could ruin relationships with parents and other family members.

Source: David K. Johnson, *The Lavender Scare: The Cold War Persecution of Gays and Lesbians in the Federal Government* (Chicago: University of Chicago Press, 2006), pp. 119–147.

On the morning of March 13, 1953, "Miss Blevins," a fifty-five-year-old, sin-gle secretary-clerk at the State Department, read in her morning paper that eight homosexuals had been dismissed from the department in the last week. The *Washington Post* called it "the first major cleanup" under the newly inau-gurated Eisenhower administration, which had campaigned under the slogan "Let's Clean House." Blevins had long harbored suspicions about her boss, Miss McCoy, the recording secretary for an inter-departmental trade agreements group. Blevins found McCoy to be difficult to work for and felt "nauseous" and "uncomfortable" in her presence. Blevins was particularly suspicious of McCoy's relationship with an older female co-worker with a "mannish voice. . . ." Although Blevins found McCoy's general appearance to be feminine, she noted certain anomalies—"peculiar lips, not large but odd-shaped." Prompted by the newspaper story, Blevins typed an anony-mous memorandum to the new head of State Department security: "I have thought about this for at least two years," she wrote. "I have not been able to get the prodding ideas out of my head that (God forgive me if I am wrong) Miss McCoy tends toward lesbian characteristics." Having read that the new administration was dismissing a moral deviate every three days, Blevins wanted to "contribute something to help get them out of the government." She added a postscript to underscore the seriousness of the charge, noting that McCoy worked on "very secret matters."

A civil servant since 1933, Blevins had only been working for Miss McCoy for the last three years. Unsatisfied with her performance, McCoy had recently placed her on probation. A State Department investigation quickly revealed that Blevins's anonymous note was the result of this "personality situation." Despite their determination that Blevins was a disgruntled employee of "questionable reliability," security officials pressed her for more information about McCoy and her co-workers. Pleased to be taken seriously, Blevins unburdened herself of all the suspicions she had accumulated. She told officials she had a "funny feeling" about one man she described as having "a feminine complexion, a peculiar girlish walk." She cast suspicion on a female co-worker for having "a deep voice, an unusual face for a woman, not at all feminine.". . .

Blevins's cooperation with security officials reflected how the Eisenhower administration institutionalized within the executive branch the security concerns that Republican politicians had been railing about since February 1950. Security officials rather than legislators would take the lead in overseeing the new security program, as the focus on security shifted from congressional hearing rooms to agency interrogation rooms. The Eisenhower administration expanded the government's security apparatus from a few federal agencies to cover the entire federal workforce while simultaneously broadening its focus from specific concerns about loyalty to vaguer notions of "national security." Blevins's anonymous note illustrated how the notion that homosexuals posed a threat to national security, once the rationale of a few politicians and security officials, was becoming the common assumption of average Americans who saw it as their duty to assist the government in weeding them out. . . .

After the [1952] election, with Republicans in the White House for the first time in twenty years, they began in earnest to implement their mandate to "clean up the mess in Washington." Within three months of taking office, [President Dwight] Eisenhower issued an executive order replacing [his predecessor President Harry] Truman's loyalty system with an entirely new security system, with new criteria and procedures for ensuring that the employment of every federal employee was "clearly consistent with the interests of national security." Executive Order 10450 signaled a change in emphasis from issues of political loyalty to broader notions of general character and suitability. . . . An individual would be disqualified for [federal] employment for "any behavior which suggests the individual is not reliable or trustworthy." The order went on to delineate specific proscribed behaviors: "Any criminal, infamous, dishonest, immoral, or notoriously disgraceful conduct, habitual use of intoxicants to excess, drug addiction, or sexual perversion." Although the generic language of "criminal" and "immoral" conduct was drawn from preexisting civil service policies—and had already been used to bar homosexuals—the inclusion of the more specific reference to "sexual perversion" was unprecedented. . . . Under the Eisenhower administration, national security would require not only political loyalty but also proper morality.

During his first television appearance, Eisenhower had his Attorney General, Herbert Brownell Jr., explain the new program to the American people. Broadcasting from the Conference Room at the White House, Brownell explained how loyalty and security were very different types of risks. "Employees could be a security risk and still not be disloyal or have any traitorous thoughts, but it may be that their personal habits are such that they might be subject to blackmail by people who seek to destroy the safety of our country." In a subsequent presidential news conference, Eisenhower singled out the same example: "We are talking security risks: if a man has done certain things that, you know, make him, well, a security risk in delicate positions—and I don't care what they are—where he is subject to a bit of blackmail or weakness." Eisenhower's halting and embarrassed language suggested that what made one vulnerable to blackmail was unspeakable, but anyone who had followed the previous three years of publicity about homosexuals in the State Department understood. In the privacy of his presidential memoirs, Eisenhower was more explicit: "Many loyal Americans, by reason of instability, alcoholism, homosexuality, or previous tendencies to associate with Communist-front groups, are unintentionally security risks." He then seemed to single out homosexuality for special consideration, writing how, "in some instances, because of moral lapses, they become subjected to the threat of blackmail by enemy agents."

The press was somewhat more explicit in its explanations. As Joseph Young, the *Washington Star* reporter on the civil service, explained, "Security risks have little or nothing to do with communism or Communist membership or sympathies." They included several types, such as "a person who drinks too much," an "incorrigible gossip," "homosexuals," "neurotics," as well as persons with large debts or those who "run around with a disreputable crowd." All might reveal secrets to the enemy, either inadvertently or under duress. . . .

As the new head of the State Department's Bureau of Security and Consular Affairs, R.W. Scott McLeod personified the Eisenhower administration's aggressive approach to security. The department's outspoken new enforcer of security regulations, McLeod quickly became a "bogeyman" to employees, "a shadow that lurk[ed] over every desk and over every conference table at [State Department headquarters in] Foggy Bottom," as one columnist described him. His tactics were said to have struck fear in the hearts of foreign service officers and brought eavesdropping and informing to new levels. Tales of steam opening of mail were rampant, and allegations of a Gestapo mentality pervaded discussions of McLeod's operation. . . .

To "clean up" the State Department, McLeod intensified the campaign against homosexuals. During his first appearance before a congressional committee, McLeod articulated the new priorities of the Bureau of Security and Consular Affairs. Second only to a general call for tighter investigative procedures and terminology, McLeod promised a crackdown on homosexuals. "The campaign toward eliminating all types of sex perverts from the rolls of the department," McLeod assured congressional leaders, "will be pressed with increased vigor. All forms of immorality will be rooted out and banished from the service." Within ten days of his appointment, sixteen employees had been terminated as "moral deviates" and five as "security risks." The swiftness of the firings suggested that the Truman administration had protected homosexuals and highlighted a new "get tough" policy aimed more at immorality than disloyalty. As his friend John Haines remembered, McLeod [a former FBI agent] "was deeply suspicious of the things in the State Department that he didn't understand, like the intellectuals. He knew shortly from his own records and investigations what he had suspected viscerally—there was a part of the foreign service that had been infiltrated by fairies." According to Haines, McLeod's approach to the issue was influenced by his experience in law enforcement. "Scotty had the essentially simple approach to a fairy that you will find in a cop who has never had the benefit of, let us say, courses in abnormal psychology at Yale. Scotty had a very black and white kind of approach—and this wasn't white."

In both public presentations and internal meetings, McLeod treated homosexuals as a special class of security risks. Meeting for the first time with department security officials, he outlined a fairly liberal policy concerning the evaluation of much employee behavior. He cautioned evaluators to weigh the behavior of employees in the distant past against their more recent conduct, implying that a brief association with a Communist-front organization during the Depression would not necessarily disqualify someone who otherwise had a clean record. But his tolerance did not extend to moral issues. With regard to homosexuality, the standard was to be absolute—one offense meant expulsion. Since one homosexual act made one susceptible to blackmail, McLeod reasoned, no amount of intervening good behavior could compensate. In a much-publicized speech to the American Legion convention in Topeka, Kansas, McLeod discussed the security risks to which he was giving top priority—Communist agents, fellow travelers, and homosexuals. He made no mention of alcoholics, blabbermouths, or any other risks. Nor did he couch his clean-up campaign in euphemisms. "I have attempted very frankly and honestly," McLeod told this sympathetic audience, "to face the issue of sexual perversion—the practice of sodomy—in the State Department." Calling it both a "security risk" and a "condition which calls for psychiatric treatment," he assured the audience that he was doing all in his power to remove such practices from the department. Since 1947 allegations concerning such behavior had led to the removal of more than five hundred department employees. To replace these security risks, McLeod was looking to recruit men "well-grounded in the moral principles which have made our Democratic republic a model form of government." The ideal candidates, according to McLeod, would be "red-blooded men of initiative." He made no mention of women. . . .

Within McLeod's security office, a special investigative branch known as the "Miscellaneous M Unit" handled homosexual cases. Although responsible for investigating any type of moral deviation, the unit had a caseload that was overwhelmingly focused on homosexuality. During one three-month period in 1954, all but one of the Miscellaneous M Unit's twenty-seven separations [firings] were for homosexuality. . . .

The Miscellaneous M Unit used many techniques to detect homosexuals, but the most successful were personal interviews and polygraph tests. According to the State Department, *Investigative Manual,* all male applicants were to be personally interviewed to help detect sex deviates. Investigators were to note "any unusual traits of speech, appearance and mannerisms." Such personal observations, the manual predicted, could provide a "tip-off" indicating "sex deviation," which might lead to other information. If information suggested an applicant or an employee was homosexual, the Miscellaneous M Unit would confront the individual and attempt to procure a confession, offering the "opportunity" of a polygraph examination to the recalcitrant. Since its first use of the polygraph in 1950, the State Department had used it almost exclusively in morals cases. Although the State Department denied that it confined use of the polygraph to such cases, internal records suggest that by 1955, of the twenty-four persons subjected to such an examination, all but two were suspected of immorality, which almost always meant homosexuality. . . .

To the Miscellaneous M Unit staff, there were only two possible results from a homosexual investigation—they cleared the person of charges or forced him to resign. Fred Traband, special agent in charge of sexual deviation investigations, told a conference of regional security supervisors in 1953 that 80 percent of homosexual investigations ended in confessions. Failure to answer charges was considered virtually the same as an admission. In addition to a confession of guilt, interrogators sought detailed descriptions of homosexual acts and the names of participants. Using a classic "good cop/bad cop" technique, they threatened to reveal the employee's homosexuality if he didn't name names. . . .

Despite their coercive tactics, State Department investigators believed they were helping the men and women whose careers they were ending. In a lecture to administrative officers about the security program, John F. Ford, head of the department's office of security, boasted about the "assistance" his office had given to the homosexuals it encountered in its investigative work, even as it engineered its dismissals. He characterized his office's treatment of suspected homosexuals as "similar to interrogations made by psychiatrists." Ford even cited "letters of praise and gratitude" the security office had received from "confessed homosexuals" who had lost their jobs. He insisted that his investigative staff was justified in being "proud of the assistance they [had] afforded in straightening out the lives of these unfortunate people."

The publicity surrounding the State Department's aggressive security stance toward homosexuality led many in the department to inform on their fellow employees, effectively widening the gaze of the security officers. Anonymous letters poured into the security office implicating individuals or giving general advice on where to search for homosexuals. . . .

Not content with removing from its own ranks anyone who had ever engaged in a homosexual act, officials in the State Department pressured international organizations to carry out similar purges. The United Nations had long been a favorite target of conservatives and anti-Communist crusaders, who associated it with [Franklin D.] Roosevelt, Yalta, and threats to American sovereignty. [Democrat of Nevada] Senator [Patrick] McCarran's Internal Security Subcommittee and a federal grand jury had already conducted investigations into the employment of Communists among the U.N.'s American delegation. Shortly before leaving office, President Truman had signed an executive order requiring loyalty checks on American citizens working for international organizations, and the U.N. had agreed to remove employees who were found to be "disloyal" to member nations. . . . But the Eisenhower State Department . . . took on the extralegal function of forwarding information regarding the "suitability" of employees, exerting considerable pressure to have its recommendations followed. During the first year of the Eisenhower administration, the State Department furnished the U.N. with derogatory "suitability" information on 238 employees, but the U.N. terminated only 41 of them. U.N. authorities did not consider such information "definitive" and often found it to be "irrelevant." This failure to follow the State Department's security advice raised the hackles of officials, prompting them to raise the pressure.

State Department officials were particularly concerned that homosexuals fired from the State Department were finding refuge with international organizations. They feared a homosexual scandal at the United Nations would be blamed on them. . . . While even McLeod had to acknowledge that "in large and important parts of the world homosexuality apparently does not excite the same degree of opprobrium as in the United States," he wanted the U.N. to understand the "pitfalls" of employing homosexuals fired from the U.S. government. Desperate to avoid such a public relations scandal, officials argued that fired homosexuals—unlike others fired as unsuitable—showed no remorse, resented their dismissals, and therefore should be considered untrustworthy. . . .

The State Department undertook an extensive lobbying campaign to ensure the ouster of homosexuals from all international organizations of which the United States was a member. In their routine briefings to twenty-six specialized international agencies, such as UNESCO, department officials included appeals for the need to purge homosexuals. They called on their security colleagues at the Treasury Department to deliver the same message to the World Bank and the International Monetary Fund. McLeod made it clear to U.N. officials that a homosexual scandal in their organization could threaten U.S. financial support. "Notoriety accompanying some revelation of homosexual conduct among U.N. personnel," warned Scott McLeod, "scandalous to the American public, might very easily have echoes in Congress unfavorable to the U.N." Henry Cabot Lodge, U.S. Ambassador to the United Nations, conveyed this message directly to U.N. Secretary General Trygve Lie, noting that U.S. support would be "seriously undermined" if the U.N. retained homosexual American employees. The Secretary General agreed to the request, but insisted that the department provide definitive information, such as a criminal conviction record, documenting homosexual activities. The Secretary General had already dismissed nineteen of twenty-seven employees about whom the State Department had forwarded derogatory homosexual information. Unrelenting in its pursuit, the State Department wanted the remaining eight employees—all in clerical positions—removed as well, even though the charges against them were mostly "allegations and rumor." It promised to reopen investigations to find more definitive proof. Although the U.S. government had no authority to provide such suitability information to international organizations, it continued to do so until 1972.

The Eisenhower administration also put pressure on its allies to exclude homosexuals from government positions. As early as 1951, officials in the British Foreign Office had informal contacts with State Department officials about their policies and procedures regarding "the homosexual problem." A few years later an interdepartmental committee looking into the control of military information found deficiencies in the British personnel security system, specifically its lack of attention to "personal associations and to defects in character and personal traits." Britain's unique relationship with the United States and a series of homosexual scandals among British government officials led the United States to put extreme pressure on the British to follow its lead in matters of security and pay closer attention to the issue of homosexuality in its personnel security program. In 1953, a top-ranking member of Scotland Yard spent three weeks in Washington consulting with FBI officials on a plan to weed out homosexuals from the government. The British, Canadian and Australian security agencies all studied and copied, to varying degrees, the antigay policies and investigative procedures developed by the United States government. Whether or not they subscribed to the same beliefs about homosexuals, each feared that the disclosure that one of their secret agencies employed a homosexual would jeopardize their close relationship with American intelligence officials. . . .

In his 1954 State of the Union Address, President Eisenhower announced the preliminary results of his administration's efforts to "clean house": 2,200 security risks had been removed from the federal workforce. . . . Many used the figures as vindication of [Senator Joseph] McCarthy's first charges against the government. Given the freewheeling manner in which Republicans used the figures, the press sought clarification. Reporters wanted to know what agencies the employees worked for, when they had been hired, whether they were male or female, and the specific grounds for their removal. . . .

Though he admitted that many security dismissals involved issue of blackmail and weakness rather than disloyalty, Eisenhower resisted pressure from the press to give more specific information. As politicians had long known, using the generic term "security risk" was a very useful way to invoke treason, espionage, and disloyalty while referring to less serious indiscretions. Giving a precise breakdown would reveal the wide range of behaviors covered under "security." Administration officials and congressional allies argued that there was no need for such a disclosure. "I, as a taxpayer, am not interested in whether a person was discharged for being disloyal or for being a drunk, and I don't think the average person is," asserted Philip Young, chair of the Civil Service Commission. On a speaking tour through Wyoming, McLeod insisted that people "aren't interested whether loyalty risks are drunks, dope fiends, sex perverts or Communists." They just wanted them out of the government, he argued. "What difference does it make if a man is no good because he cannot keep his mouth shut on atomic secrets, or does the same thing because he is a drug addict, pervert, or just a plain sap?" inquired Congressman George Bender (Republican-Ohio). . . . Like many defenders of the administration's security program, Bender blurred the lines even further between loyalty and security. His examples presumed that alcoholics, blabbermouths, and other security risks were fired because they had *already* committed treasonous acts—not because of their *potential* to do so.

The press continued to criticize the administration for lumping together serious cases of espionage with minor incidences of drunkenness. . . . Joseph and Stewart Alsop [of the *Washington Post*] charged that . . ."there was not a single case of actual subversion in all the State Department's security firings—and it is doubtful if there was one such case throughout the Government." Journalists like Joseph and Stewart Alsop criticized McLeod and the rest of the Eisenhower administration for what they called "palpably dishonest" tactics in the numbers game. Pointing out that in the vast majority of cases there was no question of disloyalty or pro-communism, Alsop charged that nineteen out of twenty cases were for "drinking, temperamental unsuitability, or the like."

This increased scrutiny of the security program also revealed some of its excesses, furthering angering the public. It became apparent that even some heterosexuals were charged with immorality under the system. In a Pulitzer Prize-winning, seven-part series on the security system for the *Washington Daily News*, Anthony Lewis disclosed that a female language specialist at the State Department had been discharged for "immorality" because she had conceived a child out of wedlock, even though she had subsequently married the child's father. Acknowledging that the practice of considering immorality a security violation had originated with the Truman administration, where it applied principally to homosexuals, he noted that application of this principle had broadened. As Lewis concluded, "The Eisenhower security program's strictures on immorality apply not only to sexual perversion, as has been well publicized, but to intimate heterosexual (normal) relations out of wedlock.". . .

Perhaps the most celebrated case of a federal employee being charged with heterosexual sexual immorality was that of Marcelle Henry.

A French-born, naturalized American [citizen], Henry worked for the Voice of America. She had been investigated under the loyalty program for Communist sympathies and exonerated. But under the security program, State Department security officials called her in again. "Have you ever had sexual intercourse without being married?" they asked her during an hour-and-a-half interrogation. "When did you last buy contraceptives?" the security agents continued. "When did you last have sexual intercourse? With whom?" She was told that sexual relations outside of marriage were both illicit and illegal, and that the moral standards of this country were not those of France. In May 1953, Henry was "separated" from the service because she had "manifested a disregard for the generally accepted standards of conventional behavior and that this has resulted in criticism of the Department." Having admitted to "having sexual relations with a number of men," Henry posed a threat not to security but to the reputation of the department. What was extraordinary about the Henry case was not the sexual nature of the questioning but the heterosexual nature of the relationships. "I am not accused of being a Lesbian," Henry noted, "I am accused of loving the other sex too much." By contrasting herself with the standard, well-accepted type of security risk—the homosexual—she sought to highlight the ridiculousness of the charges against her. Not only was she not a homosexual, she was claiming the opposite, someone whose attraction to the other sex was manifest. How, Henry wondered, could both homosexuality and heterosexuality be dangerous to the nation?

The Eisenhower security program came under increasing criticism not only because it was affecting heterosexuals, but also because it was affecting millions of Americans, even those who did not work for the government. An independent study in 1958 estimated that one of every five employed adults in America had been given some form of loyalty or security screening.

Questions for Discussion

1. As we saw, Marcelle Henry was an unmarried woman dismissed from government service because of her sexual involvement with men. She wondered how *both* heterosexual and homosexual activity could be "dangerous to the nation" during the Cold War. How would you answer that question?
2. How did Eisenhower administration officials distinguish disloyalty from "national security risks"? Why did they consider homosexuals security risks? What evidence did they present to justify firing homosexuals? What methods did they use to force them from their jobs?
3. In your opinion, why would the issue of sexual morality come to the surface in the United States during the Cold War era? Was it viewed as a threat to family life? To American survival in the Cold War?
4. In 1954, as part of the Cold War effort to distinguish American values from those of "godless" communism, the United States government added the words "one nation under God" to the Pledge of Allegiance. In your opinion, was the government's campaign against homosexuals and other "sex offenders" linked to religious

values? If so, did it undermine the ideal of separation of church and state? Can you think of other times in American history, before and after the Cold War, when state and federal governments passed legislation based on religious values that targeted the behavior of specific groups?

For Further Reading

Edward Alwood, *Dark Days in the Newsroom: McCarthyism Aimed at the Press* (2007); Dominick Cavallo, *A Fiction of the Past: The Sixties in American History* (1999); John D'Emilio, *Sexual Politics, Sexual Communities: The Making of a Homosexual Minority in the United States, 1940–1970* (1983); John Diggins, *The Proud Decades: America in War and Peace, 1941–1960* (1988); Benita Eisler, *Private Lives: Men and Women of the Fifties* (1986); Michael Freeland, *Hollywood on Trial: McCarthyism's War Against the Movies* (2008); Richard Fried, *Nightmare in Red: The McCarthy Era in Perspective* (1990); John Lewis Gaddis, *The Cold War: A New History* (2006); Herbert Gans, *The Levittowners: Ways of Life and Politics in a New Suburban Community* (1967); James Gilbert, *Another Chance: Postwar America, 1945–1968* (1981); William Graebner, *The Age of Doubt: American Thought and Culture in the 1940s* (1991); Godfrey Hodgson, *America in Our Time* (1976); Maurice Isserman, *If I Had a Hammer: The Death of the Old Left and the Birth of the New Left* (1987); Kenneth Jackson, *Crabgrass Frontier: The Suburbanization of the United States* (1985); Marty Jezer, *The Dark Ages: Life in the United States, 1945–1960* (1982); David K. Johnson, *The Lavender Scare: The Cold War Persecution of Gays and Lesbians in the Federal Government* (2006); Landon Jones, *Great Expectations: America and the Baby Boom Generation* (1980); Harvey Klehr, *The Heyday of American Communism: The Depression Decade* (1984); Walter LaFeber, *America, Russia, and the Cold War, 1945–2000*, 9th ed. (2002); Elaine Tyler May, *Homeward Bound: American Families in the Cold War Era* (1988); Douglas Miller and Marion Nowak, *The Fifties* (1977); Ted Morgan, *Reds: McCarthyism in the Twentieth Century* (2004); William O'Neill, *American High: The Years of Confidence, 1945–1960* (1986); James T. Patterson, *Grand Expectations: The United States, 1945–1974* (1996); Ellen Schrecker, *The Age of McCarthyism: A Brief History with Documents* (2002); Stephen Whitfield, *Culture of the Cold War* (1991).

14

Race, Gender, and the Civil Rights Movement

The Struggle in Mississippi

Steve Estes

In the years following World War II, the booming economy and the crusade against communism were defining features of American life. But few post-war developments changed the country more profoundly than the Civil Rights movement.

There were many reasons the Civil Rights movement surfaced at this time. Responses to events abroad were part of it. During World War II, large numbers of African Americans served in the armed forces and worked in defense plants. They did their part in defeating fascist tyranny abroad, and many saw no reason they should continue to be victimized by the tyranny of racism at home. Also, as the Cold War heated up in the late 1940s, the United States presented itself as the main defender of the "Free World" against communist oppression. At the same time, American laws sanctioned racial segregation and prevented most blacks from voting. Civil rights activists pointed to this contradiction as they challenged those laws.

Events inside the country forced racial issues to the surface as well. In sports, Jackie Robinson joined the Brooklyn Dodgers in 1947, breaking baseball's "color line" to become the major league's first black player. In politics, President Harry Truman issued an executive order the following year, ending segregation in the armed forces. In court, a lawsuit was brought by the

Alabama state trooper beating Student Non-Violent Coordinating Committee (SNCC) leader John Lewis in Selma on March 31, 1965. How does the photograph reflect various notions of "manhood" described in Chapter 14?

National Association for the Advancement of Colored People (NAACP) that challenged laws requiring "separate but equal" schools for white and black children. In 1954, the Supreme Court said the schools were unequal and the laws unconstitutional. And in public transportation, another long-standing southern racial ritual was challenged. When buses became crowded, black passengers were supposed to relinquish their seats to whites. On December 1, 1955, Rosa Parks, a forty-two-year-old Montgomery, Alabama, department store clerk and NAACP member, refused to give her seat to a white person. Parks was arrested. Montgomery's black citizens organized a successful bus boycott that lasted one year. The boycott's leader was a then unknown twenty-six-year-old minister, Martin Luther King Jr. An admirer of Gandhi, King preached the ideal of nonviolent resistance to oppression. He emerged from the boycott as the nation's most articulate and charismatic civil rights leader.

These and other events were positive developments. But they did not end segregation or give southern blacks the right to vote. And the Supreme Court's 1954 decision against segregated schools meant little in Deep South states like Mississippi, where authorities ignored the decision and less than 5 percent of blacks finished high school. Nor did they do anything to improve the economic situation of black Americans nationwide. During the greatest burst of prosperity in the country's history, more than 50 percent of African Americans were mired in poverty. In the 1950s, they were almost three times as likely as whites to be unemployed. The black exodus from the South continued after World War II: by 1970, 47 percent of black Americans lived outside the South, compared with 23 percent in 1940. But northern blacks were barred from most labor unions, and discrimination kept the majority of them from good jobs and decent housing.

The Civil Rights movement that eventually addressed these problems gained momentum in 1960 with the sit-in movement. Like much of the Civil Rights movement, the sit-ins arose spontaneously, from the "bottom-up." They were developed by "ordinary" people no longer willing to tolerate the daily humiliations of the country's racial caste system.

On February 1, 1960, four black students from the North Carolina Agricultural and Technical College, a small black institution, entered a Woolworth's department store in Greensboro. Blacks could shop at the store, but the lunch counter at Woolworth's was reserved for "whites only," as was the case throughout the South. The four students—Ezell Blair Jr., Franklin McCain, Joseph McNeil, and David Richmond—acted on their own, although they were inspired by the Montgomery bus boycott and by Martin Luther King's strategy of civil disobedience and commitment to nonviolent resistance. They sat down at the lunch counter, ordered something to eat, and were refused service. They returned the next day, this time with twenty-three other students. Still no service. On the fourth day, some white women students from a local college joined the black students at the lunch counter.

The sit-in strategy was contagious, and within weeks spread to fifty-four cities in the South. By the end of the year as many as 70,000 demonstrators had taken part in them. Most were black, although white sympathizers joined in. The majority were students. Thousands were arrested; many were beaten. But a spark was ignited. The next year came the Freedom Rides, followed by King's campaigns against segregation in Georgia, Florida, and Alabama. By the mid-1960s, the movement was successful in ending legally mandated segregation in public facilities (the Civil Rights Act of 1964) and discrimination in voting (the Voting Rights Act of 1965).

In the next essay, Steve Estes describes the activities of the Student Non-Violent Coordinating Committee (SNCC) in Mississippi during the early 1960s. SNCC (pronounced "Snick") was organized in April 1960 by African American students, in response to the success of the sit-in protests. SNCC activists challenged the racial status quo in the South by organizing black people to demand their rights as American citizens. They worked in states like Mississippi and Alabama, where whites were prepared to use massive violence in defense of their way of life.

Estes's essay is a concrete example of the ways private issues and public events are linked. On the surface, the Civil Rights movement attempted to deal with "public" policy issues such as segregation, voting rights, and poverty. As Estes shows, however, just below the surface lurked "private," family-related issues, like sexuality and gender, that were closely connected to the "public" ones.

For example, Estes points out that the involvement of black men in the Civil Rights movement was a way of asserting their "manhood." But white racists felt *their* manhood was tied to the racial status quo. What, then, did Americans mean by "manhood" in the 1950s and 1960s? And how was the issue of "manhood" related to the debate about nonviolence within the Civil Rights movement? What about women—whether white or black? Estes shows that while male activists risked their lives to promote racial equality, they usually assumed men were superior to women. That raised the issue of gender equality within SNCC in the early 1960s, years before the appearance of the women's liberation movement in the late 1960s. Finally, sexuality was inseparable from civil rights issues. White racism was grounded in fears and stereotypes about black sexuality—and in unspoken knowledge of the historical exploitation of black women by white men.

Of course, the goals of the Civil Rights movement were to improve the lives of African Americans and to achieve racial equality in the United States. But because the movement raised fundamental questions about American values such as equality, freedom, democracy, fair play, and opportunity—as well as the right to protest—it planted the seeds for other protest movements of the 1960s. Once African Americans and their white sympathizers, including the young women discussed in Estes's essay, began to ponder the meaning of words like "equality," the door was open for others to do the same. The women's, gay rights, and anti–Vietnam War movements of the 1960s owed much to the Civil Rights movement that preceded them.

Source: Steve Estes, *I Am a Man: Race, Manhood, and the Civil Rights Movement* (Chapel Hill: University of North Carolina Press, 2005), pp. 61–63, 66–76, 81–83.

As Charles McLaurin walked down the street in Ruleville, Mississippi, during the summer of 1964, he chatted with anyone who would listen about the importance of registering to vote. A field secretary for the Student Nonviolent Coordinating Committee (SNCC), McLaurin had just begun a voter registration drive in the sleepy Delta town. The mayor of Ruleville and a local police officer confronted the stranger and the small group of black citizens that surrounded him. Mayor Charles Dorrough was a white man. He had been elected without the support of Ruleville's black residents, less than 2 percent of whom could vote in 1962. Dorrough ordered the people listening to McLaurin to get off the street and go home. When

McLaurin told them to stay put, the Mayor had him arrested. McLaurin was released later that day, and he returned to the very same street to talk to the very same people about their right to vote.

As a black Mississippian himself, McLaurin understood why most of the folks he spoke with were reluctant to join him on the trip to the county courthouse. He knew that when these folks got home from trying to register, they would be fired, evicted, or even jailed. But despite the threats of retaliation, or perhaps because they were no longer beholden to the white men who once paid them little more than subsistence wages, three older women from Ruleville agreed to ride with McLaurin down to the courthouse in Indianola. There they would face a hostile white registrar in the birthplace of the Citizen's Councils of America [a white supremacy organization].

Early in the morning of August 22, McLaurin took the three brave women to register. Their car rolled south from Ruleville, passing cotton plantations where "men, women, and children, moving to the rhythm [and] beat of the hoe," labored for the arch-segregationist Senator James O. Eastland and other wealthy planters. McLaurin followed the women up to the daunting white columns that stood like silent sentinels guarding the Indianola courthouse. He waited anxiously while they tried to register and drove them home after the registrar rejected them because they were black. McLaurin brought dozens of Ruleville residents down to the courthouse that summer. Among them was a sharecropper named Fannie Lou Hamer, who became one of the most powerful advocates for the rights of women, minorities, and the poor. Looking back, that first trip to the courthouse remained one of McLaurin's most enduring memories. "I will always remember August 22, 1962," he said years later, "as the day I became a man."

Charles McLaurin's reminiscences might seem strange at first. He himself did very little. He did not register to vote or face the white registrar; the women did. Yet McLaurin found his strength that day by helping the women find theirs. He claimed his manhood by helping the women reclaim a bit of their dignity. Coming of age in Mississippi, where respect for black men was all to rare, it is not surprising that McLaurin and other SNCC men look back on their activism as a rite of passage into manhood. Responding to segregationists who had demonized black masculinity, young men in the movement created militant new models of black manhood. The rite of passage for SNCC activists and other young men in the southern movement avoided many of the traditional trappings of manhood that rested on power and domination. These men were leaders whose primary goal was to find local leaders to replace them. Though SNCC men occasionally used masculinist rhetoric, their advocacy of participatory democracy led them to an inclusive, humanistic organizing strategy that welcomed both men and women into the leadership of the movement.

The Mississippi movement and especially the summer project of 1964 raised broad questions about the gender, racial, and sexual mores of the segregated South. During the summer project, hundreds of young white men and women lived with and worked alongside black activists in an attempt to replace segregation with the "beloved community," a society based on equality, democracy, and love that knew no racial boundaries. For segregationists, it surely must have seemed that the "race mixing" apocalypse had arrived. This made local men's participation in the struggle especially difficult as their attempts to challenge white male supremacy alongside white women elicited particularly violent responses from the white community. Local blacks and civil rights organizers fought back against racial violence and oppression both with armed self-defense and nonviolent political protest. Armed self-defense safeguarded activists and the black community, fending off attacks of white vigilantes. Local men and more than a few women took up arms in self-defense as a practical necessity. For the men in particular, this was also an important way to reclaim their manhood by protecting their families. However, because it was by nature defensive, this strategy could never produce lasting change in the southern social order. Nonviolent activism, perhaps seen as a more "passive" form of resistance, was actually the potent moral force and savvy political strategy that brought about real change in the southern society. Southern civil rights organizers showed that nonviolent activism could be courageous and even manly. Above all, they demonstrated that nonviolent protest was an effective way to undercut the violence upon which white male supremacy rested and also a way to gain political power for disenfranchised African Americans in the South. . . .

VIOLENCE AND NONVIOLENCE

Though many rural black southerners accepted nonviolence as a tactic for demonstrations, most did not adopt it as a way of life. Local activists, especially black veterans, viewed armed self-defense as a practical necessity in the fight against white vigilantes. National civil rights leaders, on the other hand, understood that black activists could not outgun both vigilantes and southern authorities, and they feared that harmed self-defense would undermine the movement's moral high ground. The debate came to a head in 1959. That year, the national leadership of the NAACP [National Association for the Advancement of Colored People] denounced the militant stance taken by Robert Williams. A veteran of the Marine Corps and director of the local NAACP chapter in Monroe, North Carolina, Williams had led black activists armed with shotguns and hunting rifles in fending off attacks by Klan nightriders. During an NAACP convention in 1959, Williams demanded that national officials reconsider their position against self-defense: "We as men should stand up as men and protect our women and children. I am a man and I will upright as a man should, I will not crawl.". . .

As SNCC moved its voter registration drive into the Mississippi Delta in 1962 and 1963, student organizers had to make peace with local activists who, like Robert Williams, believed strongly in armed self-defense. Among the most visible advocates of self-defense were the men of Holmes County, Mississippi. Though it had been difficult for Charles McLaurin to persuade large numbers of Ruleville men to try to register, the men in Holmes County practically dragged SNCC organizers to the courthouse. Holmes County had been the site of a New Deal land grant experiment that helped black tenant farmers become landowners. Independent farmers could challenge white authority in ways that other men could not. Haitman Turnbow was one of the black landowners who accompanied fourteen other Holmes County residents on a trip to the courthouse. The sheriff met them at the door. Patting his side arm, he said, "Now, who will be first?" Turnbow stepped forward. Late one night, about a week after his unsuccessful registration attempt, gunshots poured into the windows of Turnbow's house and firebombs exploded outside. As his wife and daughter ran for cover, Turnbow grabbed his rifle and trained it on his assailants. The attackers quickly fled. "They can't stand it when a black man go to throwing fire," one black resident from Holmes County remembered. "When you stop and return fire, they move." Though white officials arrested Turnbow the next morning for supposedly firebombing his own house, vigilantes in Holmes County probably thought twice about attacking his house in the future.

Haitman Turnbow and Robert Williams believed that it was a man's duty to protect his wife and children against racial violence. The rationale that black men had a responsibility to protect their women and children was, in fact, very similar to the Citizen's Council argument that white fathers needed to fight against integration to protect their wives and daughters. For both black and white men, civil rights historian Tim Tyson notes, "the rhetoric of protecting women was fraught with the politics of controlling women." Though the gender politics may have been similar in the two instances, the parallel breaks down when one considers that black children, armed with only books and pencils, posed much less of a threat than white vigilantes with bombs and guns. As the attack on the Turnbow home illustrates, there were times when African American men had real reasons to defend their wives and children with arms, whereas white men's armed defense of segregation primarily protected their control of southern society, not the lives of women and children. . . .

Tragically, it was not always possible to anticipate or protect against vigilante violence. Earlier in the same summer [of 1963] when Haitman Turnbow stood his ground against nightriders in the Delta, an assassin gunned down Medgar Evers, a field secretary for the NAACP, in front of his home in Jackson. The only prints found on the rifle belonged to Byron De La Beckwith, a member of a Delta Citizens' Council, who reportedly later said, "We're going to have to do a lot of shooting to protect our wives and our children from bad Negroes and sorry white folks and federal interference." Armed self-defense alone might slow this sort of violent suppression of the movement, but as a purely *defensive strategy*, it could not transform the landscape of the state.

THE FREEDOM VOTE AND FREEDOM SUMMER, 1964

Evers's assassination and the concerted attacks against voter registration drives in the summer of 1963 forced civil rights leaders to reevaluate their strategies. "We were getting smashed by violence [and] terrorism," remembers Reverend Ed King, a white activist minister at predominantly black Tougaloo College in Jackson. "We either had to withdraw or move in a new direction." Mississippi activists refocused their energies on the gubernatorial campaign of state NAACP president Aaron Henry. As Henry's campaign manager, SNCC's Robert Moses asked Ed King to sign on as a candidate for lieutenant governor, creating the first biracial ticket in Mississippi since Reconstruction.

King and Henry solicited "freedom votes" from black Mississippians, who were excluded from the official election by white registrars. The Henry campaign hoped to garner enough of these alternate ballots to prove to federal authorities that black Mississippians wanted to participate in the electoral process but were denied solely on the basis of race. According to the U.S. Commission on Civil Rights, just over 6 percent of the eligible nonwhite voters in Mississippi in the early 1960s were registered to vote . . . .

Henry's campaign for governor attracted powerful allies and fresh ideas to the Mississippi movement. Allard Lowenstein, a Stanford professor and political activist, came to Mississippi in 1963 and proposed the idea of bringing white college volunteers into the state to help with the freedom vote. . . . He suggested to Bob Moses that university students could help staff the movement in places where many of the local organizers had been jailed or intimidated. At the urging of Lowenstein, dozens of students, most of them young white men from Yale and Stanford, traveled south to help recruit potential voters for Henry and King. As one volunteer remembered, he and his fellow students were "long on naïve idealism with little real sense of the larger history and risks," but they supplied necessary labor for the freedom vote.

The freedom vote [not officially counted because most blacks who voted were not allowed to register] proved a success, tallying more than 80,000 ballots from black citizens across the state. In the spring of 1964, SNCC leaders assessed the lessons of the campaign. The white Democratic candidate, Paul Johnson, had won, but according to SNCC organizer Ivanhoe Donaldson, this was almost beside the point. The freedom vote "showed the Negro population that politics is not just 'white folks' business.". . .

In the wake of the freedom vote, SNCC's small cadre of Mississippi organizers began to plan a much bigger campaign for the summer [of 1964]. . . . As the strongest proponents of the summer project, SNCC's Bob Moses and Charlie Cobb argued that student volunteers could staff a massive voter registration campaign and teach summer classes for the state's black children, who attended substandard, segregated schools during the year. Many local organizers, however, worried that the volunteers' educational advantages would overwhelm and intimate local activists. Yet SNCC staffers and local organizers finally agreed that the skills and financial support that volunteers could bring outweighed the dangers they posed to struggling local movements. More importantly, such a project would show America that whites and blacks, men and women, northerners and southerners, could work together to heal the deep wounds cut by segregation and disfranchisement.

SNCC struggled to recruit a truly integrated cadre of volunteers for the Mississippi summer project. Many black students simply could not afford to pay their way to Mississippi. The resulting pool of volunteers was integrated but dominated by upper middle-class white students from elite universities outside of the South. Gender, as well as race and class, factored into the composition of the volunteer staff that traveled to Mississippi. As the sociologist Doug McAdam suggests, gender formed a barrier to white women's participation in the summer project as both their parents and SNCC organizers worried about the response of white southerners to the integrated movement. Protective parents often refused to let their daughters go to Mississippi, but because of society's double-standard, this was less of an issue for male volunteers, whose parents were more likely to assume that their sons could take care of themselves. SNCC recruiters also felt that the presence of young white men in an integrated movement might be less likely to provoke the wrath of white southerners than the presence of white women. While the social double-standard partially explains the bias against white women volunteers, this was more of a practical response to the sexual and racial taboos of southern culture than an example of chauvinism in SNCC.

The very dangers that restricted white women's participation in the summer project may actually have spurred men's participation. Men were more likely to sign up and be accepted, McAdam observes, because working in the summer project was similar "to any number of other traditional challenges that were available to young men as part of the process of 'becoming a man.' "...

For the volunteers who joined the summer project, the road to Mississippi led through Oxford, Ohio, where Bob Moses and other movement veterans offered an orientation on racial oppression in the South and a crash course on nonviolence. Traveling in an old, tan Volkswagen van, Donna Howell and two other volunteers subsisted on bread and peanut butter as they trekked from the University of New Mexico to the orientation in Oxford. Along with hundreds of other volunteers, Howell listened to Bob Moses discuss SNCC's allegiance to nonviolence. To volunteers and veterans alike, Moses represented the model movement organizer, one who held fast to his ideals through countless beatings. "We don't preach that others carry guns or refrain from carrying them," Moses told the volunteers, "but no COFO [Council of Federated Organizations] workers, staff, or volunteers would be permitted to carry guns." The gentle power of his belief in nonviolence guided the paths of countless activists, yet Moses himself eschewed the leadership role. His soft-spoken demeanor and humility only reinforced the mystique that surrounded him. Volunteers remembered Moses as a "very poetic, sort of Gandhian-like figure who commanded a tremendous amount of respect but didn't have an overtly macho male leadership style." Amzie Moore, the local NAACP leader who originally invited Moses down to Mississippi, admired his young colleague because people followed him even though he never said, "I'm the man, you do this, that, and the other." Like Charles McLaurin and other men in SNCC, Moses was a hard worker, an organizer, and an idealist who represented a new type of militant, nonviolent manhood. . . .

Stepping off the train in Canton [Mississippi], JoAnn Ooiman was one of the earnest volunteers who received a warm welcome from half a dozen COFO staffers and icy stares from angry local whites. A white college student originally from Denver, Ooiman had never been to Mississippi, and her introduction began with a barbeque at a black minister's house. Just as Ooiman and the other volunteers began to dig into the heaping plates of food, police sirens brought the welcome party to a screeching halt. The sheriff hauled the volunteers down to the station, took their mug shots, and then played a taped speech from the district attorney, warning that "the women would be raped by blacks in town and the men would be beaten up." It was a welcome befitting the "closed society."

Despite the warnings of Canton's district attorney, many of the volunteers stayed in the houses of local black families during the summer without incident. In the rituals of everyday life, volunteers and local activists got to know one another as people. "Rise, shine, and give God glory," Ms. Hattie Bell hollered every morning to wake up Ooiman and another volunteer staying in her small house. A domestic worker in white homes for most of her life, Bell had saved up enough money to buy her own place. Since she had retired, she was no longer beholden to whites for income and so was freer to join the movement. She cooked large meals for the young women who stayed with her. Though she grew close to the volunteers over the summer, she never ate with them, abiding the dictates of segregation even in her own home.

As the volunteers and host families soon learned, the careful deconstruction of such racial barriers was an important part of the summer project. For young black men in Mississippi, this was especially difficult given the taboo against their interactions with white women. Explaining her son's reticence to a volunteer, one local woman said, "Jus' one boy touch a white girl's hand, [and] he be in the river in two hours. We raised them never to even look at one as they passes on the street, don't even look, that's the way down here." Veteran activists warned volunteers to be wary of southern white taboos. The SNCC staff sent a few female volunteers home because they began romantic relationships with members of the communities in which they worked.

Volunteers worked on three projects throughout the summer: voter registration drives, "Freedom Schools," and a smaller "white folks" project [aimed at attracting sympathetic Mississippi whites to the movement]. The voter registration workers walked some of the same dusty, rural roads traveled earlier by Charles McLaurin. . . . Black farmers would nod and often agree that they should be allowed to vote. . . . Some might agree to come to mass meetings. A few might even agree to try to register. But most just listened. "There's a great amount of fear there," said SNCC field secretary Willie Peacock. "They will tell you that they don't want to become registered to hide the pride, which says, 'If I say I'm afraid, then I'm less than a man.' So we've been working on trying to cut through this fear."

Occasionally, organizers used the rhetoric of manhood to push past the fear. When Charles McLaurin led a group of volunteers on a voter registration drive in the small town of Drew, he found many of the local men reluctant to participate. At one mass meeting outside of a small church, McLaurin harangued a crowd of men who looked on in silence. Referring to a group of white police officers who also stood nearby, McLaurin said, "What they're afraid of is that you're gonna rise! That you're gonna say, 'I'm a man! Treat me like a man!' Are you gonna let them see that you're afraid? That you won't join these kids and women?" McLaurin then turned to his supporters and began to chant "Which Side Are You On," an old labor organizing song adapted by the movement. Those at the meeting joined in, shouting in unison:

> Oh people can you stand it,
> Tell me how you can.
> Will you be an Uncle Tom
> Or will you be a man?

At that moment, the police arrested the young organizers. Evidently, they *were* afraid that the men who had remained silent might rise.

At the same time that voter registration work and mass meetings began to cut through adults' fears, the Freedom Schools had a similar effect on the young. As in many southern states, Mississippi's segregated public school system heavily favored white schools over black ones, allocating an average of $81.66 per white student as compared to $21.77 for each black pupil in 1964. Many black Mississippians had grown up attending split-session school years, implemented by white planters to ensure that they had enough additional child labor to plant and harvest their crops. To make up for these educational deficits, SNCC's Charlie Cobb had proposed Freedom Schools, in which volunteers would teach summer courses in social studies, black history, drama, art, French, English, and nonviolence. . . .

GENDER AND SEXUALITY IN THE MOVEMENT

Though SNCC valued Freedom School teaching and voter registration work equally, volunteers had preconceived notions of the work they wanted to do, and some questioned the gender breakdown of work assignments. A female volunteer recalled that she felt "shoved to the side" as a teacher, while male volunteers were "being macho men," facing violence out in the field. One male canvasser said that, although teaching was important, "it wasn't the same kind of, if you want, macho adventurism that I was into." Sociologist Doug McAdam used volunteer interviews and staff rosters to estimate that women were nearly twice as likely as men to be assigned to teaching, whereas men dominated the ranks of voter registration workers. At the beginning of the summer, SNCC organizers did make strategic placement decisions. They originally kept white volunteers from doing voter registration in the extremely dangerous counties and restricted white women's roles in the field for fear that their presence would provoke more hostility from local whites, but as the summer progressed, these restrictions slackened. Many women did work in voter registration even in tough rural counties, and those who worked as teachers also risked violence simply by working in the movement. Regardless of their assignments or their gender, all of the volunteers and staff members "put their bodies on the line." To white Mississippians bent on defending the racial status quo, teachers were no less of a threat than voter registration workers.

No one in the movement was immune to the violence and racism in the Magnolia State. Away from the glare of media cameras, police officers felt no compulsion about beating activists or threatening them with language that revealed the sexual subtext of white male supremacy. Bessie Turner, a black woman from Clarksdale, told SNCC workers about a police officer who took her to jail and made her disrobe and lay face down on the concrete floor while he whipped her with a leather strap. "Turn over and open your legs," he ordered, "and let me see how you look down there." Then, the officer hit Turner "between the legs with the same leather strap." When Mary Lane, George Johnson, Phillip Moore, and Paul Klein, a black female volunteer and three white male volunteers, went to the police station in Greenwood to report harassment by a local white man, they received similar treatment. Officer Logan (who did not give the volunteers his first name) kept Lane, Johnson, and Klein occupied while Moore spoke to officers in another room. Logan, off duty and out of uniform, asked how the white male volunteers liked "screwing that nigger," referring to Lane. Then he took out a long knife, and as he began to sharpen it, he said, "Sounds like rubbing up on nigger pussy." He brought the sharpened knife to bear on Klein's ribs and asked, "Think it's sharp enough to cut your cock off?". . .

The gender and sexuality of movement volunteers and SNCC veterans has been the focus of much popular and scholarly attention since the summer [of 1964] itself. The frenzied fear of interracial sex, whipped up by the Citizen's Councils and other proponents of massive resistance, contributed to the sexually charged atmosphere of the summer. From the beginning, SNCC organizers warned volunteers to avoid such interracial liaisons. As a [SNCC] project director in Greenwood, Stokely Carmichael admonished white volunteers to be conscious of the history of white men taking sexual advantage of local black women, and "as far as white girls with Negro boys—of course none of that on the other side of town." Carmichael opposed staff dating, feeling that it would only complicate matters during the summer, but he did not prohibit dating altogether. Given the close quarters of communal living arrangements, the stress and strain of daily organizing, and the young age of most movement volunteers and veterans, it is understandable that civil rights workers formed intimate relationships that summer.

Due to the highly politicized nature of interracial sex, such relationships could both bring activists together and tear them apart. . . . Liberated sexuality also represented the logical extension of SNCC's ideals—a truly free society or "beloved community." The taboos against interracial sex made it that much more enticing. "For black men," historian Sara Evans writes, "sexual access to white women challenged the culture's ultimate symbol of their denied manhood." For white women, who "had experienced a denial of their womanhood in failing to achieve the cheerleader standards" popular at that time, sexual interest from black men was especially empowering. White men and black women also experienced the liberating power of love that summer. But activists found that the personal politics of interracial sex could damage the movement. Black women, at times, grew angry when black men flocked to white women, reinforcing American society's racist standards of beauty. White women may have felt trapped in a Catch-22 of being labeled as racist if they declined black men's advances and opportunistic if they accepted. Despite all of the complications that arose from interracial sex during the movement, it is important to remember that these intimate relationships were born out of a faith in love (both platonic and passionate) and a hope that movement ideals were harbingers of a more egalitarian and open society. As one volunteer wrote in his journal, the people in SNCC "already *have* the 'beloved community' and they rightly see the aim of the movement to be the inclusion of the whole of America into *this* community. Our aim is indeed miscegenation, more profoundly so than they think."

SNCC actually came closest to embodying the utopian ideal of the beloved community before the summer of 1964. The influx of volunteers during the summer project, and the high retention rate of new staff members afterwards, exacerbated what had been relatively minor philosophical differences in the organization. As SNCC attempted to deal with these growing pains, deciding between a highly centralized structure and a more loosely affiliated group of "floating" field secretaries, several female veterans also began to question why they were relegated to what was seen, stereotypically, as "women's work." [SNCC] Executive Secretary Jim Forman remembered that discussions of gender roles had begun before the summer in Atlanta, when women protested assignment to secretarial tasks. . . . This issue cropped up again during Freedom Summer when some women felt that they were assigned to teaching and office work because of their gender. A spy from the [Mississippi] Sovereignty Commission, eager to expose divisions within the beloved community, reported, "The 'strong' females on the permanent staff have told me earlier of a revolution among females, 'the women's fight for equality with men.' I have watched it gain momentum over the past months. There are many male supporters of this new thing."

Among the strong women fingered by this spy was Casey Hayden, a stalwart movement veteran who later coauthored a paper on the position of women in SNCC. In the paper, Hayden and Mary King, another veteran white staffer, compared the oppression of women in the organization to the oppression of African Americans. "The average white person finds it difficult to understand why the Negro resents being called 'boy,'" they wrote, "because the average white person doesn't realize *that he assumes he is superior*. So too the average SNCC worker finds it difficult to discuss the woman problem because of his assumption of male superiority." Initially, the position paper received little serious discussion. It provoked Stokely Carmichael's infamous quip that "the position of women in SNCC is prone." Mary King, who heard Carmichael make this comment, later argued that it was clearly a joke and that he was in fact relatively progressive on gender issues. At the time, such jokes may have deflected the thrust of the women's arguments. Yet Hayden and King's position paper would become an influential document in the history of women's liberation. . . .

The tensions between the egalitarian ideal in SNCC and the reality of gender relations in 1964 led women in the movement to challenge both racism and sexism. Feminism, according to historian Belinda Robnett, "did not evolve from the sexist treatment within SNCC" but from the organization's liberating philosophy and open structure that fostered challenges to authority. The structure of the organization, which was founded on principles of participatory democracy, gave both men and women a voice in decision-making. Martha Prescod Norman, an activist who worked with SNCC in Mississippi and Alabama, remembered that both men and women in the organization inspired her "to be brave, to be smart, to be intellectual—to be all of the things that are stereotypically not female." Empowering women as it did, SNCC was far more progressive than other movement organizations and most parts of American society in 1964.

Yet there were times when the civil rights group did reflect society's gender bias in work assignments and formal leadership. Charles Scattergood, a summer volunteer who worked with Charles McLaurin in Sunflower County and stayed in the Delta until 1965, later acknowledged that tension on the local project was due, in part, to sexism. "I saw racism spreading all over Mississippi. But I also saw male chauvinism spreading out pretty bad too," he said. . . . As [historian] Sara Evans originally argued, the women in SNCC experienced both liberation *and* oppression. To acknowledge this paradox is not to single out the organization or male leaders for special critics; it merely captures the historical reality of 1964. Despite the pervasiveness and intractability of racism and sexism in America during the mid-1960s, the men and women of SNCC attempted to fashion a movement in which all people could gain personal and political power.

Questions for Discussion

1. The word "manhood" was used differently by various groups. Describe what "manhood" meant to (a) white segregationists, (b) black male civil rights activists, (c) black residents of Mississippi, and (d) white female and black female activists. How do you account for the differences? How was it related to the debate over nonviolence within the movement?
2. The focus of the Civil Rights movement was to challenge laws that prevented blacks from voting and that mandated segregation in public facilities. According to the author, in the minds of white southerners, these racial issues were connected to gender and sexuality. Why?
3. What did the Student Non-Violent Coordinating Committee mean by the "beloved community"? To what extent do you think they succeeded in achieving it within their organization?
4. Describe the Mississippi Summer project of 1964. What were its goals? Was it successful? To what extent did issues of gender and sexuality within SNCC undermine or enhance the summer project?
5. In your opinion, what role did the Civil Rights movement play in the development of other "rights" movements of the 1960s?

For Further Reading

Taylor Branch, *America in the King Years*, 3 vols. (1988); Clayborne Carson, *In Struggle: SNCC and the Black Awakening of the 1960s* (1981); Bettye Collier-Thomas and V. P. Franklin, *African American Women in the Civil Rights–Black Power Movements* (2001); Vicki Crawford, Jacqueline Anne Rouse, and Barbara Woods, eds., *Women in the Civil Rights Movement: Trailblazers and Torchbearers, 1941–1965* (1993); Raymond D'Angelo, ed., *The American Civil Rights Movement: Readings and Interpretations* (2000); John Dittmer, *Local People: The Struggle for Civil Rights in Mississippi* (1994); Sara Evans, *Personal Politics: The Roots of Women's Liberation in the Civil Rights Movement and the New Left* (1980); David Garrow, *Bearing the Cross: Martin Luther King, Jr., and the Southern Christian Leadership Conference* (1986); Jack Greenberg, *Crusaders in the Courts: How a Dedicated Band of Lawyers Fought for the Civil Rights Revolution* (1994); Henry Hampton and Steve Fayer with Sarah Flynn, *Voices of Freedom: An Oral History of the Civil Rights Movement from the 1950s through the 1980s* (1990); Steve Lawson, Charles Payne, and James T. Patterson, *Debating the Civil Rights Movement, 1945–1968* (2006); George Lewis, *Massive Resistance: The White Response to the Civil Rights Movement* (2007); Peter Ling and Sharon Montieth, *Gender and the Civil Rights Movement* (2004); Ann Moody, *Coming of Age in Mississippi* (1968); Howell Raines, ed., *My Soul Is Rested: Movement Days in the Deep South Remembered* (1977); Renee Romano and Leigh Raiford, eds., *The Civil Rights Movement in American Memory* (2006); Juan Williams and Julian Bond, *Eyes on the Prize: America's Civil Rights Years, 1954–1965* (1988).

15

Young Americans Fighting—and Protesting— the War in Vietnam

Two Days in October 1967

David Maraniss

The next essay portrays two days in the history of important features of American life during the 1960s: the war in Vietnam and student protests over the war. Young people were the central players in both.

Four issues about the Vietnam conflict and its consequences are important to keep in mind. First, the war was a result of the anticommunist crusade discussed in Chapter 13. Just as McCarthyism was the domestic expression of fear about the spread of communism internally, Vietnam was a manifestation of fear over its spread internationally. Beginning with President Harry Truman in the late 1940s, the foreign policy of the United States revolved around stopping the spread of communism, of containing it within nations where it already existed. Any president in office when a country "went" communist, as China did in 1949 during President Truman's first full term, would be labeled by many as "soft" and unfit for reelection. Truman did not seek reelection in 1952. That lesson helped shape the policies of the four presidents who followed Truman and who committed the United States to the longest war in its history: Vietnam.

A second important feature of the Vietnam conflict concerns those who fought it. More than 80 percent of the 2.1 million Americans who served in Vietnam, and 88 percent of the infantry riflemen who saw combat, were young men from working-class and poor family backgrounds. The military

Two views of American youth in the 1960s: young soldiers carry a wounded comrade to safety in South Vietnam's swampy terrain (top photo), while hundreds of students protest the war (bottom photo). How do these photographs reinforce or undermine stereotypes of young people in the 1960s?

draft that existed during this time exempted college students from military service; until 1968, it exempted graduate students as well. College students tended to come from middle- and upper-class families. World War II and Korea were fought by Americans from all social classes and ethnic backgrounds, and a majority of those eligible for the draft actually served. Not so for Vietnam. Of the 26.8 million baby boomers who were eligible for the draft age during the war, only 2.1 million served in Vietnam. Their average age was nineteen, compared with twenty-six in World War II. More than 58,000 of them were killed during the war, and 270,000 experienced wounds, many of them disabling. As many as 500,000 veterans suffered from posttraumatic stress disorder. And unlike veterans of World War II, those who survived Vietnam were not given victory parades when they returned home.

A third thing to keep in mind about this conflict is its impact on the Vietnamese people. Whether or not the war was justified has been debated endlessly. Beyond dispute is that in pursuit of its war aims, the United States unleashed the largest and most technologically advanced weaponry in history on a peasant society. Three times as many bombs were dropped on North and South Vietnam than the total exploded by *all* combatants during World War II. By 1970, the tonnage of bombs dropped on Vietnam exceeded the total used in every war in history to that point. This included 400,000 tons of napalm, invented by Harvard chemists during World War II. Napalm was a jellied substance made of gasoline, benzene, and polystyrene; it clung to skin, burning it at temperatures ranging from 2,000 to 5,000 degrees. In addition, more than 20 million gallons of the herbicide Agent Orange were sprayed in jungle areas of South Vietnam, destroying one-half of its trees. In time, it seeped into the water supply and food chain. Agent Orange contains chemicals that cause cancer, birth defects, and other diseases.

It is difficult to know precisely how many Vietnamese were killed during the war. Estimates range from 1.5 million to 3 million, about 900,000 of whom were combatants on one side or the other. In other words, many of those killed, perhaps even a majority, were civilians. Also, the use of chemical weapons such as Agent Orange means the death toll did not stop with the American departure in 1975. It has been estimated that since 1975, more than 100,000 Vietnamese have died from diseases associated with Agent Orange.

It was this devastation as well as the war itself that led to the fourth issue: the antiwar movement. The most widespread, sustained antiwar effort in American history, this movement began with President Lyndon Johnson's escalation of the conflict, in spring 1965, and continued into the 1970s. Contrary to stereotypes, most college students did not protest the war; nor were most young people opposed to it. Educated young people between the ages of twenty and twenty-nine were the demographic group most likely to support the war; minorities and the least educated the most likely to oppose it. The antiwar forces included clergy, members of labor unions, women's peace groups, poor people, Vietnam veterans, traditional liberals, college professors, and others. But college students opposed to the war were the most passionate, most daring, most vocal, and most provocative of the antiwar forces. Those who attended the nation's elite colleges and universities were the most likely young people to oppose the war.

In the next essay, David Maraniss describes two days in the lives of young people: some who fought in Vietnam and others who opposed the war. On October 17, 1967, a corps of elite riflemen on a "search-and-destroy" mission was ambushed in dense jungle terrain northwest of Saigon. Maraniss provides a dramatic portrait of the attack, which killed many of the riflemen. His description of what took place that day is an accurate snapshot of how the war was fought and its brutality.

Maraniss quotes from some of the letters these young soldiers sent home, and it is important to note that while many of them went along with American policy in Vietnam, many of them were either personally opposed to the war or thought it not worth fighting.

Across the world in the United States, the week of the ambush was also "Stop the Draft Week." It was the latest effort by antiwar forces to "bring the war home" and make it difficult to maintain social order in the United States as long as the war continued in Vietnam. The October 18 event described by Maraniss took place at the University of Wisconsin, one of the most active antiwar campuses in the country. Antiwar activists were trying to stop the manufacturer of napalm, Dow Chemical, from conducting job interviews on campus. Like his description of the ambush the day before, Maraniss's portrait is a "ground-level" description of events. The antagonism between the young protestors and the police is especially vivid. It is also an accurate portrayal of how people felt at the time—and of the pervasive violence, both physical and emotional, at loose during the 1960s.

As he did with the soldiers in Vietnam, Maraniss's portrait of some antiwar activists includes comments on the relationship between values instilled by parents and others as they were growing up in the 1940s and 1950s and their antiwar stance in the 1960s.

Source: David Maraniss, *They Marched into Sunlight* (New York: Simon and Schuster, 2003), pp. 141–143, 145, 147, 154, 156–157, 260–261, 268, 270, 275, 277–279, 316–319, 322–324, 367–369, 374–375, 378.

[Company Commander] Clark Welch was in a spirited mood as he sat in his small hideaway office at the Delta base camp in Lai Khe and wrote a letter home to Florida. His natural tendency was to share virtually every experience with his wife, Lacy, good or bad, trivial or exciting, but this was something special. It was the first day of the second week of training for his new rifle company, and he was exuberant about the budding esprit de corps. "This is going to be one hell of a fine combat rifle company," he wrote. "I talked to the whole company yesterday and when I said—we had a new company and could make it what we wanted to, and what I *wanted* and would *have* would be the best damned company in the Big Red One—the company that would be the first in and the last out, the company that would be called on when any other company needed help, the first combat rifle company in the 1st Infantry Division—all the men started yelling and cheering. It sounds kind of silly written down here, but if you could have seen them, you'd know why I'm here and what this is all about. These are good men, Lacy. Sometimes I don't like to think about what must happen to some of them before the year is over, but to see these men now—this is America at its finest."

Life is all in the perspective. Greg Landon, one of Welch's new men, wanted to be a good soldier and for his platoon to function effectively, but he also expressed hope that his company commander would not be too "gung ho.". . . The question of whether Delta was going to be the best damn company in Vietnam seemed less relevant to him than the fortitude of the enemy. On the same day that Welch wrote Lacy about his spirited ambitions, Landon sounded a note of concern. "The possibility of the war ending before my time is up, although present, is not very large on the horizon," he wrote to his parents. "The determined V.C. [Vietcong] counter every new strategy with a new one of their own. His monumental patience leads me to believe that he actually likes living in his tunnel reading his newspapers and occasionally going out to tend his manioc [tropical plants] or set up an ambush."

At the *New York Times* bureau in Saigon on that very day, correspondent R.W. Apple was filing a dispatch that offered a perspective close to Private Landon's. After interviewing dozens of military experts and "disinterested observers," Apple presented a grim assessment of U.S. military prospects in Vietnam as of August 6, 1967. His conclusion was neatly summarized by the headline that would appear over the front page article—"Vietnam: The Signs of Stalemate." The number of American troops in Vietnam had increased from 50,000 to nearly half a million in two years, Apple wrote, yet there was a growing sense that "the war is not going well. Victory is not close at hand. It may be beyond reach. It is clearly unlikely in the next year or even the next two years, and American officers talk somberly about fighting here for decades." The war was now draining the federal treasury of $2 billion a month, Apple noted, and there was a far larger human cost—74,818 Americans wounded and 12,269 dead.

Three reports to America on the same day: one bursting with pride, one cautious, one skeptical. Welch, the optimist of the three, was not naïve. . . . But he nonetheless had a subtle grasp of his Vietnamese experience and was flexible enough to balance seeming contradictions. He was unflinching in his belief that he was fighting the good fight with the good guys. "There's no doubt about whether or not we should be here," he wrote home. "The VC are murderers and assassins and just plain thieves. The Vietnamese people want us here because for the first time in 20–30 years they are protected by someone who is not taking advantage of them." Yet at the same time Welch worried about what the war was doing to this beautiful, alien land and to its people. He could be angry and heroic, sardonic and reflective. . . .

And these soldiers of whom Welch was so proud, were they as determined as their commander to achieve "success in combat"? It depended, for many, on one's definition of success. If it meant staying alive and getting back home, certainly.

"Right now I am back in the tower," guarding the perimeter, Mike Taylor wrote home to his parents in Alaska. "I am getting tired of this crap. I should jump out of the tower and break my leg. It's worth a six-month profile, which means easy work. Christ, I'll probably break my neck. I do the same crap every day & night. I can see now why you got out of the %*#% Army, dad. Anybody that stays in this outfit has to be crazy."

Greg Landon, with characteristic sarcasm, told his parents that he was "hoping for a slow-healing, painless wound in a couple of months that will clean up around springtime of next year."

Jackie E. Bolen Jr., the oldest of six children who grew up hunting and fishing in rural West Virginia, wrote home with increasing concern. He had arrived in Vietnam a few months [earlier]. His comrades respected him as a skilled soldier, and Lieutenant Welch had already made him a squad leader, but Bolen wanted to leave. Vietnam was nothing like he expected, and war was worse than he could have imagined. "You don't know what it is to have to kill men or watch your friends die," Bolen said in a letter to his grandmother. "It's even worse to have to carry them off the battlefield when you can't even find a part of the body. Grandma, I don't know what I have ever done to deserve the hell that I am in."

It was "just a Chicken Shit War," Mike Troyer wrote home to his parents in Ohio. "The V.C. have everything in their favor, why should they resign to a peace treaty?". . .

Clark Welch, the soldier's soldier, was driven by his vision of an ideal, but he was not unaware of war's chaotic effects. One night, as he was writing Lacy a letter, a call came about a reckless shooting on the perimeter. "You won't believe what happened," he reported later. Two men from the battalion's communications section, who had been assigned for that night to Delta Company, got in a fight. One hit the other, "so naturally the second loaded his M-16 and shot the first thru the heart.". . . By the time Welch arrived, all he could do was fill out forms, answer questions, and ruminate on why it happened. "I just don't understand. No, I guess I do understand. Both men, I just found out, were pending discharge for being unsuitable for military service. They both had jail records and have IQ's under 100. All this shooting and dying just got to be too much for some people and they react in odd ways.". . .

For the U.S. Army rifle companies in Vietnam, combat usually took place during what were known as search-and-destroy missions. In later years this terminology would evoke images of soldiers searching Vietnamese villages and destroying them, thatched roofs set aflame with Zippo lighters or napalm. The original concept, when the phrase was coined by [Commander of American forces in Vietnam] General [William] Westmorland and his aides at MACV [Military Assistance Command, Vietnam] headquarters, was no less violent but more precise in its military connotation. Search and destroy meant sending infantry into the jungle and countryside in search of enemy units and base areas, finding them and fixing them in place, engaging them if possible, and destroying them with massive firepower, preferably from a distance through artillery and air. . . .

The other side was fully aware of the American search-and-destroy strategy, according to Vo Minh Triet, deputy commander of the First Regiment of the VC's Ninth Infantry Division. His response was: *If they can't find us, how can they destroy us?*

There was a touch of bravado to his boast, for his First Regiment had been roughed up in several major battles with the Americans over the previous two years, but it was valid in one sense. The Viet Cong had a far easier time finding the Americans than the other way around. Their advantage was obvious long before the moment of combat. Among the Vietnamese living inside the village of Lai Khe were people who secretly worked for the Viet Cong and regularly provided information. One such informant, whose loyalties were misjudged by the Americans until they killed him in an ambush firefight, was the man who had served as the barber for Jim George's Alpha Company. Some VC supporters inside Lai Khe communicated with the Ninth Division by leaving messages in a bottle at a pickup point in the jungle nearby. . . .

There were two keys to success for communist forces facing American search-and-destroy missions, Vu wrote. The first was to get so close to the enemy during battle that artillery and air power could not be effective. In the metaphorical language of the Vietnamese, this tactic was popularized by a saying: "Grab the enemy by the belt and hang on." The second element was surprise. "The side which is caught by surprise will be embarrassed and unable to capture the initiative will be at a loss and will be quickly annihilated. . . ."

THE AMBUSH

[Editor's note: On October 17, 1967, the Black Lions and its Alpha Company of riflemen, led by Clark Welch, were on a search-and-destroy mission. Operating in a terrain of dense jungle approximately forty-four miles northwest of Saigon, they believed they were about to trap a group of enemy forces. But the other side had already set a trap of its own.]

The fresh tracks along the trail, the sighting of enemy soldiers in the distance—these were lures designed to draw the Black Lions deeper into a trap. Scouts from Vo Minh Triet's First Regiment and Rear Service Group 83 had been watching the American soldiers for two days. From [Captain] Jim

George's point patrol all the way to the last man in Clark Welch's rear platoon, every step the Americans took from the perimeter through the tall grass and into the ever-denser jungle had been noticed. Triet was back in his command post a few hundred meters south of the point where Alpha's lead platoon saw the trees move. He was receiving constant updates on the approaching force over a telephone line. Through hand signals, scouts stationed high in trees sent word down to camouflaged comrades below, who then reported the American positions to the command post.

The tree scouts armed with AK-47s and captured American radios, some of them tied to positions with ropes and vines, were instructed to look and listen only. They were not to use their radios until Triet told his communications officer to flip the switch so everyone could talk. That order came simultaneously with the signal to attack. When the trap was set, when the American soldiers were just where Triet wanted them to be, moving down and to the right, on a line facing his camouflaged bunkers and the machine guns and preset claymore mines, two of his battalions ready on the west and the third moving into positions from the east—at that moment he gave the signal. . . .

Private First Class Breeden was the first to die. Clifford Lynn Breeden Jr., aged twenty-two, from Hillsdale, Michigan. . . . A burst of enemy fire struck him as he was setting up his own hasty ambush. Six bullets ripped open his chest and guts. He fired a clip from his M-16 and slumped to the jungle floor. . . .

The opening fusillade echoed back through the woods to the rear platoon of Delta. What was it? Some soldiers in the rear assumed it was Alpha springing its ambush. It sounded like the sort of skirmish the Black Lions had been getting in day after day that October. Contact, a quick fire-fight, the Americans pulling back to call in artillery and air, the Vietnamese disappearing as suddenly as they came. But this time, up and down the line, sniper fire started pinging down from the trees. . . .

The Black Lions certainly had found what they were searching for. Now what? Was this an offensive operation or defensive? Would they destroy or be destroyed? How many Viet Cong were out there? Would the enemy stand and fight? That George's lead company had walked into an ambush became apparent to Clark Welch as soon as he heard reports over the radio that machine-gun fire at that point was coming from enemy bunkers. This signified more than a sniper attack; it meant the Viet Cong had been ready and waiting. But Welch did not yet feel that his own Delta Company at the rear was hopelessly outmanned. Though the enemy fire began simultaneously up and down the line, with Triet's knocks on the wood block, the opening minutes of the battle had been somewhat less intense in Delta's area. Only a few men had been wounded in the initial volley. . . . Welch figured that he was dealing primarily with some well-placed machine guns and a squad of snipers high in the trees to his right. He shot the first one himself. "I got that sonofabitch!" Big Rock [Welch's nickname] yelled to a platoon sergeant who had pointed toward the tree. Private [Melesso] Garcia, a rifleman on the right flank, took out another sniper. . . . One by one, Delta was quieting the trees, but for every sniper killed it seemed three others appeared. . . .

The second wave of the enemy attack, when it finally came, started near the front and moved back through the battalion columns with awful fury. Delta was hit from both sides and even some from the rear, but this time the worst was coming from the left, or east. Triet had taken advantage of the pause to bring more elements of his third backing battalion across the draw from the east. He also had moved more men on line from the south and west. The U ambush was complete. With fire pouring in from three sides, it became difficult to distinguish enemy fire from friendly fire. A machine gun pounding at the battalion command area from the east sounded like an American gun and further confused the situation. First Sergeant [Clarence] Barrow heard [Black Lions' Commander] Terry Allen and other officers shout, "Cease fire! Cease fire! You're shooting your own men." Welch thought differently and began yelling "Fire! Fire!" Confused soldiers decided for themselves. Most returned fire. . . .

Though the machine-gun charges proved futile in the face of such a large enemy force, they at least involved clear action with a defined goal. For most Delta men most of the time, the battle was undefined and the enemy unseen. They were pinned down, confused, woozy with fright, fighting to save themselves and their buddies. Dwayne Byrd, the young Texan leading the second platoon, had a sharpshooter's eyes, but could never find the face of the enemy. He saw only flashes that seemed to be coming out of the ground.

Jack Schroder was one of the first men wounded when the second round of shooting started. "Airborne Schroder's hit in the leg," platoon sergeant Luther Smith shouted, and members of his squad crawled over to help, dragging him toward the battalion command area, which they assumed was secure. "I'll be all right, I can make it," Schroder said. A few meters away a rocket grenade hit Sergeant Smith, blowing off much of his left leg. He was still conscious when Faustin Sena reached him. Sena took out his first aid kit and lit a cigarette and gave it to Smith, then moved back when a bullet pinged off his helmet and he heard his squad leader tell him to take over the radio. Machine-gun fire struck Sena in the wrist, making it difficult for him to work the radio and painful for him to crawl. . . .

There was no longer any question as to who held fire superiority. The Black Lions' lone advantage was artillery support, but that was minimized by close fighting—the enemy's trademark tactic of hugging the Americans by the belt and holding tight—and by confusion over when and where to stop the artillery to bring in air power, which never came close to the actual battle site in any case. The Viet Cong stayed within fifty meters at all times and often came within ten meters. They were blowing claymore mines, sending in rocket-propelled grenades, and firing down from the trees with AK-47s. . . .

While many around him were ducking for cover, Clark Welch remained on his feet. Since Alpha's command was knocked out early in the fight, he had been working with [Second Lieutenant Harold] Durham to call in artillery fire. He had wanted more artillery support from the beginning, and now he was calling in all that he could. He was also "shooting like a madman." He killed one rocket-propelled grenade gunner with his .45 and shot another sniper out of a tree. The body didn't fall this time, just a water-fall of blood. . . . For a brief time the battle seemed like Clark Welch against an entire regiment. It was not long before he was hit. The first bullet pierced his back and cut between two ribs, causing a sucking chest wound. If he leaned over, he could not breathe. If he stood straight, he could breathe. So he stood during the battle, his uniform drenched in blood. Men were moaning all around him. He estimated that fifty percent of his company was down by then, dead or wounded. . . .

Welch passed through again on his way north to his rear Delta platoon. He glanced over and saw that [Sergeant Major Francis] Dowling was dead, battalion operations sergeant Eugene Plier was dead, the radioman was dead. [Terry] Allen was "covered with blood," working the radio, talking to officers in the air above. Allen saw Welch and yelled out orders: *Start getting your company out of here. Move back on a 360 [full retreat]!*

Welch found his medic, Doc Lovato, and instructed him to come forward and assist the battalion commander [Allen]. Lovato said, "yes, sir," started crawling toward Allen with his bag, and was killed [Allen died shortly thereafter]. . . .

Upright and hurting, Welch kept moving. . . . There was a ten-yard clearing that he wanted to cross. Halfway to the other side, he was hit, this time in the arm. Machine-gun fire ripped through him with such power a biceps flew out and fell to the ground, a piece of muscle wriggling like a hooked fish. He looked down and thought, *what the hell is that?* He assumed a biceps muscle would be red, but it was blue. Scott Down— company radioman Paul D. Scott—came up, removed C-ration tins from a sock, and used the sock as a tourniquet on Welch's arm. . . . He slumped down behind a tree and passed out briefly. . . . At one point he came to and in the haze he thought he saw Sergeant Barrow pointing a machine gun directly at him and firing. In fact Barrow aimed slightly above Welch and killed a Viet Cong soldier who was trying to remove the lieutenant's shoulder strap. . . .

Welch, struggling to keep conscious, had called and told [platoon leader Lieutenant David] Stroup to leave on a 360. "We're getting the hell out of here," Stroup said to his platoon sergeant, George A. Smith, and his radio-telephone operator, David Laub. They started moving back, every soldier "crawling more or less on his own," a few inches at a time. On the way, as he encountered more soldiers, Stroup passed the word about the 360. He came to an area where many of the wounded had been treated, just in front of the battalion command area. The machine-gun fire seemed fiercest there.

The Viet Cong were zeroing in on the wounded. Unarmed and unconscious soldiers were being hit a second, third, fourth time. Sergeant Barrow witnessed it and could not clear his mind of the savage tableau—the bodies "bouncing up and down" as rounds hit them. . . .

OCTOBER 18, 1967: STUDENTS PROTEST THE WAR AT THE UNIVERSITY OF WISCONSIN

[Editor's note: In 1967, the Dow Chemical Company was the government's sole supplier of napalm. Napalm is a gelatinous chemical compound explosive designed to attach itself to flesh and then sear it at temperatures between 2,000 and 5,000 degrees Fahrenheit. American forces dropped thousands of tons of napalm on Vietnam. Student antiwar activists tried to prevent Dow Chemical job recruiters from interviewing students on college campuses. One such attempt occurred at the University of Wisconsin at Madison, on October 18, 1967.]

Jim Rowen and Susan McGovern returned to Madison for the 1967 fall semester so late that they had no luck finding a place near the university. . . . They had been married almost two months, a merger of two families of the liberal Washington establishment, though such a description, while perhaps unavoidable, was not how the young couple defined themselves. Susan McGovern, the daughter of Eleanor and Senator George McGovern of South Dakota, was a senior in sociology. Jim Rowen, the son of Alice and Hobart Rowen, an economics writer at the *Washington Post*, was in his first year of graduate school in English. They were a compact and tight-wired pair who shared a love of books and movies and had two preoccupations: their studies and Vietnam. As "liberal Democratic kids, raised to be tolerant and respectful of other cultures," the war to them seemed both unnecessary and indefensible. Whether the United States was fighting in Southeast Asia "on behalf of some half-baked imperialist extension of power or this outdated notion of anticommunism . . . it just seemed so ridiculous," Rowen thought. . . .

Rowen's first political stirrings, like those of most antiwar activists who came of age in the fifties and first half of the sixties, before Vietnam and the cultural revolution, involved civil rights. His parents had taught him to respect other races and to avoid or challenge people and institutions that did not. When he was ten and his elementary school in Bethesda was being integrated, a teacher screamed at Joe High, a black classmate Rowen had befriended, and the incident upset Rowen and helped fix his sense of self as "an enemy of people who treated blacks badly." When a bowling alley in the community, Hiser Lanes, was reluctant to allow "negro" patrons, Rowen's parents would not allow him to go there. . . .

The transition from civil rights to the antiwar movement seemed natural and seamless, but by 1967, with Vietnam now dominant, Rowen found that opposing the war intellectually was easier than figuring out how to respond to it physically. Along with many of his classmates, he spent a considerable amount of time during his senior year at the University of Wisconsin debating what to do if he got drafted, and he viewed the draft dilemma, among other things, as another manifestation of racism. He saw the war "as a reflection of domestic racism," both in how "the draft was taking minority kids no●in college," and in how "the government, in our name, was making war on Asians with dark skins, the endless talk about gooks and slopes, our technological military destruction of life and culture across Southeast Asia— it all went hand in hand."

Rowen eventually joined the Wisconsin Draft Resistance Union and signed a petition saying that he would not serve if drafted, but how exactly he would not serve was something that he and Susan "talked about endlessly" with no resolution. . . .

By the fall of 1967, Rowen was waking up every day "angry that the war was still going on" and determined to do something to stop it. At the time, he said later, the "anger seemed so reasonable" that he never "slowed down to analyze it. It was just wake up, feel that anger, get dressed, go to a meeting, get in the streets." That was the frame of mind early on the morning of October 17 as he and McGovern got into their little red Opal Kadett and drove to campus to participate in the first day of protests against Dow. They had attended many of the organizational meetings of the Ad Hoc Committee to Protest Dow Chemical and had talked about Dow with their friends at night around one of the heavy wooden tables in the Union Rathskeller. These were the two days they had been waiting for all fall. The war was escalating, the draft was escalating, the level of violence was escalating, in America and Vietnam, Dow had been on campus once before, the previous February, and Dow was coming back, and Dow made napalm. Dow and its napalm were not just symbolic targets, Rowen felt, but rather were directly responsible for some of the worst violence of the war.

The issue was not whether they would protest Dow's presence on campus but how much they were willing to risk in that protest. They argued about whether civil disobedience was "a correct or legitimate tactic," whether people had a right to obstruct other people's free access into a building. Some of their friends contended that napalm "wasn't the right issue around which to make such a large personal commitment, which might lead to arrest, jail, and possibly expulsion. But finally they decided that they had talked enough, that "the university should not permit itself and its facilities to be used for war-employment recruiting," and that they would try to stop the process. But not yet, not on this day of peaceful picketing; the civil disobedience could wait one more day.

The demonstration [on October 17] began at nine thirty at the front of Commerce [home of the Business school] with twenty "well-groomed picketers," as the *Capital Times* described them, then grew to a hundred or so and "got progressively rowdier and gruffer." The number of participants waxed and waned over the next several hours, with late arrivals and people leaving for class. They marched in the autumn sunlight, in a loose loop, chanting rhythmically, "Down with Dow! Down with Dow!" and holding handmade signs.

"Dow's Malignant, Cut It Out," read one.

"Who Would Make A Bomb for a Buck? Dow," read another.

And "Vietnam for the Vietnamese."

And "Let's Get Out."

And "Stop the Bombing."

A few signs had no words, only pictures of napalm-ravaged Vietnamese civilians. One young man marched holding not a protest sign but his infant son. There was a table where students could sign up to ride the bus to Washington later in the week for the big national protest against the war. No effort was made to prevent students from going inside to be interviewed by Dow. . . .

Shortly before noon the demonstrators gathered for an hour of speeches. The audience stood on the cement plaza outside Commerce, looking up at the collection of campus speakers on the ridge to the east who were angling for position in front of a bullhorn. Someone held a sign above their heads: From Protest to Resistance . . .

Three poems were read in honor of the fallen Che Guevara. Up stepped sociology professor Maurice Zeitlin, a charismatic young sociologist, his hair neatly trimmed, wearing a coat and tie and cool dark shades. It was Zeitlin who had presented the losing motion to the faculty senate the previous spring that attempted to ban corporations with military ties from recruiting on campus. . . . Zeitlin now said that "we live in a sad time, because it is a time in which as Americans the transparency of our government's attempts to contain and crush the aspirations for democracy and social revolution abroad have become so clear. That's why we meet here. It is the United States government, under Democratic and Republican administrations alike, which has intervened, interfered, toppled democratic governments, destroyed democratic and reform administrations and prevented their fulfillment."

Next came a few brief denunciations of Dow and napalm, followed by an existentialist rap from [student Robert] Cohen. "Now we have the corporate structure," he said. "We have uni-processed students. You go to work for them. You bring home your bacon. Nine to five every day. Pay the mortgage. Let yourself up. You're a lawyer, doctor, teacher, what have you, and are now set to accept this society. What I'm saying is we've got to understand that society, we've got to analyze it, and indeed we've got to negate it. That society is keeping two-thirds of the people in the world in the Stone Age. It's keeping us from relating to one another as human beings. It's alienated us from ourselves.". . .

[Editor's note: The student activists decided to stage a sit-in on October 18 to prevent the Dow recruiter from interviewing students in the Commerce Building. University officials warned protesters that if they interfered with classes or prevented students from being interviewed, they faced arrest by the Madison city police and expulsion from the university. The students decided to stage a sit-in. They assumed that if they were arrested for nonviolent civil disobedience, the process would be routine and equally nonviolent on the part of the police. Early in the afternoon, University Chief of Security Ralph Hanson warned protesting students that if they did not end the sit-in immediately, they would be arrested.]

Hanson found his way out [of the building] and walked across the street to the police formation under the tower. He had given a final warning to the students, to no avail, he said. William Bablitch, the law student observer, had by then slipped outside to monitor the action and was standing near Hanson. He thought he heard Hanson say, "Let's take a crack at 'em." [Chief of Madison police Wilbur] Emory turned to his men and said, "All right, let's go and carry it out." Hanson, in civilian clothes and without a helmet, led the way back toward the front of Commerce, followed by Sergeant [Kenneth] Buss [of the Madison police force] and his men. . . .

Not more than two minutes after Hanson issued his final plea for the students to leave, here came Sergeant Buss and the wedge of cops, marching through the first set of glass doors. [Officer] Al Roehling, at Buss's flank, thought his state of mind was typical of the officers at that moment. He was, he said later, "full of piss and vinegar and ready to go." They reached the narrow vestibule, then moved through the second set of doors into the foyer. There was no space to gain footing, just a wall of people, and the human wall surged forward, pushing up against the oncoming force. The officers started flailing with their nightsticks but fell backwards into the vestibule. Chief Hanson was propelled "over and around bodies" and found himself "spilled outside the double doors." He could not get back inside and was unable to lead or control the police force for the next several minutes. Sergeant Buss braced himself with his feet and arms against the corner of a door in the vestibule and remained there. One officer stumbled against a floor-to-ceiling plate glass window, accidentally breaking it into jagged shards with his nightstick, a frightening sound that added to the panic of the moment. As people around him backed away, the officer kept swinging his club at the window frame, now apparently attempting to clear it of sharp edges of glass. Some in the crowd saw only the raised nightstick, assumed the police were on the attack, and started another surge forward in an attempt to keep them away. . . .

Inside, in the few minutes after the glass broke, there was an eerie silence. Then the police regrouped and reentered the foyer, this time without Hanson and with nightsticks raised. Once inside, they felt pressed against a wall, according to Buss, and then "really started using clubs.". . .

Jim Rowen and Susan McGovern, two-thirds of the way down the corridor, could see and hear this commotion at the other end. It was an eerie phenomenon, Rowen recalled, all noise and light moving their way, the screams of students and the lights of television cameras. And on top of this a sound Rowen had never heard before, one that he could not immediately place. Then, perhaps ten seconds later, he realized what it was—"the sound of people having their heads hit. It was like a basketball bouncing on the floor. Or hitting a watermelon with a baseball bat. It makes a sort of *thunk*." It all became clear to Rowen at that moment. "Civil disobedience wasn't working on our terms. They weren't arresting people, they were beating people. That's how they were clearing the hallway. Just going through like a machine and beating people." Tom Beckman, a business student from Whitefish Bay [Wisconsin], was taking a pop quiz at that moment in a classroom one floor above the melee. The door to the room was closed, but still Beckman and his classmates could hear it all. "We could hear kids being hit on the head with nightsticks. It was gut-wrenching. It sounded like somebody taking a two-by-four and slamming it on a table."

From his place amid the students halfway down the hallway, Jack Cipperly, the assistant dean of students, saw police helmets bobbing above the heads of the crowd and "nightsticks rising and falling, rising and falling." He heard "a series of cries emanate from the group" and tried to move forward toward the police to warn them that they were approaching an area occupied by many young women protesters. Cipperly pleaded with the officers to refrain from using their clubs. "At this point it must be explained that a certain amount of hysteria and panic was apparent with the group," he reported later. "In many cases the officers and the students appeared to be acting independently. Several curses were reciprocally exchanged between the police and the demonstrators. In my direct observation I witnessed many policemen who pulled students to their feet without using their nightsticks; at the same time, I witnessed individual policemen who struck students who were on the ground." Some cops were restrained, Cipperly said, but some were not. When he saw one officer wind up as though he were going to strike a young woman, Cipperly "grabbed him, like hockey players do." It turned out to be Jerry Gritsmacher, with whom Cipperly had gone to Catholic grade school and high school.

"Jerry, what are you doing?" Cipperly asked.

"Jack, what are *you* doing?" the officer responded.

As people in the hallway retreated, Michael Oberdorfer [a student], who had been sitting outside the [Dow] interview room, moved forward. He heard a woman screaming "Stop! Stop! I'm hurt! I'm hurt!" and moved toward the screams, finally reaching a young woman who was bent over, clutching her knees, sobbing. She had been clubbed in the abdomen and uterus. Oberdofer picked her up and carried her toward the foyer and the front entrance. He was enraged, acting on reflex, shouting madly as he moved through a phalanx of police clubs. *What the hell's wrong with you guys!*

Can't you see I'm trying to help someone who's hurt! He brought the young woman out the double doors, swinging his elbows furiously as he went, knocking an officer to the ground. . . .

In the heat of the confrontation, cops versus students, individual human beings tended to be seen only as representatives of a type, and the intense hatred on one type for the other now was overwhelming. But [student] John Pickart felt conflicting emotions. He was furious about the police attack, by their use of nightsticks . . . yet he was also disturbed by the mass psychology of the angry crowd. . . . "The policemen charged with their clubs. I left again. This time for good. I couldn't stand to see 2,000 people acting like animals. I still can't believe it, in my home town! On my university! It was terrible. I have never seen such hysteria and hatred in so large a group of people. On my way out, I looked back to see the whole crowd screaming 'Dirty Fascist Honky' at the police."

Questions for Discussion

1. How would you describe the attitudes of soldiers toward the war in Vietnam? How would you compare them to those who fought World War II?
2. What was the strategy behind search-and-destroy missions? How did the Viet Cong and North Vietnamese respond to it?
3. What are your impressions of the motives and values of the student antiwar activists? On balance, were their protests carefully planned or improvised? Was the war in Vietnam their only concern? What impact did the Civil Rights movement have on some antiwar activists?
4. The author describes attitudes of some young soldiers; he also describes the attitudes of some young war protesters. Taken together, how do these descriptions affect the impressions you had of young people in the 1960s?

For Further Reading

Terry Anderson, *The Movement and the Sixties* (1995); Christian Appy, *Working Class War: American Combat Soldiers and Vietnam* (1993), *Patriots: The Vietnam War Remembered from All Sides* (2004); Mark Atwood, *The Vietnam War* (2008); Loren Baritz, *Backfire* (1985); Dominick Cavallo, *A Fiction of the Past: The Sixties in American History* (1999); Robert Dalleck, *Flawed Giant: Lyndon Johnson and His Times* (1998); Charles DeBenedetti and Charles Chatfield, *An American Ordeal: The Antiwar Movement of the Vietnam Era* (1990); Gerald DeGroot, *A Noble Cause* (1999); Frances Fitzgerald, *Fire in the Lake: The Vietnamese and the Americans in Vietnam* (1971); Michael Foley, *Confronting the War Machine: Draft Resistance during the Vietnam War* (2003); Todd Gitlin, *The Sixties: Years of Hope, Days of Rage* (1987); David Halberstam, *The Best and the Brightest* (1973); William Hammond, *Reporting Vietnam: Media and Military at War* (1998); Michael Hunt, *Lyndon Johnson's War* (1996); Arnold Isaacs, *Vietnam Shadows* (1997); Maurice Isserman and Michael Kazin, *America Divided: The Civil War of the 1960s* (2000); Rhodri Jeffrey-Jones, *Peace Now!* (1999); Stanley Karnow, *Vietnam: A History*

(1997); Gabriel Kolko, *Anatomy of a War* (1985); Michael Lanning, *The Only War We Had: A Platoon Leader's Journal of Vietnam* (2007); Michael Lind, *Vietnam: The Necessary War* (1999); Robert Mann, *The Grand Delusion: America's Descent into Vietnam* (2001); Bao Ninh, *The Sorrow of War* (1996); W. J. Rorabaugh, *Berkeley at War* (1989); Neil Sheehan, *A Bright Shinning Lie* (1989); Tom Wells, *The War Within: America's Battle over Vietnam* (1994); Marilyn Young, *The Vietnam Wars* (1991), Young et al., *The Vietnam War: A History in Documents* (2003).

16

The Women's Movement

Ruth Rosen

Like the rebellion of young people, the women's movement of the 1960s and 1970s surprised most Americans and shocked many others. And as Ruth Rosen points out in the next essay, just as the youth rebellion was split between political radicals (New Left campus critics of the Vietnam War and American society) and cultural radicals (hippies and others), the women's movement was divided into "liberal" and "radical" factions. One of the strengths of Rosen's essay is that she shows how the views of radical and liberal feminists complemented as well as opposed one another. Together, the feminism they pioneered—rooted for most in their personal experiences—transformed gender relations in the public arena, from the courtroom and the legislature, to the workplace and the media, as well as in the home.

In the years following World War II, there was a revival of nineteenth-century gender roles. By the early 1950s, the ideal family—portrayed in the media and elsewhere as white, middle class, and suburban—consisted of a husband/father/breadwinner and a stay-at-home wife/mother/homemaker. After fifteen years of economic depression and war, Americans were determined to immerse themselves in the stability and security they associated with family life. Clergy; politicians; magazines such as *Ladies' Home Journal* and *McCall's* (where the phrase "family togetherness" was coined in 1954); and television programs such as *Ozzie and Harriet*, *Father Knows Best*, and *The Donna Reed Show* portrayed the suburban middle-class family as a haven of love and affluence. Parents never raised their voices and they did not divorce. Men did not experience stress at work, and children were well adjusted.

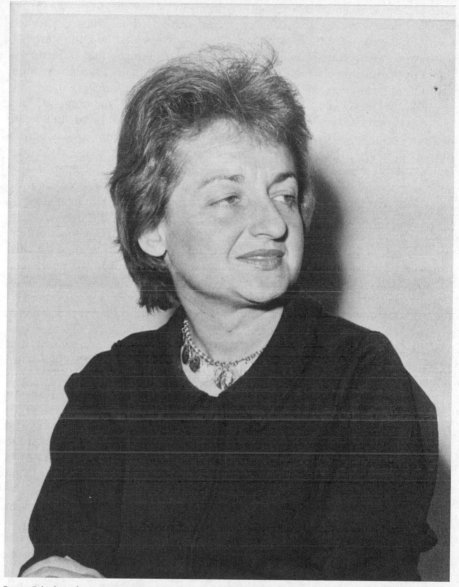

Betty Friedan, founder of the National Organization for Women, in the early 1960s. What were the main causes of friction between "liberal" feminists like Friedan and younger "radicals" in the women's liberation movement?

Most of all, mothers were always understanding, always comforting, always there with a smile.

In her 1963 bestselling book, *The Feminine Mystique*, Betty Friedan presented a very different picture of the suburban housewife's lot. Friedan argued that in devoting themselves entirely to raising children and maintaining the home, these women were leading frustrated lives of secluded desperation. Friedan did not suggest there was anything wrong with marriage or motherhood; on the contrary, for most women they were essential to a fulfilling life. But, she claimed, women should also have the same educational and employment opportunities as men. There was no reason, said Friedan, women should not enjoy both fulfilling marriages and rewarding careers.

When *The Feminine Mystique* was published in 1963, most upscale bars and restaurants in New York City would not serve women unless they were escorted by men. Many colleges either barred women from graduate programs in medicine, law, economics, engineering, and the sciences or had quotas that limited their admission. "Help Wanted" notices in newspapers had separate columns for male jobs (the ones that paid well) and female jobs. School teaching was one of the few professions open to women—unless they became pregnant, in which case they could be fired, even if they were married, as most were. There were no female airline pilots, construction workers, firefighters, or bus drivers. A married woman could not get a credit card unless her husband co-signed the application. Even when a woman managed to break into a profession usually reserved for men, the "glass ceiling" hung low. In 1960, Felix Frankfurter, a liberal Supreme Court justice appointed by Franklin Roosevelt, rejected a woman who applied for one of his clerkships. She graduated first in her class at Columbia University. But Frankfurter, who was dedicated to equal rights for minorities, did not think women should work in the Supreme Court. Thirty years later, the rejected applicant, Ruth Bader Ginsburg, would be appointed as a justice to the Court.

In 1967, Friedan and others founded the National Organization for Women (NOW). NOW's purpose was to lobby state and federal governments to enact laws guaranteeing women equal access to education and employment opportunities. The NOW "Bill of Rights" demanded an end to sex discrimination in employment. It called for government-funded child day care for working mothers, passage of the Equal Rights Amendment, and the "right of women to control their reproductive lives."

As Rosen points out, NOW's support of equal opportunity—such as equal pay for equal work—was well within the American liberal mainstream. But by the late 1960s, younger feminists, many of whom had been involved in the New Left, antiwar, and Civil Rights movements, developed a radical feminist perspective. They did not assume marriage (which some of them called "legalized rape") and motherhood were necessary for a rewarding life. Instead of seeking to "integrate" women into the American mainstream, radical women sought to "liberate" women from it. For most radical feminists, by definition the family, heterosexuality, and established political and economic systems were male-dominated, patriarchal institutions. Radical women raised issues feminist liberals mostly avoided, including lesbianism, abortion, and violence toward women.

When the women's liberation movement surfaced in the late 1960s, most states would not pursue rape cases unless there was at least one corroborating witness. Judges were often required to tell juries in these cases that "rape is the easiest charge to make and the most difficult to prove." In one state, North Carolina, only virgins could claim to have been raped. A husband who raped his wife anywhere in the United States could not be prosecuted (hence the radical's charge that marriage was "legalized rape"). There were no rape crisis hotlines. "Sexual harassment" did not exist as a legal term, and women were routinely exposed to it on the job and in the street. Abortion was illegal. Psychiatrists and psychologists usually blamed "frigid" wives when couples experienced unsatisfactory sex lives.

Radical feminists also protested stereotypical views of female beauty (in 1968 they disrupted the Miss America Beauty Pageant); media views of women as sex objects (female students at Grinnell College in Iowa staged a "nude-in" to protest the presence on campus of a *Playboy* magazine representative); and the ogling, suggestive remarks and groping they were subjected to in the streets (New York City feminists conducted a "whistle-in" aimed at men working at a construction site).

The women's movement, whether liberal or radical, did not speak for all women. The movement was overwhelmingly white and middle class. It largely ignored the experiences and needs of minority, poor, and white working-class women. These women had *always* worked—because they had to. Nor did they have the educational opportunities of white feminists, most of whom had attended elite colleges and universities. Friedan, for example, was a graduate of Smith College. During the 1960s and 1970s, tens of thousands of poor Puerto Rican, Native American, and African American women were subjected to forced sterilizations because they were welfare recipients. Most of the operations were funded by the federal government. For these women, demands for "birth control" and "reproductive rights" might have meant something very different than it did for white, middle-class feminists.

Yet, as Rosen shows in the next essay, the modern women's movement was a full-scale assault on post–World War II gender roles. Its legacies remain both pervasive and controversial.

Source: Ruth Rosen, *The World Split Open: How the Modern Women's Movement Changed America* (New York: Viking Press, 2000), pp. 71–79, 84–93.

After President Kennedy's assassination in November 1963, Congress began considering the comprehensive civil rights bill. Congressman "Judge" Howard Smith, the southern chairman of the House Rules Committee, offered an amendment to add "sex" to Title VII, the section of the bill that prohibited discrimination in employment on the basis of race, color, religion, or national origin by private employers. A longtime supporter of the Equal Rights Amendment, as well as an ardent segregationist, Smith saw his amendment as purely a win-win proposition. A prohibition on sex discrimination would give northern representatives a reason to vote against the act without the accusation of being racists. And if it passed, at least he wanted to be sure that "white women" would be the beneficiaries.

At first, Smith's colleagues did not even take the amendment seriously. In an excessive display of chivalric oratory, Smith regaled the House [of Representatives] with a letter from a woman who complained of the paucity of men available as husbands. Playing for laughs, he asked the House to take their "real grievances" seriously. The House erupted in riotous laughter. Emmanuel Celler, the liberal New York chairman of the Judiciary Committee, added to the jocular spirit when he announced that it was he—never his wife—who always had the last two words in his household, and those words were "yes, dear."

When the laughter subsided, coalitions began forming for and against Smith's amendment. Prodded by the Virginia members of the National Women's Party—never known for its progressive views on race—these women now turned to Smith as a natural ally. Democratic representative Edith Green, the sponsor of the 1963 Equal Pay Act [which required equal pay for women who did the same work as men], worried that the amendment would gather opposition to the civil rights bill and risk African-Americans' chance to win their civil rights. She decided to vote against Smith's amendment. On the other hand, yes votes came from those representatives who had decided they would not endure another "Negro hour"—the post–Civil War moment when suffrage was granted to black men [the Fifteenth Amendment], but not to black or white women. Representative Martha Griffiths, a Republican who had long sought to include a prohibition on sex discrimination in the civil rights bill, helped forge a bizarre coalition of southern congressmen and their feminist supporters who seized the unexpected opportunity. The amendment passed. . . .

Nearly every American social movement can point to some specific legal victory that decisively raised their members' sense of entitlement. For black Americans, it was *Brown v. Board of Education of Topeka*, the 1954 Supreme Court ruling against "separate but equal" education. For the women's movement, it was Title VII of the 1964 Civil Rights Act. The legislation created a new agency, the Equal Employment Opportunity Commission (EEOC), charged with investigating complaints of racial and sexual discrimination. But women quickly discovered that its director, Herman Edelsberg, considered sex discrimination a joke, or at least a distraction from the more important work of assisting black men. Edelsberg called Title VII "a fluke conceived out of wedlock." "There are people on this commission," he informed the press, "who think that no man should be required to have a male secretary and I am one of them." When it was signed into law at the White House ceremony, no women were present, and the *New York Times* account of the bill did not even mention that the new legislation prohibited sex discrimination in employment.

When someone at a White House Conference on Equal Opportunity openly wondered if Playboy clubs would no have to employ male "bunnies," the press quickly picked up the joke and dubbed the sex amendment the "Bunny Law." A *New York Times* editorial coyly suggested that

> Federal officials may find it would have been better if Congress had just abolished sex itself. Handyman must disappear from the language; he was pretty much a goner anyway, if you started looking for one in desperation. No more milkman, iceman, serviceman, foreman or pressman. The Rockettes may become bi-sexual, and a pity, too. Bunny problem, indeed! This is revolution, chaos. You can't even safely advertise for a wife anymore.

Title VII remained a joke. In August 1965, the EEOC shocked women activists when it ruled that sex-segregated help-wanted ads were perfectly legal. The *New Republic*, a liberal journal of opinion, agreed. "Why should a mischievous joke perpetrated on the floor of the House of Representatives be treated by a responsible administration body with this kind of seriousness?" The idea of banishing sex discrimination challenged deeply held ideas about gender and elicited much nervous ridicule. The *Wall Street Journal* asked its readers to imagine "a shapeless, knobby-kneed male 'bunny' serving drinks to a group of astonished businessmen or a 'matronly vice president' lusting after her male secretary.". . .

Nonetheless, by 1965, working women began flooding the EEOC with their grievances. In some parts of the country, nearly half the complaints came from working women who identified acts of discrimination. Shocked by the volume of these grievances, the EEOC nevertheless remained committed to monitoring only racial discrimination. Mired in the Vietnam War and unsettled by race riots in American cities, neither President [Lyndon] Johnson nor Congress gave women's complaints any attention. On June 20, 1966, Representative Martha Griffiths, a tireless fighter for women's rights, denounced the EEOC for its "specious, negative, and arrogant" attitude toward sex discrimination. "I would remind them," she announced on the floor of Congress, "that they took an oath to uphold the law, not just the part of it that they are interested in."

No one seemed to care—except members of the [EEOC] state commissions who had convened for their third annual conference in Washington, D.C., ten days after Griffiths attacked the EEOC. Within their respective states, the commissions had supported more flexible working hours, the repeal of discriminatory laws, equal pay, and dozens of other "women's issues." The state commissions had also created a national network of women who, by gathering and sharing data about women in their respective states, had gained expert knowledge about women's subordinate status in American society. But by themselves, as delegates to the third conference on state commissions, they were almost powerless. As Betty Friedan later noted, "It is more than a historical fluke that the organization of the women's movement was ignited by that law, never meant to be enforced, against sex discrimination in employment."

THE NATIONAL ORGANIZATION FOR WOMEN

They did have one vital resource to call on—what Betty Friedan called "an underground feminist movement" that existed in the nation's capital. Friedan was in constant contact with women who risked their government jobs to promote women's issues in the nation's capital. . . . Frustrated by the government's unwillingness to influence the EEOC and angered by the EEOC's unwillingness to address sex discrimination—especially sex-segregated "want ads"—fifteen women finally agreed to meet one evening during the [1966 EEOC state commission's conference] in Friedan's hotel room to discuss the possibility of starting a new women's organization. . . .

At the [EEOC] conference the next day, a group of delegates presented a resolution insisting that the EEOC enforce Title VII of the Civil Rights Act. Conference officials, worried about pressuring the Johnson administration, refused to allow the resolution to come to a vote. The delegates, from various state commissions, grew furious. They were tired of talk; they wanted action.

At lunch, a group hastily gathered around two tables to discuss their next move. Time was running out, because, as Friedan later explained, "most of us had plane reservations that afternoon, when the conference ended, and had to get back in time to make dinner for their families." In conspiratorial fashion, they whispered, passed around notes on paper napkins, and discussed forming a new organization. On one of those paper napkins, Friedan wrote down a name—the National Organization for Women. Its purpose, she scribbled, would be "to take the actions needed to bring women into the mainstream of American society, now" and to fight for "full equality for women, in full equally partnership with men." As they left to catch their planes, the conspirators agreed to call a formal meeting to create the new organization that fall. . . .

By creating a feminist civil rights organization, NOW members did more than assert their independence from male-dominated liberal politics; they publicly acknowledged that liberal political culture was inadequate to address the reality of women's lives. By declaring their autonomy from a liberal government, they also freed themselves to consider the question of women's rights from a more radical perspective. "Everything was different," Friedan recalled. "The problems *looked* different, the definition of the problems, the solutions sought, once we dared to judge our conditions as women by that simple standard, the hallmark of American democracy—equality, no more, no less." As she drafted a "Statement of Purpose" for NOW, Friedan found herself "forced to spell out in my own mind the implications of 'equality for women.'" One thing was certain, "separate but equal" was out of the question. How should one define equality and liberty for modern women? . . .

Like most activists of the time, Friedan shunned arguments based on difference [between the sexes]. "The time has come," she wrote, "to confront, with concrete actions, the conditions that now prevent women from enjoying the equality of opportunity and freedom of choice which is their right, as individual Americans, and as human beings." Friedan recognized

American women's right to shape their own lives as well as their right to self-fulfillment. These values, she explained, were "simply the values of the American Revolution . . . applied to women." "The logic," Friedan wrote, "was inexorable."

> Once we broke through that feminine mystique and called our-selves human—no more, no less—surely we were entitled to the enjoyment of the values which were our American, democratic human right. All we had to do was really look at the concrete con-ditions of our daily life in the light of those lofty values of equality which are supposed to be every man's birthright—and we could immediately see how unfair, how oppressive, our situation was.

But that wasn't possible without challenging many fundamental aspects of liberal political culture. Women's rights, as it turned out, were not just another ingredient you could add and stir into the American Dream. The citizen whose rights the state protected had always been imagined as a man, and his biological and work lives were dramatically different from those experienced by a woman. The right to pursue happiness, for example, took on new meaning when it included a woman's right to control her own body and reproductive future. Equal opportunity meant something quite different when it involved sharing domestic work, ending sexual harassment in the workplace, and ending all forms of violence against women. When applied to women, individual rights, which most Americans considered the touch-stone of American political culture, turned out to threaten men's authority in the family and challenge all kinds of social and cultural traditions. It was not at all clear—to many women and men—that these were "individual rights" that the state should consider protecting. For liberal political culture to recast the citizen as a woman and embrace fundamental economic and social trans-formations in the home and the workplace required nothing less than an ex-pansion of the definition of democracy.

In 1966, the radicalism of this challenge to American political culture was not yet fully grasped by Betty Friedan, by young feminists in the women's lib-eration movement, nor even by their opponents. Although feminists would long debate whether to emphasize women's difference from or similarity to men, neither choice fully embraced the reality of women's lives. Women were both like and unlike men. Any society that didn't honor a woman's ability to bear and raise children was clearly violating their rights to fully participate in society. Any society that equated equality with women living as men could not be viewed as a genuine democracy. A true "gender democracy" would have to honor the life of the family as much as it honored the life of work. Men would no longer be the frame of reference. But nor would women. The revolutionary thrust of feminism required an extensive expansion of democracy at work, in the home, in public, in private. Nothing less would do.

On October 29, 1966, NOW convened its official founding conference in Washington, D.C. . . . NOW's "Statement of Purpose" declared that women's demands for equality were "part of the world-wide revolution of human rights now taking place within and beyond our national borders." The writers were determined to avoid the kind of separatism just then emerging in black activist organizations, so the first sentence of the "Statement" began, "We men and women," and called for "a fully equal partnership of the sexes." . . .

NOW's statement challenged American society to heed women's grievances. One of those issues was that despite the optimistic social programs of Kennedy's New Frontier and Johnson's Great Society, the economic status of women had actually declined. By 1966, the wages of full-time year-round women workers averaged only 60 percent of those of men, a drop of 3.6 percent in a decade. Black women, burdened by the double discrimination of sex and race, earned even less. In addition, although 46.4 percent of American adult women now worked, 75 percent of them labored in routine clerical, sales, or factory jobs or as household workers, cleaning women, and hospital attendants.

In all the professions, women were also losing ground. Though they constituted 53 percent of the population, they represented less than 1 percent of federal judges, less than 4 percent of lawyers, and only 7 percent of doctors. In addition, since World War II, men had been replacing women in professions once considered "women's fields"—as administrators of secondary and elementary schools, librarians, and social workers. This hidden and "dangerous decline," NOW's "Statement" declared, had to be "recognized and reversed by 'the power of American law' [and the] protection guaranteed by the U.S. Constitution to the civil rights of all individuals." . . .

The "Statement" pointedly criticized the United States for lagging behind other industrialized countries in providing the kinds of social welfare—health care, child care, and pregnancy leave—that supported women's domestic and work needs. Women "should not have to choose between family life and participation in industry or the professions." . . .

Contrary to later accusations that feminists ignored the issue of child-rearing and denied women the choice of remaining full-time mothers, NOW's "Statement" called for a nationwide network of child care centers, as well as programs to provide retraining, after their children grew up, "for women who have chosen to care for their own children full-time." The "Statement" also urged recasting traditional gender roles within marriage, proposing that "a true partnership between the sexes demands a different concept of marriage, an equitable sharing of the responsibilities of home and children and of the economic burden of their support."

CONFLICT WITHIN THE WOMEN'S MOVEMENT

A certain wilder spirit of protest began to enter NOW, thanks in part to younger women who by 1967 were creating loosely affiliated small groups collectively known as the women's liberation movement. Though NOW and women's liberation groups often joined forces for specific protests, efforts to form coalitions between the two branches of the movement frequently failed. The demons that haunted the daughters of the fifties never fully disappeared. Meredith Tax, an early activist, realized how much the female generation gap influenced the culture of the young women's liberation movement:

> My friends and I thought of NOW as an organization for people our mother's age. We were movement girls, not career women; NOW's demands and organizational style weren't radical enough for us. We wanted to build a just society, not get a bigger slice of the pie. Besides, we were generational sectarians; we didn't trust anyone over thirty.

Influenced by the anti-hierarchical spirit of New Left groups, as well as by the theatrical thrust of the counterculture, the younger women's liberation movement was not particularly concerned with proving their respectability; on the contrary, they wanted to shake things up as much as possible. . . .

The "Valerie Solanas affair" intensified some of the conflicts between older and younger feminists in New York's NOW, where tensions were already high. In 1968, a disturbed artist in New York's avant-garde art scene wrote—by herself—a document she called the "SCUM Manifesto," an acronym for the Society for Cutting Up Men. Her manifesto not only blamed men for every evil in the world, but also argued for their collective annihilation. Shortly afterward, Solanas shot and wounded pop artist Andy Warhol, whom she blamed for her own marginality. She was arraigned for attempted murder and consigned to psychiatric observation.

A few younger feminists turned Solanas into a cause celebre; others viewed her as a disturbed women in need of sisterly assistance. When Ti-Grace Atkinson, the president of New York NOW, publicly appeared at Solanas's trial, some NOW members worried about being identified with "man-hating" women. NOW's board [of directors] consisted of university professors and administrators, state and national labor union officers, local and federal government officials, business executives, physicians, and members of religious orders, all of whom were dedicated to preserving NOW's public reputation and credibility. Atkinson, already dissatisfied with what she considered NOW's "elitist" structure, then resigned to form her own organization, the October 17th Movement (named after the day she left), later renamed "The Feminists."

Collisions between the women's liberation movement and NOW were frequent and probably inevitable. In November 1969, a year not remembered for youthful deference, NOW attempted to gather disparate groups from the mushrooming women's movement at a Congress to Unite Women in New York City. For three days, over five hundred women from a wide range of groups and organizations debated feminist issues, but it was clear that the young women dominated the agenda and that their rebellious spirit ruled the meeting. Betty Friedan, for instance, would never have convened a workshop to discuss "whether women's liberation would end sex or make it better." As she later wrote:

> I didn't think a thousand vibrators would make much difference— or that it mattered who was in the missionary position—if unequal power positions in real life weren't changed. It was the *economic* imbalance, the power imbalance in the world that subverted sex, or made sex itself into a power game where no one could win. . . .

In the first evening, a group of women from Boston's Female Liberation took the stage and formed a semicircle around one woman who proceeded to cut off the luxurious long hair of another. Wearing short hair, the women explained to the audience, was a rejection of the conventional feminine image cultivated by society. The audience was electrified. Some women shouted that they shouldn't cut their hair, that long hair was lovely and countercultural. Other women denounced the image of the long-haired, hip, radical movement "chick."

Betty Friedan looked on in horror. To her, the hair-cutting demonstration perfectly captured the differences that separated NOW from the women's liberation movement. To Friedan, as to most other NOW members, the highest priority was to change social policy and to eliminate legal sex discrimination. After women gained economic independence, NOW members reasoned, they would have the power to make changes in their private lives as well.

To older women, transforming oneself was not, by itself, a political act. Friedan loathed "the abusive language and style of some of the women, their sexual shock tactics and [their] man-hating, down-with-motherhood stance." Their message, she argued, "was to *make yourself ugly*, to stop shaving under your arms, to stop wearing makeup or pretty dresses—any skirts at all. . . .

Despite NOW's determination to maintain its respectability, the women's liberation movement continually nudged the organization in new directions. Initially, NOW scorned the idea of consciousness-raising, arguing that feminism was about action, not talking. But as new women entered the organization, unfamiliar with politics of any sort, let alone feminism, older members discovered that "rap groups" helped such novices "catch up" on movement issues.

The truth is, both branches of the movement were essential. NOW activists promoted leadership and the organizing skills that made them effective lobbyists, organizers, and strategists. They also provided the modern women's movement with the staying power it needed to withstand backlash after backlash. . . . Some younger liberationists characterized NOW as "liberal" or "reformist," an organization that merely wanted a piece of the pie, rather than entirely new ingredients. But it is much too simple to categorize these two branches of the new women's movement as liberal versus radical, or legislative versus revolutionary. NOW's struggle for equal opportunity, especially in employment and education, required a *collective* solution to individual women's problems. . . .

Young feminists contributed something equally important—a radical critique of patriarchal culture, visions of alternative lifestyles, and the unmasking of the hidden injuries women had suffered. Although they generally chose to work outside established institutions, they created a network or alternative, grassroots, self-help, nonprofit services—rape crisis centers and battered women's shelters, for example—that eventually became established institutions themselves. Sometimes the injuries these younger women unmasked changed laws; sometimes NOW's legislative efforts altered the nation's consciousness. In many ways, the differences were really about the targets and the style in which the struggle was waged. At times, ideological or generational differences bitterly divided feminists, but neither branch of the movement, by itself, could have brought about the staggering changes that swept through American culture during the remaining decades of the twentieth century. . . .

In 1972, Congress quickly passed the Equal Rights Amendment and sent it to the states for what many assumed would be a quick ratification. In the same year, Congress passed Title IX of the Education Amendments of 1972, which denied funds for men's sports unless an equal amount were provided for girls' and women's sports, a piece of legislation that instantly altered women's relationship to athletics and sports. In the same year, *Ms.* Magazine made its debut; women for the first time became floor reporters at political conventions; the Equal Pay Act was extended to cover administrative, executive, and professional personnel; NOW and the Urban League filed a class action suit against General Mills for sex and race discrimination; NOW initiated action against sexism in elementary-school textbooks with *Dick and Jane as Victims;* and women theologians called for the "castration of sexist religions" at the largest and most prestigious gathering of biblical scholars in history.

One year later, in 1973, the Supreme Court ruled in *Roe v. Wade* that abortion was constitutionally protected by a woman's right to privacy; Billie Jean King beat Bobby Riggs in a much-hyped "Battle of the Sexes" tennis game; AT&T signed the largest job sex discrimination settlement—$38 million—in the nation's history; the U.S. Printing Office agreed to accept "Ms." as an optional title for women. . . .

In 1974, approximately one thousand colleges and universities offered women's studies courses; the steel industry settled a sex discrimination suit that gave $56 million in back pay and wage adjustments to 386,000 women workers; Congress passed the Equal Credit Opportunity Act, which allowed married women, for the first time, to obtain credit in their own names, and the Educational Equity Act, designed to eliminate sexist curricula and achieve equity for all students regardless of sex; and Helen Thomas, after covering the White House for thirty years, became the first woman to be named a White House reporter.

So many successes in so few years. Yet, the speed of change masked a strong strain of resistance that grew alongside the women's movement. Signs of an instant backlash appeared everywhere. After the election of Richard Nixon in 1968, legal challenges met stiffer resistance from a Republican administration. It was not until 1970, for example, that the Justice Department actually pressed its first sex discrimination case. In 1970, former vice president Hubert Humphrey's personal physician, Dr. Edgar Berman, sparked a fierce national debate when he announced that women were unfit for the presidency because they might be "subject to curious mental aberrations." In the same year, the Catholic Church established the National Right to Life Committee to block liberalization of abortion laws; [Protestant evangelist] Billy Graham called feminism "an echo of our overall philosophy of permissiveness.". . .

AUGUST 26, 1970: THE WOMEN'S STRIKE

To commemorate the fiftieth anniversary of the ratification of the women's suffrage amendment (August 26, 1920), Friedan called for a national "Women's Strike for Equality." Although she hoped women would abstain from their usual work, Friedan viewed the strike as a symbolic gesture. Word went out that local chapters should decide how to participate in the "strike." After considerable squabbling, feminists finally agreed upon three central demands: the right to abortion, the right to child care, and equal opportunity in employment and education. (Radical feminists, however, carried banners demanding "free abortion on demand and 24-hour child care centers.")

Here, then, were the core demands of the feminist revolution in 1970. Riding high on a string of legal victories and widely publicized demonstrations, for twenty-four hours feminists laid aside their factional differences and mounted the largest women's demonstrations held since the suffrage movement. In cities and towns across the country, women marched, picketed, protested, held teach-ins and rallies, and produced skits and plays. Some women actually refused to work. A common poster urged, "Don't Cook Dinner—Starve a Rat Today." Another reminded women, "Don't Iron While the Strike is Hot.". . .

The 1970 Women's Strike was a stunning success. In the months to come, NOW's ranks swelled by 50 percent. Many feminists remembered the day as a peak experience in their lives. Across the nation, feminists in coastal cities, as well as those in the heartland, no longer felt isolated. Unity, if only achieved for a day, filled participants with exhilaration. For a brief moment, the banners "Sisterhood is Powerful" and "Women of the World Unite" seemed to describe the future. At the end of the day's whirlwind events,

Betty Friedan's keynote speech solemnly expressed the spiritual transformation many women experienced that day:

> In the religion of my ancestors, there was a prayer that Jewish men said every morning. They prayed, "Thank Thee, Lord, that I was not born a woman." Today I feel, feel for the first time, feel absolutely sure that all women are going to be able to say, as I say tonight: "Thank thee, Lord, that I was born a woman, for this day."

Questions for Discussion

1. What was Title VII of the 1964 Civil Rights Act? Why was it proposed? Why did the press and others at the time refer to Title VII as the "Bunny Law"? What role did it play in the emerging women's movement?
2. Describe the goals and strategies of the National Organization for Women. How did it propose to change the legal and occupational status of women?
3. What were the most important disagreements between Betty Friedan's "liberal" and "radical" feminists? According to the author, how did the two points of view complement one another?
4. What were the most important long-range consequences of the modern women's movement?

For Further Reading

Susan Brownmiller, *In Our Time: Memoir of a Revolution* (1999); Nancy Cott, *The Grounding of Modern Feminism* (1989); Barbara Crow, *Radical Feminism: A Documentary Reader* (2000); Alice Echols, *Daring to Be Bad: Radical Feminism in America, 1967–75* (1990); Barbara Ehrenreich, *Hearts of Men* (1983); Sara Evans, *Born for Liberty* (1997), *Personal Politics* (1983); Peter Filene, *Him/Her/Self: Gender Identities in Modern America*, 3rd ed. (1998); Estelle Freedman, *No Turning Back: The History of Feminism and the Future of Women* (2003); Betty Friedan, *Fountain of Age* (2006), *The Feminine Mystique* (1963); Stacy Gillis, Gillian Howe, and Rebecca Munford, eds., *Third Wave Feminism*, 2nd ed. (2007); bell hooks, *Feminism Is for Everybody* (2000), *Ain't I a Woman: Black Women and Feminism* (1999); Daniel Horowitz, *Betty Friedan and the Making of the Feminine Mystique* (2000); Alice Kessler-Harris, *In Pursuit of Equity: Women, Men, and the Quest for Economic Citizenship in 20th Century America* (2003); Robin Morgan, *The Word of a Woman: Feminist Dispatches*, 2nd ed. (1994); Susan Oliver, *Betty Friedan: The Personal Is Political* (2007); Ruth Rosen, *The World Split Open*, rev. ed. (2006); Benita Roth, *Separate Roads to Feminism: Black, Chicana, and White Feminist Movements in America's Second Wave* (2003); Vicki Ruiz, ed., *Unequal Sisters: A Multicultural Reader in U.S. Women's History* (1999).

Against the Women's Movement

The Defeat of the Equal Rights Amendment and the Rise of the New Right

Donald T. Critchlow

By the mid-1970s, a massive backlash against the various protest and liberation movements of the 1960s gathered steam. Eventually the backlash coalesced into a new and dynamic conservative movement, a "New Right" or "Religious Right," as it was variously called. It would dominate the Republican Party and much of American political life into the twenty-first century.

There were multiple reasons for the backlash. Many whites resented the Civil Rights and Black Power movements. Also, most people were outraged by the antiwar movement, which they felt was unpatriotic. They were equally disturbed by long-haired young hippies and the provocative flaunting of their sexuality, their raucous music, their public displays of drug use, and their obvious rejection of the American work ethic. In addition, there were widespread fears about the future of the family. Millions of Americans, many of them women and most of them religious, placed much of the blame for what they called the "decline" of the family on the women's movement.

For years, conservative Roman Catholics and fundamentalist Protestants had been disturbed by secular trends in American society. A Supreme Court decision banning prayer in public schools was deeply offensive to many,

According to the author, why did many women oppose the Equal Rights Amendment and how did their opposition help create a new conservative movement?

especially fundamentalist Protestants; so were the Court's decisions that required the teaching of evolutionary theory in high school biology classes. But nothing stirred those with deeply felt, powerful, and personal religious beliefs to action more than their fears about the family's decline.

In 1970 California became the first state to pass a "no-fault" divorce law (supported by many feminists), which made divorce relatively easy to obtain. Most states followed suit, and by 1980 the rate of divorce had doubled. Many social conservatives placed the blame for the surging divorce trend on the sexual hedonism of the 1960s counterculture and the antimarriage rhetoric of radical feminists. The feminist demand for "reproductive rights" became explosive in 1973, when the Supreme Court declared most abortions legal in the landmark *Roe v. Wade* case. By the late 1970s, the abortion rate in the United States was four for every ten live births, perhaps the highest in the nation's history.

Religious conservatives responded to *Roe* by organizing groups such as Focus on the Family (1977), which opposed abortion and sex education in public schools, and the Moral Majority (1979), which claimed to be "pro-life, pro-family, pro-morality, and pro-American." There was a cluster of related issues that bothered religious conservatives, most of them dealing with sex. They included easy access to the birth control pill, which effectively divorced sex from procreation; the enormous popularity and profitability of the pornography industry; the prevalence of sexual imagery in advertising and the media; a blossoming gay rights movement, including the demand by some gays for the legalization of same-sex marriage; and the steady increase of households composed of unmarried couples.

In the next essay, Donald Critchlow describes an opening salvo in the "culture war"—the battle between religious and social conservatives on one side and secular and women's rights groups on the other—that continues to this day. The focus of Critchlow's essay is opposition to the Equal Rights Amendment (ERA). The amendment, first proposed in the 1920s, had gathered dust in Congress for a half-century. In 1972, at the behest of feminists, Congress passed the ERA by wide majorities. The proposed amendment contained a single sentence: "Equality of rights under the law shall not be denied or abridged by the United States, or by any State, on account of sex." By 1977, with the feminist movement still a powerful force, it was approved by thirty-five of the thirty-eight states necessary for ratification. It seemed certain that ERA would become part of the Constitution.

Critchlow shows how a relatively unknown midwestern anticommunist crusader, Phyllis Schlafly, became the leader of the anti-ERA forces. Schlafly was an attorney, a mother of six, and a devout Roman Catholic. She was also an extremely astute organizer and articulate polemicist. Schlafly worked with antifeminist allies like Beverly LaHaye, founder of the "pro-family" organization Concerned Women of America. But more than anyone else, Schlafly led the battle against the ERA in the 1970s by organizing antifeminist women around the country. In the process, she helped lay the foundation for rise of the Religious Right. The ERA was defeated in 1982.

Source: Donald T. Critchlow, *Phyllis Schlafly and Grassroots Conservatism* © 2005 by Donald T. Critchlow. Published by Princeton University Press. Reprinted by permission of Princeton University Press.

After [President Richard] Nixon resigned from office, the Republican party stood arguably at its lowest point in its 120-year history, even lower than when [President Herbert] Hoover left office in 1933. In 1974, only 18 percent of voters identified themselves as Republican. Yet within six years, many voters came to see the GOP not as a party of big business and the wealthy, but as a party of the little guy, the regular American Joe and his wife, while the Democratic party belonged to elitists who imposed schemes for social engineering, social privilege, and special interest—all at the expense of the hard-working middle-class. The catalyst for this transformation was found in the grassroots reaction against feminism, legalized abortion, ERA [Equal Rights Amendment], and the ban on prayer in school. Writing after the ERA had been lost, feminist Sylvia Ann Hewlett observed, "It is sobering to realize that the ERA was defeated not by Barry Goldwater, Jerry Falwell, or any combination of male chauvinist pigs, but by women who were alienated from a feminist movement the values of which seemed elitist and disconnected from the lives of ordinary people."

When ERA passed Congress in 1972, nobody expected it would have such strange political repercussions or become the epicenter of a political earthquake. The proposed amendment made its first appearance in Congress soon after the adoption of the Nineteenth Amendment enfranchising women in 1920. In July 1923 the ERA was unanimously endorsed by the National Women's Party at a convention in Seneca Falls, New York, but feminists divided over the amendment because some feminists, such as the National Consumer League's Florence Kelley, believed it would undermine legislation protecting female workers. The amendment gained momentum when the 1940 Republican platform endorsed the ERA, and four years later the Democratic party platform endorsed the ERA. When reintroduced in Congress in 1947, support for the ERA extended across party lines. . . .

In 1947, opposition arose immediately to the proposed amendment from conservative women's groups, a point sometimes neglected by historians who have tended to look only at divisions within the feminist movement. Representative James Wadsworth's office, for example, received many petitions and letters from women in his state [New York] opposing the ERA. Many of the arguments raised would be echoed in the 1970s. . . . Typical of this opposition was Cecilia Yawman, representing the Rochester Diocesan Council of Catholic Women, who wrote Wadsworth that 20,000 Catholic women in her city opposed ERA because "great danger lies in it. We do not confuse equal rights with identical rights.". . .

The emergence of a new women's movement in the late 1960s imparted new life to the ERA. In October 1967 the newly formed National Organization for Women (NOW) voted overwhelmingly to endorse the Equal Rights Amendment. . . . On August 10, 1970, after only one hour of debate, the House [of Representatives] approved the amendment by a vote of 352 to 15. . . . [On March 22, 1972,] the ERA passed the Senate by 84 to 8. Congress granted seven years for the amendment to be ratified by three-fourths of the states. Then on January 22, 1973, the U.S. Supreme Court legalized abortion, a decision that was to have profound implications in debates over women's rights in the 1970s and 1980s.

Within the first year after passage by Congress on March 22, 1972, thirty states ratified the ERA; only eight more states were needed for ratification. ERA appeared headed for speedy ratification when Phyllis Schlafly organized the STOP ERA movement in September 1972. Her involvement came about serendipitously in December 1971, when she was invited to a debate sponsored by a conservative forum in Connecticut. She suggested that the debate focus on national defense, but was told the club wanted to address the Equal Rights Amendment, then pending in the U.S. Senate. Claiming she did not know much about ERA, she asked for material to be sent to her. After reading the material, she decided she was against the amendment.

Prior to this Schlafly had not taken much interest in feminism. This turn to feminism, or more exactly antifeminism, reflected a turn in grassroots conservatism to social issues that would no longer be linked to communism or defense. In the 1960s, the Supreme Court's ban on prayer in school sparked the first signs of Christian political mobilization. Some Republicans joined in this opposition, as seen when Senator Everett Dirkson (R-Illinois) proposed legislation to allow prayer in school. Schlafly had supported this legislation, but her major interest remained defense. Schlafly's response to the ERA initiated a direct response to the feminist challenge from Christian women who saw traditional culture under attack. The ERA issue introduced large numbers of Christian women to politics and tapped into their fears that their values were being threatened by the secular Left.

Schlafly took the lead in rallying this festering opposition when she published "What's Wrong with 'Equal Rights' for Women?" in the *Phyllis Schlafly Report* in February 1972. In this antifeminist manifesto, Schlafly articulated the basic principles that would guide the anti-ERA forces for the next ten years. In doing so, she laid out the fundamental reasons for opposing the women's liberation movement, arguing that the family is "the basic unit of society, which is ingrained in the laws and customs of our Judeo-Christian civilization [and] is the greatest single achievement in the history of women's rights." The family, she argued, "assures a woman the most precious and important right of all—the right to keep her own baby and to be supported and protected in the enjoyment of watching her baby grow and develop." This opening declaration was a direct challenge to feminist Betty Friedan, who had argued in her bestselling book, *The Feminine Mystique* (1963), that American women had been taught to accept traditional, middle-class gender roles of homemakers and housewives, and that kept them from pursuing self-fulfillment in the workplace, largely out of social pressures and fears of being labeled an "improper mother." To the contrary, Schlafly argued that women benefited from the "Christian tradition of chivalry," which obligated men to support and protect their wives and children. Furthermore, she continued, American women were the beneficiaries of the technological advances of the late nineteenth and twentieth century. She wrote that the real liberation of women from backbreaking drudgery of prior centuries is "the American free enterprise system which stimulated inventive geniuses" to provide women with labor-saving devices.

Continuing, she called ERA a direct threat to the protection that mothers and working women enjoyed in American society. Specifically, she argued that the ERA would "abolish a woman's right to child support and alimony," and would "absolutely and positively make women subject to the draft." The issue, she claimed, was not whether women should be given better employment opportunities, equal pay for equal work, appointments to high position, or gain more admission to medical schools. Such goals were desirable and she supported "any necessary legislation" to fulfill these goals. But the feminists, she said, were claiming these goals as their own in order to sugar coat with "sweet syrup" an agenda that was "anti-family, anti-children, and pro-abortion." Actually, "women libbers view the home as a prison, and the wife and mother as a slave. The women libbers don't understand that most women want to be a wife, mother and homemaker—and are happy in that role." In making this argument, her language was direct, unqualified, and bound to infuriate feminists.

A month after publishing "What's Wrong with 'Equal Rights' for Women?" Schlafly received a phone call from an excited subscriber in Oklahoma, Ann Paterson, who told her that the Oklahoma state legislature had defeated ERA after her report had been circulated to them. Schlafly knew immediately they she had found an issue to rally the grassroots. Yet, even after the Oklahoma defeat, few believed that ERA could be stopped. . . . By mid-1973, 30 states had ratified the ERA, but then ratification slowed; three more states ratified in 1974, one in 1975, and another in 1977, bringing the total to thirty-five states of the needed thirty-eight. Schlafly entered the ERA fight as an experienced organizer with a network of supporters throughout the country, but political observers believed that chances for defeating the ERA were nil. . . .

At first, Schlafly drew activists from her network of conservative Republican women across the country, particularly women who had traveled to Washington, D.C., in 1967 to vote for her as president of the National Federation of Republican Women. . . . As the campaign grew, she effectively reached out to women not previously involved in politics, especially younger, evangelical Christian women. One television producer remarked in filming a television special on ERA, "I've been surprised at the variety of women who oppose it. There are many young, attractive mothers who feel threatened by ERA, for instance, because they believe it would deprive them of special protection they now have." These evangelical Christians tended to be stay-at-home mothers, but many worked outside the home as well. What they shared were organizational and speaking skills acquired in their churches. These women brought an evangelical enthusiasm that energized the entire anti-ERA movement and impressed state legislators with their commitment to stop ERA from being ratified. Evangelical women were drawn from the Church of Christ, Southern Baptist, and fundamentalist independent churches, but Mormons, Orthodox Jews, and Roman Catholic women were effectively organized as well. For the first time, these women were brought into the larger conservative movement by social issues, rather than anticommunism. What held these groups together was Schlafly's personal leadership plus their organ of communication, the *Phyllis Schlafly Report*, which each month presented news and new arguments against ERA, kept a running tally of votes by the states, and advised on campaign strategies and tactics. The establishment of these chapters encouraged Schlafly to broaden her political base. In November 1975, she established Eagle Forum, calling it "the alternative to women's lib." By the end of the ERA battle, Eagle Forum members no longer viewed themselves as "the alternative"; [they] believed they were mainstream, even though their membership of 60,000 paled in comparison to the National Organization for Women with its 220,000 members.

Overall, anti-ERA activists mirrored pro-ERA activists, although with important differences. Both pro- and anti-activists drew largely from white, middle-class women. For example, charter members of the National Organization for Women (NOW), the leading pro-ERA group, were 50 percent over the age of thirty, 66 percent held bachelor's degrees, with approximately half of the college graduates also possessing advanced degrees. Surveys showed that support for ERA was greatest among highly educated and divorced women who did not attend church services regularly. Many ERA supporters were young, unmarried, and employed outside the home. While anti-ERA activists tended to be married women, over half in one survey reported above-average family incomes and many had college educations and worked outside the home.

The fundamental distinction between anti-ERA activists and pro-ERA activists lay in their different value systems, as indicated by religious affiliations. A remarkable 98 percent of the anti-ERA supporters claimed church membership, while only 31 to 48 percent of pro-ERA supporters did. Studies done at the time consistently showed that anti-ERA activists were motivated by a strong belief in the tenets of traditional religion. ERA supporters tended to welcome the new morality of sexual liberation and reproductive rights, and identified with progressive causes. For antifeminist activists, ratification of the ERA and legalization of abortion symbolized threats to the traditional nuclear family. They saw themselves as upholding the ideal of the two-parent family—a father, a mother working at home, and children—which they feared was being replaced in the 1970s by single-parent families and cohabiting couples, both heterosexual and homosexual. Anti-ERA activists identified themselves as politically conservative, committed to the old morality, and supporters of traditional gender roles. For fundamentalist and evangelical Protestant women, beliefs about the place of wives in the family and women in society came from biblical injunctions to uphold the authority of husbands and fathers.

Yet, many of the empirical studies of anti-ERA activists showed that these women, like their counterparts on the other side of the debate, believed that they could control their own lives and were heavily involved in the political system. As one study concluded, females who were opposed to equal rights for women were "high achievers, but closed-minded." While anti-ERA females denied significant gender discrimination, they supported equal pay for equal work, knowing that federal law already outlawed such discrimination. Such evidence suggested that anti-ERA activists were not motivated by any sense of alienation from society, urbanization, industrialization, or status anxiety caused by declining social positions—a case frequently made by later feminist scholars. . . . Moreover, while many of the anti-ERA activists held conservative beliefs that were anti-big government, anti-egalitarian, and fearful about moral disorder in society, they never had contact with the segregationist Right—the Ku Klux Klan, the Minutemen, or white separatist groups. . . .

The anti-ERA movement reflected the character of the diverse localities from which its members were drawn. In Oklahoma, many of the local activists belonged to the Church of Christ; in Utah, Nevada, and Arizona, many of the key activists were Mormon; the Southern states drew heavily from Southern Baptists, the Church of Christ, and smaller fundamentalist churches. Illinois attracted many Roman Catholics, and orthodox rabbis played an important role in the Chicago campaign. The South Dakota STOP ERA chairman was an Austrian immigrant, a refugee from the Nazis and the Communists. The North Dakota STOP ERA chairman was one of twelve children born to Hispanic parents. The Vermont STOP ERA chairman was a twenty-something who had voted for [Democratic presidential candidate] George McGovern in 1972. The head of the North Carolina STOP ERA campaign, Dorothy Slade, was a member of the [ultra Right-wing] John Birch Society. The diversity and commitment of these women were not something captured in a statistical survey.

For the most part, the women who joined Schlafly were middle-American women, down-to-earth and not given to airs of sophistication. They called one another "dear" and "honey" and referred to themselves as "girls." Even in their political correspondence they often spoke of their children and might share a recipe for banana bread. What they brought to the anti-ERA movement was an ability to talk to state legislators, many of whom they knew as neighbors or as members of their congregations, without appearing threatening. These were women who would send a thank-you card to their legislators for voting "No" on ERA with a drawing of an adoring woman with her head tilted and her laced fingers under her chin, surrounded by floating hearts with a caption reading, "For Recognizing the Difference, You are Terrific, Fantastic, and Marvelous."

Typical was Shirley Curry, the wife of a Church of Christ minister, who with anti-ERA material under one arm and the *Congressional Record* under the other, joined with "other informed Christian women to tour this state [Tennessee] talking to ladies Bible classes, telling each group which representatives they need to influence" because ERA was "a vital issue for the church and the nation." In Alabama, Peggy Alston phoned Eunice Smith to tell her that she had given birth to twin babies a month early, but "this little series of events did not interfere with her plans for attending the ERA hearings." Her fellow Alabamian Chris Collins reported to Phyllis Schlafly that she gave five speeches before the leading women of Anniston, including black church groups—"all enthusiastic. I have really stirred the town. All are agog regarding your coming to Alabama for two days." In Michigan, Elaine Donnelly, described by a local newspaper as "young, pretty, happily married" with two young children, declared that the feminists "reject the values that the majority of women hold . . . they have a very negative attitude toward the family and I don't think they understand the nature of commitment to the family." Many STOP ERAers came to the movement as political novices, so they took pride when they were able to debate effectively with a local professor or testify at legislative hearings. Anna Graham wrote Schlafly in the summer of 1973 about one such hearing, "We anticipated the proponents [of ERA] accurately and matched them point by point and person to person—youth, blacks, a lawyer, a housewife, a working gal, etc. . . . Really I was so pleased that we did so well, considering the lack of political experience most of the opposing women have."

These women were the backbone of the anti-ERA movement. To ensure that they were prepared for the battle ahead, Schlafly conducted workshops on how to debate and testify at a public hearing. Schlafly talked about the importance of good grooming and what kind of makeup to wear, what colors looked good on television, and how to be poised and smile when attacked. Above all, Schlafly emphasized the importance of conducting oneself as a lady. The president of the Florida Women for Responsible Legislation summarized the attitudes of these grassroots activists when she told a local reporter that "looking feminine is important" in winning support against ERA. Schlafly encouraged this use of femininity to win over state legislators. "Get Maud Rogers and that pretty young girl who had the baby and the nice looking redhead," she told her leaders in Arkansas, "to commit themselves to talk personally with ten legislators. That would be thirty. Pick the ones who are wavering and go for it." However much feminists deplored these tactics, they knew that in the battleground states, located largely in the South and the Midwest, such tactics were well suited to win over the middle-aged white legislators who dominated the state legislatures. The women who joined the anti-ERA campaign became unrelenting in their political activity. These were local women whom most politicians feared to alienate, because these women talked politics, volunteered in political campaigns, and wore political buttons when they came to meetings. They placed ERA as the most important issue in their political world.

In organizing against ERA, opponents portrayed the ERA as elitist, an amendment promoted by leftist feminists out of touch with and hostile to stay-at-home mothers. Typical was an anti-ERA letter, hand-typed and mimeographed, which was distributed to Ohio state legislators. "We are a group of wives, mothers, and working women vitally concerned with how the Equal Rights Amendment will affect the status of women and the fundamental respect for the family as a basic unit of our society." The letter went on to say, "Those women lawyers, women legislators, and women executives promoting ERA have plenty of education and talent to get what they want in the business, political, and academic world. WE, the wives and working women, need you, dear Senators and Representatives to protect us. We think this is the man's responsibility, and we are dearly hoping you will vote NO on ERA." Feminists were repulsed by this language that appealed to the paternalistic instincts of male legislators and they were even more disgusted when anti-ERA women showed up at state capitals, of course wearing dresses, to deliver home-baked bread and pies to their legislators. These tactics probably did not change many votes, but they did generate publicity for the STOP ERA cause.

STOP ERA women had another advantage—a capacity to attack the amendment from a variety of directions, which kept their opponents off balance. The anti-ERA movement was unified politically, even though its participants opposed the amendment for different reasons. This allowed STOP ERA to bring together women from different social backgrounds, different religious denominations, different careers, and different beliefs. Pro-ERA women were more ideologically homogeneous in that they considered themselves feminists, even though they differed on the political and legal consequences of ERA. The abortion issue was especially divisive, and many ERA leaders tried to separate reproductive rights from ERA. On the other hand, leaders in NOW and some local American Civil Liberties Union Lawyers tried to further reproductive rights by brining suit under state ERA laws. In Hawaii and Massachusetts, pro-abortion activists filed briefs claiming that their state ERAs provided the right to use tax funds for abortions based on the doctrine that "equality of rights under the law shall not be denied or abridged by the state on account of sex." Such actions allowed Schlafly to link abortion with ERA by arguing that the federal ERA was a way for feminists to push abortion-on-demand and homosexual rights surreptitiously into the U.S. Constitution. These kinds of arguments fed into Schlafly's larger point that the ratification of ERA would have unforeseen consequences when activist courts began to interpret the amendment. The Alabama STOP ERA made this point exactly in a long letter sent to each legislator: "There is no way for anyone to say positively how the Supreme Court will apply the ERA to conscription, combat duty, alimony, child support, wife support, divorce, homosexuality, public restrooms, separate gym classes and athletic teams, single sex education, sexual crimes, and prostitution. It is these women's liberationists—a well-financed and vocal minority wishing to reconstruct the American family—who have the money and are eager to bring cases to court under the ERA which would force the changes in our lives which they desire."

Schlafly argued that the amendment was also unnecessary because Congress had already enacted the Equal Pay Act (1963) and Title VII of the Civil Rights Act (1964); equal opportunity found expression in the Equal Employment Opportunity Act (1972); educational opportunity for women was ensured by Title IX of the Education Amendments Act (1972); and credit protection for women was guaranteed in the Depository Institution Amendments Act of 1974. Feminists argued that problems of inequality existed in other areas that could not be addressed through piecemeal legislation and, furthermore, without a constitutional amendment, this legislation could be repealed. As Karen De-Crow, president of the National Organization for Women, asserted in a debate with Schlafly, "Congress gave us the right to equal pay for equal work, but Congress can take it away. Congress gave us Title IX, and Congress can take it away." This kind of argument suggested, however, that progress had been made, even though it might be tenuous.

The fact is that opponents of ERA had mixed views on the meaning of social equality, which feminists might have exploited but did not. For example, many Christian anti-ERA activists believed that women held a special, yet subordinate, position to their husbands in the family. Illinois State Representative Monroe Flinn wrote anti-ERA activists Kathleen Sullivan, "I have always stated that I have no opposition to women having equal rights in every respect, but we must also respect the fact that God created us differently. To pass a law or constitutional amendment saying that we are all alike in every respect, in my opinion, flies in the face of what our Creator intended."

Too often feminists in debating Schlafly—their main opponent—instead of exploiting inconsistencies in the anti-ERA movement, turned to personal attacks on her. In battling Schlafly over ERA, many feminists manifested a personal antagonism that never emerged with the other opponents she had energetically fought, such as the anti-anticommunists and the Rockefeller Republicans. The bitter antagonism that emerged in the ERA fight reflected the politics-is-personal style that emerged in the 1970s and the fact that the ERA fight went to the heart of deeply philosophical issues over the meaning of life and lifestyle in America. Schlafly was experienced in these kinds of appeals to emotion, so as a result, these debate tactics usually backfired by allowing her to portray her opponents as the actual extremists. For example, at a debate with Schlafly in 1973 at Illinois State University, an angry Betty Friedan declared, "I consider you a traitor to your sex, an Aunt Tom" and said what became an oft-repeated line: that she would like to burn Schlafly at the stake. Schlafly calmly replied, "I'm glad you said that because it just shows the intemperate nature of proponents of ERA."

By making Schlafly the sole target of their attacks, feminists inadvertently enhanced her prominence as a media star. Schlafly became a regular guest on daytime television. . . . In 1976, the Associated Press named Schlafly as one of the ten most influential *people* in Illinois, and in 1978 the *World Almanac* selected her as one of the 25 most influential women in the United States. Starting in 1977, *Good Housekeeping*'s reader poll regularly listed her as one of the ten most admired women in the world. Feminists helped make Schlafly into a national figure and perhaps even a cultural icon. Making Schlafly into a primary target allowed the anti-ERA movement to appear more unified ideologically than perhaps it actually was.

Questions for Discussion

1. What was the Equal Rights Amendment? Why would millions of women oppose it? In your opinion, was an amendment to the Constitution necessary to ensure equality between the sexes, or was it mostly symbolic?
2. In what ways were pro- and anti-ERA women similar? In what ways were they different?

3. Did the Schlafly-led women oppose all elements of the feminist movement? Which aspects of modern feminism did they most oppose?
4. What role did Schlafly and her anti-ERA campaign play in the rise of the modern conservative movement?

For Further Reading

Peter Applebome, *Dixie Rising: How the South Is Shaping American Values, Politics, and Culture* (1996); Robert Baird and Stuwart Rosenbaum, *Same-Sex Marriage: The Moral and Legal Debate* (2004); Stephanie Coontz, *The Way We Never Were: American Families and the Nostalgia Trap* (1992); Sara Diamond, *Not by Politics Alone: The Enduring Influence of the Religious Right* (1998); Susan Faludi, *Backlash: The Undeclared War against American Women* (1991); Morris Fiorina et al., *Culture War? The Myth of a Polarized America* (2005); Frances Fitzgerald, *Cities on a Hill: A Journey through American Cultures* (1986); Robert Fogel, *The Fourth Great Awakening and the Future of Egalitarianism* (2000); David Frum, *Dead Right* (1994); Andrew Hacker, *Mismatch: The Growing Gulf between Women and Men* (2003); Gertrude Himmilfarb, *One Nation, Two Cultures* (1999); Godfrey Hodgson, *The World Turned Right Side Up: A History of the Conservative Ascendancy in America* (1996); James Hunter, *Culture Wars: The Struggle to Define America* (1991); James Hunter and Alan Wolfe, *Is There a Culture War?* (2006); Jane Mansbridge, *Why We Lost the ERA* (1986); William Martin, *With God on Our Side: The Rise of the Religious Right in America* (1996); Lisa McGerr, *Suburban Warriors: The Origins of the New American Right* (2001); James Morone, *Hellfire Nation: The Politics of Sin in America* (2002); Gary Nash et al., *History on Trial: Culture Wars and the Teaching of the Past* (1997); William Saletan, *Bearing Right: How Conservatives Won the Abortion War* (2003); Phyllis Schlafly, *Feminist Fantasies* (2003); Arthur Schlesinger Jr., *The Disuniting of America: Reflections on a Multicultural Society* (1991); Gary Wills, *Under God: Religion and American Politics* (1990); James Wilson, *The Marriage Problem: How Our Country Has Weakened Families* (2002); John Wilson, *The Myth of Political Correctness: The Conservative Attack on Higher Education* (1995); Jonathan Zimmerman, *Whose America? Culture Wars in the Public Schools* (2002).

The Columbine Shooting

Teenage Male Violence
and Contemporary America

Steven Mintz

In the following essay, Steven Mintz asks the question, "Why would two boys from stable, affluent homes try to massacre their classmates?" Mintz is referring to the infamous 1998 shooting by two students at Columbine High School in Littleton, Colorado, in which fifteen people were killed. School violence, as Mintz shows, is common. How violent are American teenagers? Are teenagers, especially males, innately prone to violence? Or do they learn it? Is it instilled in the privacy of their homes? Or is it foisted on them by a combination of the media, video games, and the extraordinary level of gun-related violence in the United States? And if their violent behavior is learned, does that mean American society is at fault? How violent is American society compared with other affluent nations?

Ultimately, Mintz presents us with a paradox. Since the late nineteenth century, Americans have viewed childhood as a time of carefree development and innocence. No stage of life is free from problems, but childhood is supposed to be relatively immune from the stresses, routines, and anxieties of adult life. Yet, according to Mintz, childhood in contemporary America is marked by levels of stress, competition, and insecurity that mirror adulthood. Might this help account for violence among teenagers?

There are no easy answers to these questions or to the paradox Mintz poses. But the questions should at least be raised, because there are some disturbing facts to ponder. As Mintz shows, Columbine may be the most famous of the school shootings, at least until April 2007, when thirty-three

The aftermath of the Columbine High School shooting. The essay points out that school violence among American male teenagers is common. In your view, are young males innately prone to violence? Or do they learn violent behavior in the home? From peers? Both?

students were killed at Virginia Polytechnic Institute (Virginia Tech). But such incidents are common in the United States. That is not the case in other industrialized, affluent societies. The United States has the highest rate of homicide by guns among those nations.

For example, in 1998, the year of the Columbine shootings, the homicide rate per 100,000 population using guns in the United States was 14.24—more than 14 of every 100,000 were killed by guns. In Japan, it was less than 1 person per 100,000, or 0.05; in England and Wales, it was 4.31; Germany, 1.24; Spain, 0.78; France, 5.15; Scotland, 0.54; and Canada, 4.31. Put another way, of all the murders with guns committed in the world's thirty-six most affluent nations in 1998, 45 percent of them occurred in the United States. In 2007, about 15,000 Americans were killed with guns—roughly forty each day.

A major reason the countries cited here have low murder rates with firearms is that they also have strict gun control laws. That is not the case in the United States. In June 2008, the United States Supreme Court ruled that the Constitution guaranteed the *personal* right of individuals to bear arms for "self-defense." This makes it difficult, if not impossible, to devise effective gun control laws.

Most of the violence—gun-related and otherwise—is committed by men and boys. In 2000, males were responsible for 95 percent of all violent crime in the United States; and nearly 90 percent of homicides committed by boys between fifteen and nineteen were by firearms. Are young males, then, in-herently prone to violence? A July 31, 2008, story on the front page of the *New York Times* was headlined, "Mangled Ear a Badge of Honor for the New Breed of Fighter." The story described teenage boys who engage in "mixed martial arts" (wrestling, boxing, and jiu-jitsu) and proudly display the cauliflower ear injuries common to the sport. "When you get cauliflower," said one fifteen-year-old from Virginia, "you're really a man." Or do they learn it from adults? According to this boy's father, the injury is "just one way you toughen up the kid."

People often associate teenage violence with some combination of inner-city youth, poverty, drugs, and single-parent households. There is plenty of violence in cities. Economic hardship, for example, is a major presence in the lives of America's children, including those who live in cities. About 40 percent of the nation's children live either in poverty or in low-income households. Living in single-parent households can also damage the young. The out-of-wedlock birthrate soared from under 10 percent in 1970 to well over 30 percent in 2005.

But the Columbine shootings, along with the other school killings described by Mintz, occurred in rural or suburban schools. They were com-mitted by white males from families with incomes ranging from comfortable to affluent. Not only did males commit the violence; they often displayed disdain, even hatred, for females. Finally, the violence usually occurred in schools, where the competition for grades was intense, as was the struggle among students for status and prestige.

Source: Reprinted by permission of the publisher from HUCK'S RAFT: A HISTORY OF AMERICAN CHILDHOOD by Steven Mintz, pp. 372–384, Cambridge, Mass.: Harvard University Press, Copyright © 2004 by the President and Fellows of Harvard College.

In 1900 the Swedish reformer Ellen Key predicted that the twentieth century would be the century of the child. Just as the nineteenth century had brought recognition of women's rights, the twentieth century would bring accept-ance of children's rights. She argued on behalf of a childhood free from toil in factories and fields, devoted to play and education, and buttressed by leg-islation guaranteeing children's well-being. . . .

During the twentieth century the United States moved a long way toward fulfilling Key's noble vision. During the Progressive era a loose coalition of child psychologists, educators, jurists, physicians, and settle-ment workers, supported by thousands of middle-class women, took the first crucial steps toward universalizing the middle-class ideal of a pro-tected childhood, through the establishment of playgrounds and kinder-gartens, the expansion of high schooling and enactment of mothers' pen-sions and a separate system of juvenile justice emphasizing rehabilitation rather than punishment. The 1920s saw a proliferation of childrearing advice based on the most up-to-date understanding of children's psychological and developmental needs. The New Deal marked another significant advance as the most exploitative forms of child labor were outlawed, an economic safety net for dependent children was established, and high school education became a normative experience, irrespective of class, region, and race. The late 1960s and early 1970s marked the culmination of Key's century of the child as fundamental legal rights—to due process, freedom of expression, gender and racial equality, and contraception and abortion—were established.

But the century of the child ended with a bang, not a whimper. On April 20, 1999, eighteen-year-old Eric Harris and seventeen-year-old Dylan Klebold, clad in long black coats, stormed into Columbine High School in Littleton, Colorado, a suburb south of Denver. The high school seniors were armed with two sawed-off 12-gauge shotguns, a 9-millimeter semiautomatic rifle, and a 9-millimeter semiautomatic pistol. They also carried fifty-one bombs, including an explosive fashioned from two twenty-pound propane tanks and a gasoline-filled canister that they placed in the school cafeteria. The bomb, filled with nails, BB's, and broken glass—contained enough propane and gasoline to kill a majority of the 500 students in the school's lunchroom. The two youths apparently timed the attack to coincide with the anniversary of Adolf Hitler's birth. Within sixteen minutes they had gunned down twelve classmates and a teacher and wounded twenty-three others. Less than an hour after their rampage began, each committed suicide by shooting himself in the head.

Before the rampage, no one noticed anything unusual about their behavior, even though the boys had left numerous warning signs. Klebold walked down his school's halls making aggressive racist remarks and wore black clothing lettered with German phrases. Police testified that the youths had left a sawed-off shotgun barrel and bombmaking materials in plain sight in one of the boys' rooms. In the weeks preceding the assault, the shooters exploded pipe bombs and fired automatic weapons in the mountains near Denver. The boys were arrested for breaking into a van and stealing $400 worth of electronic equipment. In a class in video production, they made a videotape showing trench-coat-clad students walking down the hallways of Columbine High School shooting athletes dead. Meanwhile Harris, who had been suspended for hacking into the school computing system, posted on a website drawings of shotgun-toting monsters and skulls and instructions for making pipe bombs like those he brought to Columbine. Eight times, a classmate's parents contacted the local sheriff's office with allegations that Harris had threatened their son. The complaints were ignored. Because the boys came from affluent, intact two-parent families, those danger signs were disregarded. Their mood swings and infatuation with violence and death were dismissed as if they represented typical examples of adolescent alienation and resentment. The Columbine massacre produced an unsettling picture of a suburb where adults had only the most superficial insight into the lives and mentality of the young.

Why would two boys from stable, affluent homes try to massacre their classmates? Police investigators concluded that Harris and Klebold were angry and alienated and were taking revenge for years of perceived slights from peers. . . . According to police officials, the shooters were also motivated by a desire to become cult heroes. Like [Nathan] Leopold and [Richard] Loeb [wealthy Chicago youths who kidnapped and murdered a fourteen-year-old boy in 1924], the pair felt superior to their peers. "We're the only two who have self-awareness," one wrote. In a flagrant attempt to gain publicity, the boys left a diary and videotapes for the police to find. One thread was an expectation of notoriety. "Directors will be fighting over this story," wrote Klebold.

The Columbine shooting was partly the grotesque outcome of a long-running feud with the more popular cliques at school. The "preps" and "jocks" who dominated the school apparently taunted the pair by referring to them with derogatory homosexual terms. But unlike high school misfits of an earlier generation, Klebold and Harris were willing to offend, antagonize, and ultimately kill their tormentors. Nor were they alone in expressing their resentments with violence. The Columbine massacre was the sixth multiple-victim school shooting over an eighteen-month span in 1998 and 1999. During the 1990s the number of school shootings with multiple victims climbed from an average of two a year to an average of five. In West Paducah, Kentucky, fourteen-year-old Michael Carneal told schoolmates that "it would be cool" to shoot into a student prayer group. He did as promised, killing three girls and wounding five other students who were praying in a school hallway. In Edinboro, Pennsylvania, Andrew Wurst, also fourteen, started shooting at his eighth-grade prom, killing a teacher and injuring three others. In Jonesboro, Arkansas, eleven-year-old Andrew Golden and thirteen-year-old Mitchell Johnson activated a fire alarm and shot four girls and a teacher to death and wounded ten others as they evacuated the school. In Springfield, Oregon, fifteen-year-old Kipland Kinkel killed his parents, then shot twenty-four people in his school cafeteria, killing two students. In Pearl, Mississippi, a suburb of Jackson, sixteen-year-old Luke Woodham stabbed his mother to death before shooting nine students, killing two, at his high school. In Bethel, Alaska, sixteen-year-old Evan Ramsey murdered a popular athlete and then tracked and killed the school principal.

Some commentators argued that media coverage of these shootings was overblown, since multiple-victim school shootings were extremely rare. Not only was school violence not a new phenomenon; it had actually peaked during the 1992–93 school year, when nearly fifty young people and adults were killed in school-related violence. Yet what made these school shootings especially shocking was that violence had spread from urban to rural and suburban areas and involved multiple victims. The schoolyard killings in 1998 and 1999 were not gang related, nor were they fights over money or girlfriends. The victims were chosen randomly, and the motives for the killings were obscure.

In general, explanations of juvenile violence stress a process of brutalization, involving abuse, exposure to violence, and emotional numbing; but in none of the schoolyard shootings of 1998 and 1999 was there evidence of a history of physical abuse, severe corporal punishment, or family violence. Nor could the shootings be blamed on such suspects as urban poverty, broken families, or single parenthood. The Columbine rampage was particularly unsettling, since unlike the earlier school attacks, it could not be explained as the product of southern or rural gun culture. The killings seemed to embody two characteristics: gestural suicide, intended to provoke widespread attention; and revenge fantasies, modeled on the indiscriminate violence feature on television and video games, in which the victims provide an audience for the killers to work out their needs. . . .

Popular explanations of the violence that took place in Littleton, West Paducah, and Pearl emphasized such factors as young people's easy access to semiautomatic weapons, capable of firing off dozens of pounds of ammunition in less than a minute; their exposure to video games that involved the graphic killing of human targets; a popular culture in which people settle scores violently; and a lack of adult presence in their lives. Many commentators attributed the school rampages to school status hierarchies, suburban alienation, and inadequate parental supervision. Social contagion and copycat killing, with one rampage feeding on another, certainly played a role.

Several threads linked the rampages. Each case involved a child or youths who felt unpopular, rejected, or picked upon. Many student killers exhibited signs of serious depression. Most were suicidal, writing notes before the killings assuming they would die. For many, the attack offered to end a life of torment in a blaze of terror. To varying degrees, the attackers were obsessed with violent popular culture and preoccupied with guns, death, and killing. For many school killers, the boundaries between reality and fantasy had eroded, and many of the shootings had a gamelike quality. In the Jonesboro, Arkansas, killings, and eleven-year-old and a thirteen-year-old dressed up in fatigues and hid in the bushes like snipers and killed four girls and a teacher in the crossfire. There was frequently a misogynist element in the shootings, with girls, mothers, and female teachers constituting a majority of the victims. Like Harris and Klebold, most of the shooters left a road map of warning signs pointing toward the violence to come, often in detailed writings at school. In case after case, friends and acquaintances heard boasts and muttered plans for mayhem. Many of the student killers had a history of violent behavior. Kip Kinkel set off firecrackers in cats' mouths, threw rocks at cars from an overpass, and gave a talk in speech class about how to build a bomb. But the clues were missed by parents who were unable to face the evidence of serious mental turmoil and by teachers who failed to take threats seriously.

Were the schoolhouse shootings aberrations or were they symptoms of unacknowledged failings in the ways that Americans raise children, especially boys? Precisely because the Littleton rampage could not be attributed to "broken homes," to a violent or abusive family life, or to declining job prospects in decaying working-class communities, it focused public attention on the stresses besetting the lives of privileged youths. It led commentators to focus on the social dynamics of secondary schools, where social ostracism, marginalization, and alienation are commonplace; a boyhood "culture of cruelty," where bullying, taunting, and insults are everyday occurrences; and the psychological impact of movies that feature casual cruelty and gratuitous violence, music that is fixated on death and features the abuse of women, and video games that involve the graphic killing of opponents.

During the twentieth century, high schools had become the primary arena where American adolescents tried out new styles, trends, and identities. But high schools also mimicked some of the most disconcerting aspects of adult society, including clearly defined ladders of status and prestige. At the end of the twentieth century, popular culture reexamined these status hierarchies from a much more critical perspective. No longer was the ideal simply to "fit in" or join the "in crowd." Such teen films as *Clueless* (1995), *Jawbreaker* (1998), and *Varsity Blues* (1999) portrayed high schools as brutal, Darwinian environments that were status-obsessed, materialistic, hierarchical, and savagely competitive. In real life, too, secondary schools were roiling emotional cauldrons, filled with bullying and snobbery. Middle and high schools had their own social pecking order, with a status hierarchy defined largely by looks, athletic prowess, and money.

In recent years the cliques found in middle schools and high schools have proliferated. Alongside the strutting jocks, cheerleaders, and preppies of the past, there were now skateboarders, freaks, Goths, stoners, and other outcast cliques as geeky loners banded together. Unlike yesteryear's high schools, where the nerds, wallflowers, and other outcasts felt truly powerless, their contemporary counterparts were less willing to suppress their hostilities and resentments. The social dynamics of secondary schools, where kids engage in various forms of social ostracism and casual sadism, lurked behind many of the schoolhouse shootings. It is clear that the killers felt disrespected and unnoticed and desperately wanted power and attention. While secondary schools address young people's intellectual needs, they do not do an effective job of meeting their psychological and emotional needs. They are filled with social as well as academic stresses, and many students feel a deep sense of isolation and estrangement. A recent survey of 100,000 students found that only 1 in 4 said they went to a school where adults and other students cared for them.

Gender hostility was another thread running through the school shootings. All the schoolhouse assailants were male, and over half of their victims were female. Rage or resentment against female teachers and students helped generate violence. Gender hostility was not new. Younger boys have longed pulled girls' pony tails, and adolescent male culture has long treated girls as sex objects. . . . Yet even as an antifeminist backlash against female assertiveness spread within the adult male culture, it appeared in the youth culture, too, especially among deeply disaffected middle-class adolescent males. Anger and rage at women became part of the background noise of their world. One of the harshest complaints against rap music, which found its largest and most enthusiastic audience among white suburban teenaged boys, was that it glorified sexist, misogynist, patriarchal ways of thinking and behaving. Rap lyrics frequently associated blunt sexist language and graphic descriptions of rape and violence with manliness and rebelliousness.

There can be no doubt that youth violence in the United States is highly gendered. During the 1990s, 96 percent of youths committing serious acts of violence were male. Most school killers showed signs of clinical depression, and responses to depression vary by gender. Depressed girls are more likely than boys to cry openly or talk about their problems; they are also more prone than boys to self-mutilate or attempt suicide. Boys, in contrast, have fewer acceptable outlets to express depression or frustration and rage. Depressed boys tend to withdraw socially or group together with others who feel outcast, and to act out aggressive impulses, and to succeed in committing suicide.

Sometimes isolated incidents, like bolts of lightning that suddenly illuminate a darkened landscape, can reveal stresses and contradictions otherwise difficult to discern. The school shootings point to contradictions that lie at the very heart of the contemporary conception of childhood. By most measures, the young were better off than ever. They were bigger, richer, better educated, and healthier than at any other time in history. In many ways they were uniquely privileged. They had grown up in a period of sustained prosperity, had access to unprecedented amounts of information and education, and had more private space in their homes than ever before. Girls and racial and ethnic minorities had unparalleled opportunities and role models to emulate. Yet despite genuine gains, 60 percent of all adult Americans and 77 percent of African Americans said that their children were worse off than when they were children.

Certainly, some of this anxiety reflects nostalgia for a lost world of childhood innocence, when six-year-old girls didn't wear slinky dresses, lycra, and glitter nail polish, and preteen boys didn't wear earrings or dye their hair purple. Partly adults' concern involves the problems facing poor children. Even at the height of the economic boom of the 1990s, child poverty remained a severe problem, with 13.5 million children living in poverty and 12 million lacking health insurance. Still, when the public expressed alarm about the young, it reflected their sense that for all young people, not simply the poorest, childhood and adolescence had grown riskier and more stressful. Adults worried that children were growing up too quickly and faced pressures, risks, and choices far greater than those that they experienced at a similar age. . . .

Contemporary childhood is characterized by a host of contradictions. Numerically, today's children are the largest generation of young people ever, even bigger than the baby boom at its peak in 1964. Nevertheless, with the average age of Americans over thirty-three, the United States is a more adult-centered society, deeply ambivalent toward the young. Adults mimic the styles of the young and envy their appearance, energy, and virility, but intergenerational contact is increasingly confined to relationships between children and parents, teachers, and service providers. More fully integrated into the consumer economy than ever before, and at a much earlier age, the young are, at the same time, more segregated than ever in a peer culture. Kids have more space than ever inside their homes, but less space outside to call their own.

American society romanticizes childhood and adolescence as carefree periods of exploration, a time of freedom and irresponsibility, and young people do have more autonomy than ever before in their leisure activities, grooming, and spending. Yet there has simultaneously been a countertrend toward the systematic over-organization of young people's lives, a trend especially noticeable in schools, where student behavior is much more closely monitored than it was three or four decades ago, and where many nonacademic and extracurricular activities have been eliminated. As anxiety intensifies over whether the young were prepared to compete in the global economy, many schools curtailed recess (which has been eliminated in about 40 percent of school districts), cut programs in art and music, expanded summer school programs, imposed competency testing, eliminated many extracurricular activities and assemblies, and reemphasized drill and repetition as part of a "back to basics" movement. Not surprisingly, fewer students found school intellectually stimulating or fulfilling. Instead, they found it stressful and pressured.

The underlying contradiction in youthful lives is the most disturbing. Young people mature physiologically earlier than ever before. The media prey on children and adolescents with wiles of persuasion and sexual innuendo once reserved for adult consumers. The young have become more knowledgeable sexually and in many other ways. They face adult-like choices earlier. Yet contemporary American society isolates and juvenilizes young people more than ever before. Contemporary society provides the young with few positive ways to express their growing maturity and gives them few opportunities to participate in socially valued activities. American society sends young people many mixed and confusing messages. The young are told to work hard and value school, but also to enjoy themselves. They are to be innocent but also sexually alluring. They are to be respectful and obedient, but also independent consumers beholden to no one. They are to be youthful but not childish. The basic contradiction is that the young are told to grow up fast, but also that they needn't grow up at all, at least not until they reach their late twenties or early thirties.

History offers no easy solutions to the disconnections, stress, and role contradictions that today's children face, but it does provide certain insights that might be helpful as we seek solutions. The first is that nostalgia for the past offers no solutions to the problems of the present. It is not possible to recreate a "walled garden" of childhood innocence, no matter how hard we might try. No V-chip, Internet filtering software, or CD-rating system will immunize children from the influence of contemporary culture. Since we cannot insulate children from all malign influences, it is essential that we prepare them to deal responsibly with the pressures and choices they face. That task requires knowledge, no sheltering. In a risk-filled world, naivete is vulnerability. . . .

A little more than a century ago, the American ideal of childhood as a world apart, a period of freedom and self-discovery, received its most influential and lasting embodiment in *The Adventures of Huckleberry Finn.* In superficial ways, that ideal was realized. Emancipated from traditional forms of child labor, youth has become a prolonged period of education and leisure. More than ever before, youth has come to occupy a separate and autonomous realm, free from its traditional family obligations. Yet in a deeper sense, the world we created is the polar opposite of the ideal embodied by Twain's novel. Over the past century and a half, the timing, sequencing, and stages of growing up have become ever more precise, uniform, and prescriptive, purportedly to better meet children's developmental needs, but in practice often failing them. In *Tom Sawyer* and *Huckleberry Finn,* many ties connected the young to a host of adults, some of whom were family members, but many of whom, like the fugitive slave Jim, were not. Today, connections that linked the young to the world of adults have grown attenuated. The young spend most of their time in an adult-run institution, the school, or consuming a mass culture produced by adults, but have few ties to actual adults apart from parents and teachers.

Huckleberry Finn represented a rejection of the idea that childhood was a period of life that was important merely as preparation for adulthood. Like Jean-Jacques Rousseau, Mark Twain considered childhood valuable in and of itself. We may cling to that idea in the abstract, but in practice American culture—oriented toward mastery and control—views childhood as a "project," in which the young must develop the skills, knowledge, and character traits necessary for adulthood success, which is increasingly defined in terms of academic skills, knowledge, and competencies—and the forms of discipline those require. We expect even very young children to exhibit a degree of self-control that few adults had 200 or more years ago. Meanwhile, forms of behavior that previous generations considered normal are now defined as disabilities. American society is unique in its assumption that all young people should follow a single, unitary path to adulthood. Those who cannot adjust are cast adrift, to float aimlessly in a river that threatens to sink their lonely raft.

Contemporary American childhood is characterized by a fundamental paradox. More than ever before, children are segregated in a separate world of youth. . . . Yet at the same time, children became more tightly integrated into the consumer society and more knowledgeable about adult realities at an earlier age. The result is a deepening contradiction between the child as dependent juvenile and the child as incipient adult.

In recent years, the psychological costs of this contradiction have grown more apparent. Hovering parents make it more difficult for children to separate; schools, preoccupied with testing and discipline, monitor students more closely and make education an increasingly stressful experience; demanding peer groups enforce conformity and ostracize those who fail to fit in. Our challenge is to reverse the process of age segmentation, to provide the young with challenging alternatives to a world of malls, instant messaging, music videos, and play dates. Huck Finn was an abused child, whose father, the town drunk, beat him for going to school and learning to read. Who would envy Huck's battered childhood? Yet he enjoyed something too many children are denied and which adults can provide: opportunities to undertake odysseys of self-discovery outside the goal-driven, over-structured realities of contemporary childhood.

Questions for Discussion

1. Which of the following do you think is most responsible for the spate of school shootings described in this essay: the availability of guns, stressful high school experiences, antagonisms among high school cliques, violent films and video games, male disdain for girls and women, or lack of communication between adults and children?
2. The author raised this question: "Were the school shootings aberrations, or were they symptoms of unacknowledged failings in the ways that Americans raise children, especially boys?" How would you respond?
3. The author argues that tragedies like the Columbine shootings point to "contradictions" in the ways Americans view childhood and treat children and adolescents. What are those contradictions? Do you agree with him?

For Further Reading

Leroy Ashby, *Endangered Children: Dependency, Neglect, and Abuse in American History* (1997); Rami Benbenishty and Ron Avi Astor, *School Violence in Context* (2005); Richard Maxwell Brown, *Strain of Violence: Historical Studies of American Violence and Vigilantism* (1975); Philip Cook and Jens Ludwig, *Gun Violence: The Real Cost* (2000); Alenxande DeConde, *Gun Violence in America* (2003); Delbert Elliott, Beatrix Hamburg, and Kirk Williams, eds., *Violence in American Schools A New Perspective* (1998); Donna Gaines, *Teenage Wasteland: Suburbia's Dead End Kids* (1998); Charles King, *Children's Health in America* (1993); Gary Kleck, *Point Blank: Gun Violence in America* (1991); Gregory Moffatt, *Blind-Sided: Homicide Where It Is Least Expected* (2000); Steven Mintz, *Huck's Raft: A History of American Childhood* (2004); Mohammad Shafi and Sharon Lee Shafi, eds., *School Violence: Assessment, Management, Prevention* (2001); Richard Slotkin, *Gunfighter Nation* (1998); Peter Smith, *Violence in Schools: The Response in Europe* (2002); Murray Thomas, *Violence in America's Schools* (2006); Richard Weissbourd, *The Vulnerable Child* (1996); Franklin Zimring, *American Youth Violence* (2000).

Gender and the Latino Experience in Late Twentieth-Century America

Pierrette Hondagneu-Sotelo

On October 3, 1965, at the base of the Statue of Liberty, President Lyndon Johnson signed into law the Hart-Celler Immigration Act of 1965. The law abolished the national quota system on immigration created in 1924. The quotas were designed to reduce the number of Catholics and Jews entering the country and to eliminate those from Asia. In his speech, President Johnson said the quotas violated "the basic principles of American democracy" and were "un-American in the highest sense." At the same time, he sought to reassure those who feared the law would open the floodgates to a new surge of immigration. "The bill we sign today," he said, "is not a revolutionary bill. It does not affect the lives of millions. It will not restructure the shape of our daily lives."

President Johnson had good reason to make this statement. The new law was intended to be largely symbolic, not to increase immigration. The quota system was an insult to the tens of millions of assimilated descendents of the immigrants who came from southern and eastern Europe and Asia, from the mid-nineteenth century to World War I. And in 1965, with the Civil Rights movement at high tide, overt expressions of ethnic prejudice were seen as bad form. Also, while the law did away with the quota system on ethnic groups, it retained a limit on annual immigration, capping it at 290,000.

Recent immigrants becoming American citizens. In what ways does the influx of immigrants in twenty-first-century America differ from the surge of immigration during the early years of the twentieth century?

But contrary to Johnson's words, the immigration law of 1965 would transform the ethnic composition of the country over the next forty years. A stipulation in the law allowed immigrants who became citizens (which takes about five years) to be "reunified" with family members. There was no limit placed on the number of their immediate relatives who could join them in America. For example, once a male immigrant became a citizen he could send for his wife and children, his parents, and his siblings. And once all of these individuals became citizens, they could do the same. The result was an enormous surge of "family-chain" immigration that rivaled, in numbers and ethnic diversity, that of the late nineteenth and early twentieth centuries. Between 1966 and 2000, nearly 23 million people legally entered the United States, while many additional millions came illegally. Before 2000, the greatest number of legal immigrants to enter the country in a given decade was the 8.8 million who came between 1901 and 1910; that figure was surpassed by the 9.1 million who entered between 1991 and 2000.

There are similarities and differences between those two waves of immigration. The most glaring similarity, of course, is the reason most people come to the United States—economic opportunity. Another similarity is the ambiguity Americans have toward immigrants. Today, agricultural and other low-wage industries, such as hotels, restaurants, and fast-food chains, tend to favor liberal immigration policies—just as agricultural and manufacturing concerns did in 1900. Also, those in today's America who worry about the negative impact of immigration on jobs and wages, or who dislike the racial and ethnic backgrounds of the newcomers, want to restrict immigration—repeating the fears of many early-twentieth-century Americans.

There are significant differences between the "old" and "new" immigration. At the turn of the twentieth century, the vast majority of migrants were European and male. In the recent surge, most are non-European. They include newcomers from Asia and Africa. By far, the great majority are from Mexico, the Caribbean, and Central America. For example, the United States Census Bureau reports that in 2007, 54 percent of the nation's 38.1 million foreign-born residents hailed from Latin America, with the vast majority (about 30 percent) coming from Mexico. Immigrants from Asia accounted for 27 percent of the total, while 13 percent arrived from Europe and 4 percent from Africa. A slight majority of recent immigrants are female—compared with about 30 percent in the early years of the twentieth century. The significance of the racial, ethnic, and gender differences between the two waves of immigration are enormous, as the next essay points out. Also, it should be noted that while the overwhelming majority of earlier immigrants were unskilled and had educational attainments below most Americans, a decent portion of recent immigrants possess sophisticated skills and educational attainments. Indeed, today's immigrants are almost as likely to possess college degrees as native-born Americans: 27 percent of immigrants are college graduates compared with 28 percent of native-born Americans. Asian immigrants are more likely to be college educated than those from other parts of the globe. For instance, 75 percent of Indian immigrants hold college degrees.

In the following essay, Pierrette Hondagneu-Sotelo discusses the consequences of migration on the gender and family relationships of Latino immigrants, who are by far the largest source of contemporary immigration. Hondagneu-Sotelo's work is especially important because she ties the issues of family and gender to wider social and economic issues, including modern feminism and the globalization of the American economy. Her work is an important and subtle approach to one of the most significant and contentious issues in contemporary American life.

Source: Pierrette Hondagneu-Sotelo, "Gender and the Latino Experience in Late-Twentieth-Century America," in David Gutierrez, ed., *The Columbia History of Latinos in the United States since 1960* (New York: Columbia University Press, 2004), Chapter 7, pp. 281–302. Reprinted with permission of Indiana University Press.

What topic could be more expansive, slippery, and unwieldy than a discussion of the contours and tenor of gender relations among Latino groups in the United States at the end of the twentieth century? To begin with, the title of this chapter is a misnomer: there is no one, singular Latina or Latino experience in the United States. This has always been the case, but given the diversity of individuals and groups who take shelter under the contemporary Latino umbrella, this is probably truer at this moment than ever before. . . .

After a mid-twentieth-century hiatus in immigration, the last three decades of the twentieth century witnessed a vigorous resurgence of migration to the United States. New immigrants now mostly hail not from Europe, as they did in the early part of the twentieth century, but from Asian, Latin American, and Caribbean nations. This is a diverse immigration population, not only with respect to ethnic and national origins, but also in terms of socioeconomic class and legal status. Latino immigrants in this period have entered the United States with a diversity of citizenship and legal-status arrangements, with Cubans largely granted and Salvadorans largely denied political refugee status; and Mexicans, who have migrated in the greatest number by far, living in the United State both legally and illegally. Unlike their earlier, European-origin predecessors, U.S. immigrants in the late twentieth century include not only poor, manual workers, but also substantial segments of entrepreneurs and highly educated urban professionals.

Census figures clearly demonstrate the scope of the changes that have transformed U.S. society over that period. In 1960, the U.S. Census counted a pan-Latino population (that is, both native and foreign-born) of only about 7 million. But . . . disparities in economic opportunity between the United States and Latin America, political instability in many Latin American nations, and dramatic improvements in communication and transportation technologies laid the foundations for one of the most dramatic epochs of migration in human history. By 1970, the pan-Latino population of the United States grew to 9 million, and by 1980, to 14 million. The pace of migration rapidly accelerated after that. By 1990, the combined foreign-born and native population of Latino origin grew to 22 million. By 2000, after one of the most intense periods of migration in American history, the Latino population had grown to 35 million, or nearly 13 percent of the total population of the United States—and this number did not include the 3.8 million inhabitants of the American Commonwealth of Puerto Rico.

The historical tendency of both U.S.-born and immigrant Latinos to settle in urban areas greatly magnified the effects of this massive demographic transformation. Immigrants and their families tend to settle in clusters, and, increasingly, many big cities have become Latino immigrant cities. According to the 2000 census, more than one-fifth of the entire Latino population of the United States lives in just four metropolitan areas: Los Angeles County (4.2 million), Miami-Dade County (1.3 million), Harris County, Texas (1.1 million), and Cook County, Illinois (1.1 million). In eight of the ten largest cities in the United States (New York, Los Angeles, Chicago, Houston, Phoenix, San Diego, Dallas, San Antonio) Latinos now constitute anywhere from a low of 25.4 percent of total populations (in San Diego), to highs of 46.5 percent (Los Angeles) and 58.7 percent (San Antonio). If one factors in the multiplier effect of the presence and rapid recent expansion of the Spanish-language print-media, broadcast conglomerates such as Televisa and Univision, and the number of Spanish-language radio stations that enjoy leading Arbitron ratings, the reach of Latino cultures in the United States is much greater.

Population growth was so great in the 1980s and 1990s that Latinos began to leave saturated labor markets along the U.S.–Mexico border to seek work and upward mobility in new areas of settlement. Thus Latinos, and especially Latino immigrants, are migrating to work and live in all kinds of rural and small-town areas throughout the United States. Pundits and scholars alike now frequently announce the imminent "browning of the Midwest," the "Latinization of the Southeast" and the Mexicanization of the Northwest." As the last nomenclature suggests, Mexican immigrants appear to be the ones primarily fueling this trend, as they either leave saturated labor markets and big city problems in Los Angeles or forego the Los Angeles step altogether in favor of new jobs in northwestern apple orchards, Midwestern slaughter houses and packing plants, or southeastern poultry farms and carpet factories. . . .

Although it is impossible to predict precisely how this ongoing process of demographic revolution, urbanization, and geographic dispersal will influence the way gendered relations are forged in the increasingly complex and variegated Latino population, if trends established in the 1980s and 1990s hold into the future, it seems certain that the Latino presence in the United States will now be situated far and wide, in numerous industries, neighborhoods, and institutions in every one of the fifty states. It also seems most likely that the twenty-first century will witness new levels of public participation and achievement by Latinas and fewer restrictions on women and girls in Latino families. The majority of Latinos in the United States are either immigrants or the children of immigrants, and even here, where we might expect to see more traditional patterns among recent arrivals from the Dominican Republic, Mexico, El Salvador, and Puerto Rico, we see increasing women's participation in politics, education, and employment. The reasons for these trends are complex. Some of the breakdown of more rigid traditional Latino gender roles and systems can be attributed to the cosmopolitan influences of living in urban areas in a post-feminist environment in which women routinely work out of the home, regularly contribute to their own and their families' support, and thus develop self-images and expectations that may be dramatically different from those learned in more traditional, rural environments in Latin America. The increasing fluidity of gender roles and systems can also be partially attributed to the socializing effects of American popular culture and American public education, no matter how flawed the public education system otherwise is.

But one could also reasonably argue that it is the legacy of the second-wave feminist movement of the 1960s and 1970s that has most effected change in gendered systems in the United States—and that this sea change has had a strong residual effect of creating opportunities for Latinas in their relations with men, and in the range of possible roles they can now play in society generally. Feminism has provoked far-reaching transformations on the social landscape not only in the United States, but also in Latin America, where many countries had feminist political movements in the early twentieth century. . . . Using the mid-twentieth century as a bench-mark, it is startling to acknowledge the prevalence, by the late twentieth century, of women, including married women with children, throughout the paid labor force, and even in the highly coveted professions of law and medicine. While the gendered division of labor at home seems more resist-ant to change, even on that front there have been important shifts toward greater egalitarianism. And as we shall see, those moves toward greater domestic egalitarianism have occurred even in those families believed by many to be most culture-bound and impervious to social change, Latino families. . . .

More circuitous perhaps, but still worth acknowledging, is the role of the Civil Rights Movement in pushing the nation to end all forms of legal discrimination, including racial exclusion provision in immigration law. . . .

In any case, the intersection of a more liberal civil-rights and gender-rights environment with the massive growth of the pan-Latino population of the country laid the foundation for significant changes in the structure and practice of gender relations among Latinos. This is perhaps most easily demonstrated by examining the changing relation between work and family in Latino subcultures. Again, however, in discussing these changes it is im-portant to remember that gender is not a variable like sex (female or male), but rather a relational and constantly contested social system of power. . . .

A good deal of early 1970s second-wave feminism focused on women's subordination in the home. In *The Feminine Mystique* (1963), Betty Friedan identified confinement in the private, domestic sphere as the source of oppression for women, but she was really addressing the concerns of specific women—middle-class, college-educated, white women. Women's house-work and absence from the labor force was seen as the universal source of their subordination. Posed in this fashion, "the problem which had no name" seemed readily resolvable with exhortations for women to participate in the public sphere of employment and politics.

As many commentators have since pointed out, Friedan and other 1970s Anglo-American, middle-class feminists of that ilk had overlooked that many working-class and women of color were already in the paid labor force. Employment had not spawned liberation in the home for working-class women of color. Rather, occupational exploitation and racism in the public sphere had more often made the family a source of refuge. As Maxine Baca Zinn argued in an early feminist article, for many Chicanas and other Latinas, Latino families are simultaneously sites of patriarchal dominance and racial and class solidarity.

One of the great and lasting contributions of second-wave feminism is the recognition of unpaid housework and care work as work that benefits so-ciety. Yet the ways that women of different class and racial or ethnic groups approach housework was not always specified by early feminist scholarship. Among other things, the literature tended to overlook the fact that some elite women purchase housework services, and other women—poor women of color and, today, immigrant women of color—perform this work for pay in other people's homes and without pay in their own homes.

As already noted, a dominant feminist idea held that public employment would lead to all women's liberation from sexism. This literature overlooked not only the different occupational opportunities available to different groups of women. It also ignored the fact that historically, for some poor and working-class women, remaining outside of the paid labor force and taking care of one's own home and children were seen as achievements and privileges, not as sources of subordination. This has been true for a variety of Latinas in the United States. As one Cuban American women in Miami explained to researchers after accepting employment in the garment trade only for a temporary period, and then only to advance family socioeconomic mobility,

> there's no reason for women not to earn a living when it's necessary; they should have as many opportunities and responsibilities as men. But I also tell my daughter that the strength of a family rests on the intelligence and work of women. It's foolish to give up our place as a mother and a wife only to go take orders from men who are not even part of your family. What's so liberated about that? It is better to see your husband succeed and to know you have supported one another.

When women face racial discrimination, sexism, low wages, and exploitative working conditions in the public sphere, staying home sometimes is a welcome respite from those restricted labor-market experiences. One young Mexican immigrant wife and mother of three young sons told me that when her husband requested that she withdraw from paid work in a factory, she responded eagerly. She explained her response not only in terms of her husband's cultural mandates, but also with respect to her very limited job opportunities:

> He is one of them that likes his woman in the house and coming home to find me there. That's what they are accustomed to. It seemed fine to me. I didn't have a job that I liked very much. It wasn't as though I had an important job, then perhaps I would have preferred to stay [employed].

Class, occupation, and culture mediate the different meanings women experience from public/private divides. One woman's privilege becomes another's burden.

Latinas' formal labor force participation rates *are* lower than those of women from other racial- and ethnic-group categories. According to the census data for 2000, the percentage of Latina women in the labor force reached 56. This figure represents significant upward movement from 1973, when 40 percent of Latinas were in the labor force, but both figures are probably underestimates of Latinas' income-earning activities. Historically, Latinas have worked in jobs rendered "invisible" by the ways in which they are perceived and performed. Throughout the Southwest, a long historical legacy of Mexican American women working as private domestic workers, laundresses, and migrant farm workers and in canneries has been obscured. These sorts of jobs simply do not fit with models of nineteenth- and twentieth-century industrial employment. When women hold paying jobs that are performed on a seasonal schedule, on a part-time basis, or actually in the home, as are contemporary childcare and industrial home work in the garment industry, these jobs also do not seem to "count" as jobs. . . .

What informs Latino women's and men's decisions, practices, and ideals about work and family arrangement? What explains the diversity of work and family arrangements, and what explains Latina women's relatively lower labor-force participation rates? Are cultural attitudes the driving force, or is it social structure and its attendant arrays of institutions, resources, and rules, which prove to be the determining factor? Debates over Latinas' approach to work and family negotiations have often been posed this starkly, although the answers are never so simple. On the one hand, a long legacy of Eurocentric social-science scholarship has located explanations of all factors of social life among Latinos in a paradigm of cultural deficiency. Assumptions of traditional values and fatalism have fueled a long legacy of research based on "blame-the-victim" cultural deficiency models. Chicana and other Latina social scientists writing in the late twentieth century have countered this view with one that places strong emphasis on social structure, discrimination, and material resources. . . .

While it remains true that wives, regardless of employment rates, class, and racial or ethnic group, still do the majority of household work, change has clearly occurred in recent decades. Still, compared to patterns that prevailed fifty years ago, men in the United States, acting as fathers and husbands, have begun to take on some housework responsibilities. What explains men's willingness to do so?

A large body of research suggests that the amount of money that spouses earn shapes household divisions of labor. This correlation between women's employment and men's increased involvement in household chores hold true in Latino families, although studies disagree on the extent to which these modest changes reach meaningful levels. . . . When Chicano men earn substantially more than their wives, they are less likely to perform a substantial amount of housework and child rearing. When Chicano men earn less than their wives and when their careers have been stymied, their wives seem to encourage more successfully their husbands' participation in housework and active child rearing. Consistent with a broad array of other studies, sociologists [Scott] Coltrane and [Elsa] Valdez found men taking more responsibility in the arena of child rearing and less in the poorly visible and less rewarding work of house cleaning.

However, in another study of Chicano dual-earner families the researcher found that while the earning gap between husbands and wives shapes household arrangements, it is not the only factor. This study indicates that occupational positions held by the wives also determined the extent to which Chicano men in the research sample performed housework. When this researcher compared housework arrangements among Chicana professionals, clerical workers, and blue-collar workers, she found that the professionals and blue-collar workers had the highest expectations for their husbands' participation in household labor, while women clerical workers clung closely to traditional ideological tenets that allocate housework to women. Accordingly, not only relative earnings, but also ideological stances, occupation, and work schedules influence who does what in the home.

Among a group of undocumented Mexican immigrant families residing in northern California, my own research reveals substantial modifications in household gender arrangements, mostly in the direction of greater gender egalitarianism. In general, the Mexican immigrant women seem to make great strides in achieving greater spatial mobility, greater say in family decision-making processes, and, in some important cases, in achieving a more equitable division of household labor. While other studies about gender and Latino immigrants view women's employment and earnings in the United States as the primary catalyst for these changes, I believe that migration processes themselves are also critical to the reconstruction of gender relations in the United States. When husbands and wives are separated for long periods of time during the early stages of immigration, spousal separation mandates that men will have to take some responsibility for their own daily upkeep (cooking, cleaning, laundry) and women will face new obligations previously the domain of their husbands (decision making, budgeting, mediating public encounters). These transformative experiences inform the gendered division of household labor when the family is reunited.

Latinas are not a monolithic group, however, and hence we see tremendous variety in the ways in which work and family issues are negotiated. In the last decades of the twentieth century, in an era defined by high rates of middle-class women's labor-force participation, high rates of migration from Latin America and the Caribbean, and increasingly accentuated inequalities of wealth and income, new family and work patterns began emerging among Central American, Caribbean, and Mexican migrant women. This pattern, which I have referred to elsewhere as "transnational motherhood," involves Latina immigrants' employment and residence in the United States while their children and families remain "back home" in their country of origin. . . .

Why have thousands of Central American, Caribbean, and increasingly, Mexican women left their children behind with grandmothers, other female kin, the children's fathers, or paid caregivers while they themselves migrate to work in the United States? They have responded to the exigencies of a new political economy of globalization, one that has extended the market for cleaning and caring services. Now that middle-class mothers are in the workforce, relatively privileged families can outsource the work of cleaning and caring to immigrant women from third world nations. This allows these middle-class women, mostly white mothers and wives, the privilege to opt out of their own gender oppression in the home without exhorting middle-class husbands and fathers to share the burden. This, in turn, creates new family inequalities further down the global class chain, whereby some families are denied face-to-face relations.

These are not altogether new arrangements. In fact, one precursor to these arrangements can be found in the mid-twentieth-century Bracero Program, which in effect legislatively mandated Mexican "absentee fathers," who came to work as contracted agricultural laborers in the United States. This longstanding arrangement still occurs today, although it is no longer legislatively mandated. When these men come north and leave their families in Mexico—as they did during the Bracero Program, and as many continue to do today—they are fulfilling their breadwinning obligations toward their families. When women do so, however, they are embarking not only on an immigrant journey, but on a more radical gender-transformative odyssey. As they initiate separations of space and time from their communities of origin and from their homes, children, and sometimes husbands, they must cope with stigma, guilt, and criticism from others. The ambivalent feelings and new ideological stances that emerge in tandem with these new arrangements are still in formation, but tension is evident. As they wrestle with the contradictions of their lives and beliefs, and as they leave behind their own children to care for the children of strangers in a foreign land, these Latina domestic workers innovate new rhetorical and emotional strategies.

Not all families are torn apart by immigrations and transnational processes, and some are even brought closer together through their struggles for economic survival. In the last years of the twentieth century, many Mexican and Central American immigrant families settled into permanent jobs and communities in the United States, and as they did, they helped foment a new wave of community unionism. Contrary to the predictions of anti-immigration groups, who long feared immigrant workers would depress wages and weaken organized labor, this new union movement is largely fueled by the efforts of U.S.-born *and* Latino immigrant workers from Mexico, Central America, and the Caribbean. Organizing as hotel and restaurant workers, as janitors, as drywell installers and other construction workers, and as home health aides, in the late 1990s they have created innovative social-movement strategies for winning demands from their employers. Job demands which once centered on wage and hour issues now encompass basic family issues such as family health insurance and affordable housing.

Economic restructuring . . . provides the backdrop for the emergence of these developments. As the office-janitorial industry was increasingly subcontracted to smaller firms throughout the 1970s and 1980s, small competitive office-cleaning businesses recruited Mexican and Central American immigrant men *and* women as favored employees. The wages were typically lower than those that had been paid to U.S.-born men, the former workers in this occupation. As relatively newly arrived immigrants with dire financial needs, these immigrant workers often had no alternatives but to accept these low-wage, downgraded, dead-end jobs. In the process, the janitorial occupation has undergone a radical transformation, as it is now a job, in Los Angeles at least, which is institutionally occupied by Latino immigrant men *and* women. In recent years, guided by the efforts of some very talented organizers, these workers have struggled to improve the quality of their jobs and pay, and, in the process, both labor organizing and familiar work/family arrangements have changed.

In Los Angeles, the creative, militant efforts of one very successful union, the Service Employees International Union's (SEIU) "Justice for Janitors" campaign organized vociferous street protests in some of the toniest corporate districts of southern California. Throughout the 1990s, in the shadows of high-rise corporate centers in Century City, Westwood, and in downtown Los Angeles, immigrant Latinos wearing brightly colored union T-shirts, and together with their children, have taken to the streets with demands for workplace fairness and economic justice. These protests culminated in a large general strike during the spring of 2000. In the process, old patterns of work and family relations have fallen by the wayside. . . .

As women have taken to the street to shout out their demands, men have taken on greater responsibilities for children and household. . . .

While gender egalitarianism has not been attained among Latinos or any other racial or ethnic group in the United States—we have seen, in the twentieth century, a definitive movement toward a greater plurality of gender arrangements and a general trend toward greater gender parity in the workplace and in many families. A new plurality of family and work arrangements prevails, *even within groups*, defying easy generalizing statements.

How will the complexities of globalization and the United States' position within the larger world economy shape gender and social relations among Latinos in the years that lie ahead? My speculations hinge on the growth of Latinos in the United States, their continuing geographical diversification, and on new patterns of employment promoted by globalization. The Latino population in the United States is now hailed as the United States' largest minority groups, outnumbering African Americans; most demographers believe the Latino numbers will continue to grow. Accompanying this trend, as we have seen, is increasing Latino geographical diversity and occupational diversity. This last factor, I believe, will prove critical in reconstructing and remaking Latino gender relations.

In this new context of globalization, we can expect to see still more increases in the rates of salaried and wage employment for Latinas. Many Latinas will be working in the lower echelons of our burgeoning service industry, while a few will occupy key positions in the professions and business. . . . In this regard . . . today's gendered demand for immigrant labor is quite different than nineteenth- and earlier-twentieth-century patterns, where Asian, European and Mexican *male* workers were recruited for manufacturing and primary extractive industries. Globalization has remade the United States so that it cannot function without immigrant labor, and especially without female immigrant labor. *Braceras* in homes and hospitals have replaced the *braceros* of yesterday. In this context, family and gender relations are being renegotiated in a myriad of ways.

Questions for Discussion

1. According to the author, in what ways is the current surge in immigration different from that of the late nineteenth and early twentieth centuries? In 1910 or so, the term "Melting Pot" was associated with immigration. Today the phrase "multiculturalism" is linked to immigration. How do the two differ?
2. What impact did the modern feminist movement have on women from minority and working-class backgrounds?
3. The author suggests that immigration does not lower wages. Do you agree? What evidence does she present to support her view?
4. Which factors most affect gender roles of immigrants from Latin America: globalization, "transnational motherhood," the women's movement, immigrant culture, or the wages earned by wives and husbands?

For Further Reading

Jose Alamillo, *Making Lemonade out of Lemons: Mexican American Labor and Leisure in a California Town, 1880–1960* (2006); Grace Chang, *Disposable Domestics: Immigrant Women Workers in the Global Economy* (1990); Fred Cordova, ed., *Filipinos: Forgotten Asian Americans* (1983); Roger Daniels, *Coming to America: A History of Immigration and Ethnicity in American Life* (1990); Juan Flores, *From Bamba to Hip-Hop: Puerto Rican Culture and Latino Identity* (2000); Gilbert Gonzalez and Raul Fernandez, *A Century of Chicano History* (2003); Jennifer Gordon, *Suburban Sweatshops: The Fight for Immigrant Rights* (2005); David G. Gutierrez, ed., *The Columbia History of Latinos in the United States since 1960* (2004); Nora Hamilton and Norma Stolz Chinchilla, *Seeking Community in a Global City: Guatemalans and Salvadorans in Los Angeles* (2001); Gabriel Haslip-Viera and Sherrie Baver, eds., *Latinos in New York: Communities in Transition* (1996); Pierrette Hondagneu-Sotelo, *Domestica: Immigrant Workers Cleaning and Carrying in the Shadow of Affluence* (2001), *Gendered Transmissions: Mexican Experiences of Immigration* (1994), ed., *Gender and U.S. Immigration: Contemporary Trends* (2003); Madhulika Khandelwal, *Becoming American, Being Indian: An Immigrant Community in New York City* (2002); Alan Kraut, *Silent Travelers: Germs, Genes, and the "Immigrant Menace"* (1994); Augustin Lao and Arlene Davila, eds., *Mambo Montage: The Latinization of New York* (2001); Robert Lee, *Orientals: Asian Americans in Popular Culture* (1999); Arthur Murphy, Colleen Blanchard, and Jennifer Hill, eds.,

Latino Workers in the Contemporary South (2001); Mary Romero, *Maid in the USA* (1992); Ruben Rumbaut and Alejandro Portes, eds., *Ethnicities: Children of Immigrants* (2001); George Sanchez, *Becoming Mexican American* (1993); Ilan Stavans, *The Latino Condition: Reflections on Culture and Identity in America* (1995); Marcelo Suarez-Orozco and Mariela Paez, *Latinos: Remaking America* (2002); Jere Takahashi, *Nisei, Sansei: Shifting Japanese American Identities and Politics* (1997); Milton Vickerman, *Crosscurrents: West Indian Immigrants and Race* (1999); Roger Waldinger and Mehdi Bozorgmehr, eds., *Ethnic Los Angeles* (1996).